Changing Policies, Changing Teachers

New Directions for Schooling?

EDITED BY

STEPHEN WALKER AND LEN BARTON

Open University Press

Milton Keynes ● Philadelphia

Open University Press
Open University Educational Enterprises Limited
12 Cofferidge Close
Stony Stratford
Milton Keynes MK11 1BY, England

and

242 Cherry Street
Philadelphia, PA 19106, USA

First Published 1987

British Library Cataloguing in Publication Data

Changing policies, changing teachers: new directions for
   schooling?
   1. Teachers—Great Britain
   I. Walker, Stephen, *1944–*   II. Barton, Len
   371.1′02′0941   LB1775

   ISBN 0-335-10292-1

   ISBN 0-335-10291-3 Pbk

Library of Congress Cataloging in Publication Data
Main entry under title:

Changing Policies, Changing Teachers

Based on papers originally presented at the 9th International
Sociology of Education Conference held in Birmingham,
England in Jan. 1986.
      Includes bibliographical references and index.
      1. Teaching—congresses.   2. Teachers—Great Britain—
congresses.   3. Educational innovations—Great Britain—
congresses. Sex discrimination in education—Great Britain
—congresses.   I. Walker, Stephen, 1944–   II. Barton, Len.
III. International Sociology of Education Conference
(9th:1986:Birmingham, West Midlands, England)
LB1025.2.C493 1987   371.1′02   87-11039

ISBN 0-335-10292-1

ISBN 0-335-10291-3 (Pbk.)

Typeset by Colset Private Limited, Singapore
Printed in Great Britain

Contents

Acknowledgements   v

List of Contributors   vi

Introduction   viii
    Stephen Walker and Len Barton

Part 1: New Roles for Teachers?

Introduction   1

1 Citizens or Consumers? Policies for School
    Accountability   (3)
    Stewart Ranson, Valarie Hannon and John Gray

2 Teacher Motivation and the Conditions of
    Teaching: A Call for Ecological Reform   22
    Rodman B. Webb and Patricia T. Ashton

3 Burntout or Beached: Weeding Women Out of
    Woman's True Profession   41
    Sara Freedman

4 Are Teachers Being Proletarianised? Some
    Theoretical, Empirical and Policy Issues   58
    Hugh Lauder and Beverley Yee

Part 2: New Initiatives for Schooling?

Introduction   73

5 Mandating Computers: The Impact of the New
  Technology on the Labour Process, Students and
  Teachers   75
  Michael W. Apple

6 Fixing the Mix in Vocational Initiatives?   96
  John Evans and Brian Davies

7 Teachers and the MSC   117
  Patricia Sikes

8 Studying Education Policy through the Lives of
  the Policy-makers: An attempt to Close the
  Macro-micro gap   138
  Jenny Ozga

Part 3: New Policies and New Practices?

Introduction   151

9 Bringing Gender Equality into Schools   153
  Rosemary Deem

10 Gender and Physical Education: Ideologies of
   the Physical and the Politics of Sexuality   169
   Sheila Scraton

11 The Dilemmas of Parent Education and Parental
   Skills for Sexual Equality   190
   Miriam David

Author Index   211

Subject Index   215

Acknowledgements

The articles that appear in this collection are all versions of papers originally presented at the IXth International Sociology of Education Conference held in Birmingham in January, 1986. The Conference is supported by Carfax Publishing Company, of Oxford. The theme of the 1986 meeting was 'Policy, Teachers and Education.'

We are grateful for the advice and help of our publisher, John Skelton, and also for the assistance given by Janet Cowsill and Sarah Wattison in the preparation of the manuscript. Our thanks also go to Sandra Walker and Joan Barton for their patience and support.

The article in this collection by Webb and Ashton is based on material previously published in The Journal of Thoughts, Winter 1986.

Contributors

Michael Apple Department of Curriculum and Instruction, University of Wisconsin-Madison, 225 North Mills Street, Madison, Wisconsin 53705, USA.

Pat Ashton College of Education, University of Florida, Gainesville, Florida 32611, USA.

Len Barton Department of Education, Bristol Polytechnic, Redland Hill, Bristol BS6 6UZ.

Miriam David Department of Social Sciences, Polytechnic of the South Bank, Borough Road, London SE1 0AA.

Brian Davies Centre for Science Education, Chelsea College, University of London, Bridges Place, London SW6.

Rosemary Deem School of Education, The Open University, Walton Hall, Milton Keynes MK7 6AA.

John Evans Department of Physical Education, The University, Highfield, Southampton SO9 5NH.

John Gray Division of Education, University of Sheffield, Sheffield.

Sara Freedman Boston Women's Teacher Group, PO Box 169, West Summerville, Boston, Mass 02144, USA.

Valerie Hannon c/o Institute of Local Government Studies, JG Smith Building, University of Birmingham, PO Box 363, Birmingham B15 2TT.

Jenny Ozga School of Education, The Open University, Walton Hall, Milton Keynes MK7 6AA.

Hugh Lauder Department of Education, University of Canterbury, Christchurch 1, New Zealand.

Sheila Scraton School of Education, The Open University, Walton Hall, Milton Keynes, MK7 6AA.

Pat Sikes School of Education, The Open University, Walton Hall, Milton Keynes MK7 6AA.

Stewart Ranson Institute of Local Government Studies, JG Smith Building, University of Birmingham, PO Box 363, Birmingham B15 2TT.

Stephen Walker Department of Teaching Studies, Newman & Westhill Colleges, Bartley Green, Birmingham B32 3NT.

Rodman Webb College of Education, University of Florida, Gainesville, Florida 32611, USA.

Beverley Yee Education Department, Wellington, New Zealand.

Introduction

Stephen Walker and Len Barton

The title of this book might seem ambiguous. The papers which follow are all versions of presentations originally made to the Ninth International Sociology of Education Conference held at Westhill College, Birmingham, in early 1986. In choosing *Changing Policies, Changing Teachers* as a title for this collection, we have attempted to capture the flavour of certain crucial questions, certain key ambiguities which were raised during discussion at the conference and which are further investigated in the articles which follow. The main theme of the 1986 meeting was an exploration of how recent changes in political and educational policy have influenced the ways in which teachers perceive and perform their professional work. That political and educational policy is under reform in the 1980s is beyond doubt. But the ways in which these changes will affect teachers and teaching is decidedly unclear. This is for at least three reasons. Firstly it is unclear because, as yet, we are unable to assess the *cumulative* impact the whole series of reformist projects will have upon the conditions of schooling and education. Are current policy initiatives likely to make minor modifications of teachers' classroom roles or are they likely to transform totally teachers' purposes and objectives, their social power and status and even their images of themselves? Secondly it is unclear because we do not know how teachers are likely to respond themselves to the changes which confront them. When faced with proposals for shifts in policy, practice or priorities, will teachers promote such proposals in the spirit of the policy design or will they struggle and subvert such initiatives? Thirdly it is unclear because teachers are themselves the targets of some of the attempts at achieving educational change. Thus, teachers are in the somewhat curious position of being both the victims and the agents of reform, wider educational change being inextricably related to their own metamorphosis.

That teachers themselves *feel* that, currently, they are going through a period of upheaval and change is, however, fairly certain. The following comments made to us recently by teachers from a variety of different sections of the education service reflect not only a fairly widespread impression that the conditions of teaching are undergoing some pretty profound changes but also, significantly, that these changes either accompany or even cause feelings of increased pressure and stress. Although the teachers to whom we have spoken could not be represented as a systematically constituted sample, nevertheless, when talking about how they thought teaching had changed in the last seven years, the number of teachers who used images of pressure and tension – in effect, all those involved – was almost as striking as the strength and the force of this kind of response. Their comments included the following descriptions:

> You would expect it to get easier as it goes on, but I find it harder. There's far more pressure put on you – both by parents and by the school situation. I felt I was less effective when I finished than when I started.

> We're being bombarded from all directions – it's too great a strain and some just can't take the stress.

> We're moving into a different way of learning, of teaching – it's much harder. I just don't know how to cope with the different expectations put on us . . . parents, advisers, inspectors.

> It's all pressure these days. Pressure from central government, assessment, a narrowing of the curriculum – parental pressure, government, employers, the DES.

> More and more is expected from all quarters and less and less is given from all quarters – resources, buildings, attitudes. And what was once seen by parents as a priviledge is now seen as a right.

> The good will that existed five or six years ago has disappeared and will not reappear for decades – teachers have come to expect to be in conflict with their employers.

> People at the chalk-face feel constantly under pressure but they are not always sure where the pressure is coming from.

> Accountability is the problem – but teachers feel very threatened about the question of who they are to be accountable to and for what.

These comments might be regarded as untypical expressions of the mood and attitude of the majority of teachers or they might be seen as manifestations of the kind of ritualistic griping sometimes associated with teacher culture. However, one can also identify in them certain recurring references, certain consistent themes which call for more careful scrutiny and reflection. That these teachers find their work increasingly stressful is obvious enough. But one can also sense in their accounts that this stress comes from new and unfamiliar sources – from the increased and different expectations they feel are being placed upon them, from the impression they have that powerful pressure groups from either educational management or from outside of education have a threatening interest in directing, organising and monitoring their work and from a sense of bewilderment they share about how to retain a positive assessment of themselves and their work. Of course, not all teachers share these feelings of vulnerability and alienation. However, we would want to argue that a loss of teacher power and esteem, a reformulation of teachers' main work roles and a challenge to personal ideologies and commitments are logical and inevitable outcomes of the specific policy initiative currently being applied to education, notably by supporters and politicians of the Thatcher government. And essentially, the detailed exploration of these losses, reformulations and challenges is the main focus in this collection of conference papers.

Having suggested this link between changes in educational policy and changes in the conditions of teachers' work, it is perhaps necessary to add that neither the transformations in teachers' roles and responsibilities nor the reactions such changes provoke in teachers are a consequence of a single policy initiative. One of the problems for teachers attempting to cope with everyday routines and fresh professional demands is the sheer range of policy initiatives they are being required to assimilate and the speed with which each new reform follows its predecessor. Indeed, it is difficult to think of an educational concern or an area of schooling which has not been the focus of one kind of reformist spotlight or another. Since 1980, a wave of discussion documents, DES directives, Government White papers and Parliamentary Acts – all aimed at reforming educational practice – has swamped the world of education. New criteria for the content and structure of the curriculum have been established; new modes of assessment and of public examination have been evolved; new management structures for schools have been erected; support services have been privatised; teachers conditions of service and salary structures have been redefined by dictat; the funding and resourcing of education has been carefully manipulated through control of award bodies or through the distribution of Rate and Educational Support Grants; a national core curriculum has been proposed; school accountability and teacher assessment schemes are being developed; vocational and training ideologies have come to dominate Further Education and the later end of secondary schooling: teacher training programmes have been required to conform to centrally determined criteria and principles; the list is long.

It is neither the range nor the rate of policy change, however, which make these initiatives critical in terms of their influence on teacher practice. Rather, it their radicalism – and the impact of current policy on teachers and teaching is radical in three important ways.

Firstly, current policy is radical because both its intended and unintended consequence is a fundamental shift in where and how the education system is controlled and managed. In statements on curriculum policy issued by HMI like 'Curriculum 5–16' or 'Mathematics 5–16', in the development of criteria for the new GCSE examination syllabuses and procedures, in the allocation of funds for new educational projects like TVEI or the spread of computerised learning aids, in the imposition of conditions of service on teachers – one finds a movement of power to control and define education towards the political centre. This might not be an entirely new phenomenon but what makes it radical is that the balance of decision-making power between central and local governments seems to have been abandoned, that representative decision-making bodies are being replaced by central government with non-elected boards and commissions like the MSC, the SCDC and the NAB and, that the policy central government is implementing through these control mechanism is essentially fundamentalist and reactionary.

Secondly, current policy is radical because it aims at establishing certain limited visions of what schools are designed to accomplish, at asserting certain educational priorities. In the vast majority of the policy initiatives directed towards education since 1980, it is easy to detect the deliberate and determined application of a '*market ideology*' as the major perceptual framework for educational planning and evaluation. This ideology is most obvious in the relentless drive to direct educational spending, the curriculum and teaching processes into explicitly vocational and instrumental pathways. But, it is also evident in moves to increase the influence of market forces on education like privatisation programmes or policies which, in the name of increased parental choice, force schools to compete for pupils according to some supposed notion of 'efficiency'. And, lastly, the emphasis in the mechanisms of policy implementation on management routines, on increased bureaucratic intervention and on the sanctity of official management views of issues like conditions of service or contracts or curriculum criteria or performance norms, legitimates this ideology.

Thirdly, current policy is radical because it represents a shift in how educational success and effectiveness is defined and assessed. A significant extension of the 'market ideology' mentioned above has been the development and application of accountability and appraisal programmes for schools and teachers. The importance of this development, as we see it, lies in two assumptions on which this initiative is based. The first of these would seem to be that performance of some easily identifiable, objective and measurable 'task' is the hallmark of educational achievement for either pupils or teachers. The second of these is that it has to be assumed that different parties to educational encounters are likely to agree on what these hallmarks should be or should not be. Which particular skill, task or accomplishment will be selected or given priority in these accountability programmes? Given increased central control and the operation of a market ideology as a major educational principle, it is not too difficult to speculate on possible answers to this question.

In the papers that follow the implications these radical changes have for teachers are explored in a variety of ways. We have divided the book into three section – one in which the emphasis is upon the pressures upon teachers, one in which the emphasis is upon the impact of vocational initiatives and of management principles in policy-making and, lastly, one in which the impact changing policies have upon teachers and their practices is explored through consideration of the progress of policies which challenge the reform goals of the New Right, such as those aimed at establishing gender equality. And it is appropriate that this particular discussion concludes this collection; essentially, the whole policy debate is about whether equality is either a practicable or a desirable social and educational pursuit. At present, it seems, it is not.

PART 1

New Roles for Teachers?

Introduction

In the current spate of educational policy initiatives, teachers occupy a strangely contradictory position. At the same time as they are being castigated as the likely source of any number of social breakdowns, they are also being required to accept all kinds of extensions and modifications of the professional role – often without either consultation or appreciation of the cost to teachers of the proposed role changes. Thus, whilst teachers are frequently being portrayed as individually and collectively responsible for the poor academic achievement of many school-leavers, for indiscipline and retarded moral development in young people and for the failure of the education system to foster and transmit skills specifically applicable and useful in the work-place; they are also being asked to accept that they are likely to continue in this inefficient way – unless they take on all kinds of 'new' definitions of their work roles and responsibilities – in particular, that their teaching must be skill-centred, that most educational decisions are beyond them and best left to more 'knowledgeable experts' and that they are incapable of assessing and reviewing their own performances and effectiveness.

The papers in this section of the book examine the different kinds of pressure created by criticism of teachers' role performance and by the 'new' definitions they are being required to accept. Three particular dangers are identified. The first is that the restructuring of teaching being attempted in current policy is actually dependent on teachers accepting that they have been inadequate and ineffective in the past (Freedman). The second is that the ideology on which attempts to restructure teaching is based ignores or obscures

1

explanations of these supposed inadequacies based upon the
economic conditions of schooling (Freedman) or upon alienating
characteristics of the conditions of schooling (Webb and Ashton).
The third danger is that some of the reformist policies, like accountability schemes (Ranson *et al.*) or like merit salary/master teacher
schemes (Freedman), are much more likely to increase the alienating
potential of teaching rather than reduce it.

The loss of teacher autonomy involved in the moves to restructure
the conditions and definitions of teachers' work discussed in this
section is crucially related to policies which effectively de-skill
teachers by excluding them from the processes of curriculum design
and development and of educational appraisal. However, in the
final paper in this section (Lauder and Yee), it is argued that state
interest in teachers' work need not inevitably result in the de-skilling
of teachers and that such a process can be resisted if teachers can act
together to exploit divisions which develop within the ruling capital
class.

CHAPTER ONE

Citizens or Consumers? Policies for School Accountability

Stewart Ranson, Valerie Hannon and John Gray

Introduction [1]

The 1970's saw a growing number of challenges to teachers and schools: concern was expressed by the Black Paperists about standards of achievement, industrialists doubted the appropriateness of the curriculum, while parents were reported to be worried about new teaching methods. The Great Debate aired the criticisms and it was concluded that 'education like other public services is answerable to the society which it serves and which pays for it, so these criticisms have to be given a fair hearing'[2]. There was therefore a growing demand for schools and teachers to become more accountable to the public. School should become more accessible, governing bodies made more representative of parental interests and parents accorded more choice of school for their children.

The 1980 Education Act introduced a number of measures to strengthen public accountability in education. Parental participation in governing bodies was extended and parents were to be given more information about schools (such as their exam performance) in order to inform their 'expression of preference' for particular school.

This chapter reports on research[3] which has studied the developing response of LEAs and their schools to the new duty to publish examination results as the most important means of making schools and teachers more accountable to parents and the public. We begin by developing a conceptual analysis of accountability before discussing the emerging policies towards accountability in three LEA Case Studies. We shall argue that underlying such policies are important assumptions about the working of power and authority in

3

the local polity as well as assumptions about accountable practice in local education authorities.

Understanding Accountability

Accountability is a multi-layered concept: its several layers of meaning need to be unravelled if sense is to be made of the emerging institutional forms of accountability. To be accountable is to be 'held to account' but also to 'give an account' (cf. Sockett,[4] and Stewart[5]). These elements reveal the distinctive social characteristics bound up in the accountable relationship relations of control but also of discourse. Power and purpose are brought together in the institutional arrangements of accountability.

Accountability as 'being held to account' defines a relationship of control. It implies rather formal ties between the parties, one of whom is answerable to the other for the quality of their actions and performance. Accountability, argues Lello[6] 'involves being called upon to give an account, sometimes mandatorily, but always with a clear and special responsibility'. Responsibilities have been conferred upon persons for the performance of roles and functions and on the understanding that they are answerable for the performance of their duties (Jones[7]). The interdependent elements of responsibility, answerability, evaluation and potential sanction are articulated particularly well by Dunsire[8]:

> 'Being accountable may mean . . . no more than having to answer questions about what has happened or is happening within one's jurisdiction. . . . But most usages require an additional implication: the answer when given, or the account when rendered is to be evaluated by the superior or superior body measured against some standard or some expectation, and the differences noted: and then praise or blame are to be meted out and sanctions applied. It is the coupling of information with its evaluation and application of sanctions that gives 'accountility' or 'answerability' or 'responsibility' their full sense in ordinary usage.'

To hold to account, therefore, focuses upon the dimensions of control in accountability. But even in a hierarchy the responsibilities between tiers are reciprocal. In a service which has formally divided functions and responsibilities between 'partners' to the service — central and local government, the teachers and parents — then patterns of mutual answerability are to be expected. Such multilateral discourse and negotiation within accountable relationships is further to be expected if we explore those layers of meaning in accountability that focus directly upon the interpretive procedures of the actors involved: that is, the 'giving of an account'.

The duty to provide an account is usually more than a descriptive activity. An account may include a report on the use of resources or the achievement of students but, in most cases, there will be a further expectation 'to account' for performance: that is to offer a narrative which interprets and explains performance. To be held to account invites the respondent to say why such-and-such has been accomplished and thus make intelligible that which may have remained unclear in the facts of a report.

A headteacher, for example, might seek to account for 'poor exam results' by pointing to the school's social and financial context. The head invites factors to be 'taken into account'. Yet the accounting process typically draws upon a much deeper set of interpretations and understandings which are embodied in the purposes and practices of an organisation's work. The achievements of a school have to be understood in the context of what it is setting out to achieve. Those who are held to account may be led to articulate the underlying values and beliefs which define their understandings of the educational task:

> The idea of accountability in everyday English gives cogent expression to the intersection of interpretive schemes and norms. To be accountable for one's activities is both to explicate the reasons for them and to supply the normative grounds whereby they may be justified.
>
> (Giddens,[9])

Interpretive schemes thus provide the framework which actors draw upon to make sense of educational performance: they define

* what counts as performance: defining the dimensions of achievement together with the criteria which it may be appropriate to apply;
* what counts as the conditions for effective achievement: defining how schooling is most effectively organised and delivered.[10]

Those held to account are drawn to communicate why they have been doing what they have been doing and how they have gone about it. Accountability is a court of judgement that distributes praise and blame and sometimes sanctions. But, at the centre of the process there is often a search for agreement, a sharing of a language in which to talk about purpose and practice and performance. Accountability institutionalises a discourse about purpose. The ensuing dialogue can illuminate Habermas'[11] notion of 'communicative rationality' whereby actors in an unfettered setting can explore the integrity of the reasons which have informed action and reach a common understanding about future progress.

Forms of Accountability

The elemental processes of accountability set out in the previous section are in themselves neutral as between particular educational values and interests. 'To be held to account' or 'to give an account' do not embody intrinsic value positions. But accountability is an institutionalising of relations between actors. Once we explore the specific form of the institutional arrangements of accountability then distinctive values and interests begin to manifest themselves. As Pateman[12] has argued cogently,

> 'preferences among different possible forms of accountability in education relate to and serve different possible orderings of socially available values'.

Kogan[13] has proposed recently that the central analytical task at this stage in the study of accountability is to develop a clearer understanding of the values and power invested in different institutional forms of accountability:

> 'There thus remain two central tasks upon the agenda of those pursuing a study of education accountability. The first is to get clearer about the values base of different models of accountability. The second is to establish more firmly what will be the power distributions resulting from different patterns. For the latter a surer sense will be needed of the actual flows of legitimacy and of the ways in which different organisational patterns – hierarchy as against collegium coercive as against exchange relationships – affect the actual work in schools'

The different dimensions of accountability – of 'being held to account' and 'giving an account' – have been organised in very different ways during the post-war period to reinforce particular sets of values and relations of power. There have been two significant forms of accountability – professional and market – and we shall argue that a third, public accountability, may be emerging in parts of the country. The first two may be described as follows:

> (A) *Professional Accountability*: The professional view is that exams constitute an important but narrow indicator of pupil achievement and that other dimensions of learning must be taken into account when evaluating standards: the whole cultural, social and creative aspects of school life should equally be assessed. A more comprehensive account is important for each student.

Professional values and orientations, therefore, emphasise the scope of educational achievement and a belief in the unfolding potential of each young person whose progress at any one point in time should be recognised as reflecting the quality of the relations and expectations which teachers can create within the classroom. The professional form of accountability is thus grounded in assumptions about the complexity of the educational task of developing students' capacities over time.

Given these complexities of educational process, the professionals argue that the necessary requirements of being held to account are best organised internally by teachers or by advisory and inspectorial colleagues who understand the nature of the task and can evaluate the extent of students' progress. Evaluating standards presupposes an understanding of context and, if sanctions are warranted, then professional peers are best suited to determine the improvements required without damaging the quality of the relations within the school. Power should reside with the teachers, advisers and officers. A number of LEAs – notably, the ILEA, Oxfordshire and Soli- hull – have been developing procedures for professional self-evalua- tion as a means of improving their accountability.

(B) *Market Accountability*: Proponents of this model argue that the pro- fessional interpretive schema of internal accounting distorts the essential purpose of the accountability of institutions looking outwards to the public beyond their boundaries. Schools should be answerable to their consumers, in this case the parents. The orientation of this account, it is claimed, should be upon standards of attainment rather than process. When we buy a cycle or a washing machine we are not interested in the problems of production only in the quality of the final product. Dis- satisfied consumers can shift their preferences and, at the same time, signal to the producers to improve their standards or leave the market place. Schools, no less than factories, can benefit from the cool draft of the market.

The 1980 Education Act introduced some of the conditions of the market place into schools. The Act made the publication of examination results central to the account which schools must offer their public. It provided, it was claimed, the single common currency that could be carried into the market place to test school standards. Parental affirmation or sanction, registered in the selection of parti- cular schools, was now recognised as the best instrument for holding schools to account. Consumer sovereignty was to replace the poten- tially undemocratic imposition of professional will.

Public Accountability as a critique of consumerism in education

The demand for the education service to become more accountable was a demand for teachers and schools to look beyond their profes- sional boundaries to the world beyond. The assumptions of the 1980 Education Act, indeed, form a quite radical view about public accountability because they link the accounting process to public action in the form of individual consumer choice. There is a conception here of an active public, of the agency of the public, being integral to the effective performance of public institutions. The interpretive scheme of market accountability is flawed. It proposes a limited account of educational achievement (solely in terms of exam results) while its theory of the conditions for effective schooling (consumer competition and choice) is incoherent. Effective schools arguably depend upon a complex system of curricular offering, staffing, resourcing, balance of intake, teacher morale as well as parental confidence which cannot be aggregated from individual consumer choices. Indeed, the unintended consequences of individual action may undermine the originating intentions (individual and isolated choices of parents in favour of small schools as the most desired context for learning end up creating a large school.) The recent work of Sen, Elster, and Parfit focuses upon the irrational and self-defeating outcomes of self-interest in certain decision-making contexts[14]. The critique of consumerism in education and the need to develop a more responsible form of *public accountability* has been made in a sustained challenge by Sallis[15] as well as by Kogan[16]:

> we cannot in any sense isolate our personal satisfaction from the health of the system as a whole since the quality of what is done in schools profoundly affects everybody
>
> (Sallis[15])

The important task for education, it is argued, is to develop relations and institutions of mutual accountability between public and school. Only by a partnership of parent and teacher and LEA can the learning process be enhanced for all young people.[17]

Developing LEA Policies on Exams and Accountability

By making it a duty for schools to publish information on (amongst other things) examination performance, and a duty for LEAs to enable parents to express a preference for schools, the 1980 Education Act was designed to improve the public accountability of schools and LEAs. Legislation sought to enact the principles of market accountability in secondary schooling.

Some LEAs and schools have treated the new duties required of them as an irritant an encumbrance upon the normal tasks of schooling. In other authorities, however, there has been a more vociferous response, either supportive or critical, towards the assumptions of accountability embodied in the legislation: both in terms of the values of 'the account' given of educational achievement, and the principles of power embodies in the processes of answerability ('being held to account') to consumer preference.

We discuss here three of the LEA case studies in our research and their emerging strategies towards examinations and public accountability in secondary schools. Two of the LEAs express the archetypical forms of accountability described above, and strategies to develop those forms:

- *Oceana County*: Reforming the professional form of accountability
- *Market Town*: Developing the institutions of consumer accountability

A third LEA – *Civitas City* – illustrates an Authority in transition from a professional tradition towards a mode of public accountability that recognises the public as citizens within the education polity.

(A) *Self-Evaluation in Oceana County*:

In the late 1970's exam results were published in the form of a league table in the local press, much to the consternation of teachers, advisers and officers. In subsequent years the Chief Education Officer pleaded successfully with the editors not to publish the results in such an invidious form, arguing the case of complexity whilst, at the same time, presenting the papers with a mass of necessary but unanalysed data.

More important, however, than the quiet subversion of intelligible publication of results was the increasingly articulate educational argument against exam results as the single means of accounting for young people's achievement. The argument was advanced that traditional schooling had been straitjacketed by an unduly limited conception of academic achievement. Schools needed to celebrate a much wider range of pupil achievements. Passing exams may not adequately test cognitive skills let alone other aspects of personal accomplishment which are properly the concern of schools – social, cultural and practical aspects of achievement. Thus, the Chief Education Officer:

I have become more disparaging about exams. . . . Exams are a doubtful, dubious form of assessment: they are skewed towards narrow skills; they are biased towards information retention and recall. . . . We have been running an educational system which has produced a subliminal message: if you pass 16 + exams, excellent; onto A levels and if you pass these then that is even better news; onto University and so on. The system communicates only one dimension of achievement – academic success. But this is an extremely narrow idea of educational achievement – highly intellectual and highly cognitive. It is minimally about practical skills, social and aesthetic accomplishment or attitudes etc. We must return to our conception of educational purpose.

The account which senior professionals in Oceana County provide defines not only a broad conception of achievement but a distinctive understanding of the processes of learning as the secret to improved schooling.

The key to personal development, it is argued, lies in encouraging the motivation of pupils. This points to the urgent need to reform the system of assessment. Exams are designed to fail more students than they pass and this failure undermines the very motivation which is the secret to learning:

> The assessment system should reinforce the motivation of young people in the 5th year not weaken it.

The Authority along with a number of others has begun to devise a system of assessment which provides the student with a portfolio that includes:
- examination
- graded assessments
- personal record of achievement

The portfolio of records tests and exams is designed to celebrate the positive achievements of each student the assessments can then be used formatively to reinforce confidence as well as to counsel about future learning opportunities.

At the same time as it wished to extend the procedures for assessing students. The Authority was keen to develop an institutional setting of accountability – processes of holding schools to account – that was sensitive to and enhanced the internal learning processes of schools. Oceana County began to consider procedures for school 'self-evaluation' as its response to the growing demand nationally for greater accountability of schools and LEAs. The idea of self-evaluation had been gaining ground within the education profession generally and had already been introduced in a few local authorities such as the ILEA. The Chief Education Officer of Oceana argued:

> School self-evaluation was recognised in Oceana discussions as a powerful element in the development of teachers and their institutions and it was thought more worthwhile to encourage schools, and individuals, to take up a sharper evaluative stance from within than to impose evaluation through external inspection . . .
>
> The acceptance by the Education Committee of the school's own assessment as an instrument of public accountability is an extra step and demonstrates a trust in the schools which a matter of pride. . . . Schools are judged in their own context, by their own standards, not by invalid comparisons: nor are they stultified by rigid testing.

The 'Navel exercise', as the self-evaluation is appropriately referred to, involves outsiders (the governors, officers and committee members) in later stages of the reporting process, but their role is conceived as being supportive of the teachers seeking to develop their own confidence in the internal reform of the learning process:

> It will be seen that although the evaluation starts within the school, there is an external contribution which, to some extent, validates the internal exercise.

The process of self-evaluation seeks to develop an internal, confidential, dialogue with the school to help them develop their professional practice:

> Heads produce the report in association with their staff. We use the report to create a dialogue with the school, to review their strengths and weaknesses. In one school their weakness is obsessive exam orientation: when we met the Head and his staff we never mentioned exams.
> The discussions are confidential. Why? Because of Ruskin, Tyndale, and because of our publishing examination results. Teachers and schools were worried that we were getting into a crude form of accountability.
> My role is to hold a mirror to the school, to begin a dialogue with them:
> • at the first stage to discuss with the head and his staff and chairman of governors. It is a supportive discussion. It is to do with professionals reviewing and developing practice together. Challenging, but not in front of the member.
> • at the second stage to discuss with governors and members.

The process encourages, and has developed, language codes that are appropriate for the public and private contexts of self-evaluation accountability:

> Its a code. There are things that can be said within the family (the school) and there are things which can be said outside in the public house.

The tacit agreement is established that in exchange for a restricted public language, a more elaborate, extended code is developed between professionals. The members played their supportive role in the self-evaluation process of schools. Thus a senior member of the Education Committee maintained:

> The main agenda of evaluation was to get schools to open out. The confidential nature of the process has given poor schools the confidence to open out. There have been positive achievements. The members took a learning role, not a changing role. It was the only way it could have been done. Schools were challenged by the officers. We played an enabling role: there was no confrontation. (Though on some issues – the perceptions some schools have of working class pupils and their capacity to achieve – I felt I wanted to challenge.)

The interpretive schema and institutions of accountability in Oceana County focus upon the teacher. The teachers are invited to hold themselves to account, evaluating their own performance with others drawn in to encourage and support the internal dialogue and analysis. The values which inform the account and the relations of answerability form a consistent whole: the key to improved personal achievement is believed to depend upon reform of the learning process and thus internal, knowledgeable, self-evaluation is regarded as the best means of safeguarding public accountability. Such a view of public accountability is regarded as too weak and inappropriate by our third Authority.

(B) *Consumer Sovereingty in Market Town*:
Market Town is an affluent outer London Borough with leafy areas as well as council estates that border the ILEA. The values which shape the Authority's understanding of educational performance and procedures of accountability focus upon the significance of examination results and the right of parental choice of school.

The account about what counts as educational achievement is preoccupied, almost obsessively with examination results. 'Performing well or badly in exam results' is the defining criterion of educational standards in Market-Town. Schools are evaluated in terms of their exam performance and compared in terms of the levels of passes (O level 1−2's; A level A−B's) achieved in specific subjects. The exam results are published in the public section of the Education Committee as a league table. A senior officer reported that this had made the Heads 'a little sensitive', particularly as the Authority had previously given an assurance that it would not publish league tables.

Examination results and the manner in which they are published are seen as crucial derterminants of school popularity amongst parents:

> The parental criterion for selecting schools? Exam results are the most prominent. Parents want exam results. They are always seeking information on exam performance in schools. If we want to change the catchment areas for a school and hold a meeting with parents they ask for information on exam results
>
> (Senior officer)

> Our governors look at the information on exam results very carefully. They draw up a league table. They compare it with last year's league table – they are very keen and interested. They see it as part of the marketing of the school because we are in a very competitive situation here, both in respect of the private sector and other state schools
>
> (Head)

As the senior officer concluded, 'exams provide the discipline for schools and the means of competition between schools'.

The interpretive scheme that informs accountability in Market-Town articulates a theory of competition between schools as the most effective method of improving educational performance.

Schools are to compete in the market place for consumer preferences:

> Schools are set in competition with each other. The strong survive and the weak fail
>
> (Headteacher E)

> The Chair of the Education Committee has stated publicly that schools must respond to pressures of the market place. If you don't respond and parents don't like you then schools will close
>
> (Headteacher D)

> The dominating influence in the Borough is parental choice
>
> (Headteacher A)

The Authority judges schools by their level of recruitment in the market place. The market place is constituted by the maintenance of surplus places in schools which allow parents to express their preference for a school and be reasonably sure of gaining a place. In setting the framework for the market the Director and Chair of Education had wanted to set admission limits at three or four forms of entry although Headteachers wanted to maintain six forms of entry: a compromise was in fact, reached at five forms of entry:

> The LEA deliberately keeps open a lot of secondary school places because they like to promote competition and they believe in the market economy
>
> (Headteacher C)

Each school is provided with its own catchment area of 'feeder primaries' but this is calculated to provide only two forms of entry and thus not enough to fill the admissions places. This situation has been designed intentionally so that schools have to compete for parental choices:

> I always work from an industrial model: if you lose more than fifty percent of your home market you had better close down. A school can't make up fifty percent from outside
>
> (Senior officer)

Heads, teachers are expected to 'market' their schools to parents: advertising in the press, making sure that the papers know about the achievements of the school and, in particular, exploiting the public occasions – such as speech day, prize givings, sports days and carol service – to win parental support for the school:

> marketing is essential for all headteacher here.
>
> (Headteacher C)

> To keep the demand for one's school buoyant all Heads have to do it. One has to present oneself and one's school in the most Up-market way possible.
>
> (Headteacher C)

> You need to maintain your intake. At the November meetings of parents
> . . . then you are very conscious that you have to go into the market place.
> (Headteacher B)

> Must attend to one's shop window: there is a speech day and prize giving.
> Prize giving is about image building . . . since I have become more sen-
> sitive to marketing trends and to selling positively, exam results become
> very handy. I have made it into a grand affair.
> (Headteacher C)

Schools have to watch their 'shop-window'. They have to avoid
down-market images

> We know we have a good product here, and the examinations typify it,
> but the image is too far down-market.
> I discussed it with the Director of Education and he said I should try
> and avoid a social worker image. Not to say in Parents Evenings: if
> anyone has any difficulty in providing the uniform, they have only to see
> me about it because we assist'. He said, cut that right out, because it's up
> to the parents to provide the clothes and if they don't just suspend them.
> (Headteacher B)

The pressure of the market place and the determining influence of
parental choice has also begun to have its impact upon the curriculum offerred in schools. In one school the new Head of a school
was informed by the authority that one of the reasons parents were
not choosing the school was the provision of integrated, rather than
separate sciences. Although it was against his professional judgement the Head believed he had no alternative but to respond to
parental demands.

> (parents ask) . . . whether the curriculum is up to date: does the school
> have computer education? Is CDT up to date and developed? They are
> concerned whether there is a creative element in the curriculum . . . They
> enquire about discipline, the measures used. Is there school uniform?
> What is the presentation of staff – are they in jeans?
> (Senior officer)

Some schools like to try and influence market preferences by using
the principle of 'product differentiation': 'its like putting the blue in
Daz . . . .it means that you choose something that is going to make
your school appear different' (Headteacher C). The market can
influence the 'hidden curriculum' as well. A senior member of the
Education Committee commented upon the 'failings' of one headteacher:

> He spent more time with the underprivileged child rather than the bright
> child and parents did not want that.

The 'problems' of such educational values brought an early
retirement!

The account of education performance in Market-Town defines exams as the measure of achievement and competition between schools as the condition of effective education. This interpretive schema stresses accountability of the Authority and its schools to the public which is conceived as individual parents who by their choice of school can hold the professionals to account. Sovereignty, in Market-Town, lies with the consumer.

The role of the LEA is to facilitate these relations of account-ability. They do so in three important ways. Firstly by promoting the language and beliefs of the market place, so that officers can talk of schools as 'plant', heads as 'plant managers' needing to 'market' themselves, inspectors as 'quality controllers', and schools compe-ting with each other to 'respond to the demands of the market place'. The second role of the LEA is to ensure fair play in the market place:

> my job is to give all heads fairness in the market place. Some heads are using fast selling techniques; they are actually dishonest about their exam results
>
> (Senior officer)

> I am a referee to ensure fair competition between schools
>
> (Senior officer)

The third role of the LEA, in facilitating market accountability, is to interpret the trends and movements of the market and to take appro-priate action. This might mean: imposing inspections to evaluate the internal management and organisation of a school; sending heads on management development courses to improve their marketing and management skills; and, in the last resort, taking disciplinary action. Alternatively a school might be allowed to wither and die in the cool winds of the market place if it failed to meet parental expectations.

(C) *Civitas City – Negotiating the Learning Contract*
Civitas City, like Oceana, is striving to reform the learning process, it differs in that it is more committed to the belief that learning cannot be imposed by professionals but has to be negotiated with pupils, parents and the community. In that sense they can be compared to Market Town because they desire a much more active sense of public accountability than Oceana – wanting the education service to be accountable to parents and the public. Yet they believe the assumptions of the market place to be anathema to education and are seeking to develop a notion of the public as citizens rather than self-interested consumers.

The emerging process of accounting in this LEA, more than in any other LEA in our study, focuses upon the learning needs of the student: it is argued that the system of education from teacher, school, LEA and assessment process require considerable reform if they are to become truly child-centred in their orientation. The educational challenge as one Head put it, is 'to release the creative capacity of young people'. If that is to be achieved students must be at the centre of the learning process and have an opportunity to shape what is happening: The articulate Chief Inspector of Civitas City develops the theme:

> The curriculum which is being offered should relate to the pupils. The kids should understand the curriculum and why it is offered. The pupils should be at the centre of the whole process. We need to demystify education for them . . . . Learning becomes a much more child centred process . . . Children are valued, watched, counselled.

A Head, wanting to reform his school, argued that achieving a child-centred education was his first priority:

> I need to create an environment . . . in which young people can have value, can have recognition for their achievements; where teachers can relate readily to young people, where teachers can enjoy being in lessons with young people. All this means a child-centred education.
>
> (Headteacher F)

The source of child-centred learning, in this view, lies in the need for students to understand the various dimensions of achievement, to understand the purposes of the curriculum, its outcomes and the way it relates to their needs. This not only helps to demystify the curriculum but leads to the negotiation of learning of what pupils are expected to achieve and how that is to be accomplished. Negotiation not only makes the learning experience meaningful for the student but secures their stake in the importance of learning:

> Young people need leading towards independence. But we regiment too much. We don't treat our 5th formers as young adults.
>   Young people are seeking an adult relationship with teachers, but they are constrained by rules which are designed for younger pupils. Children must have an opportunity to determine what is happening.
>
> (Headteacher B)

The argument continues that if teachers and students define the goals of learning together, negotiating what is to be achieved, reviewing what has been achieved, then learning can become a formative process, a process which is positively generating of achievement, confidence and motivation. It positively reinforces ownership of learning, self-direction and responsibility.

  The development of a child-centred education is seen to have deep implications for the work of teachers and schools:

> Teachers are into children. A school which has gone through this process – defining what they want pupils to achieve; considering how this will influence the teaching process; how to assess new forms of pupil progress; how to report – that school will develop its pupils formatively.
>
> (Chief Inspector)

Teachers and schools are challenged to acquire new skills of (non-didactic) teaching, team teaching, to develop new systems of (credit related) assessment and reporting. Some teachers may feel threatened by the loss of teacher control, while others believe they are pioneers working with young people traditionally rejected by the education system. The LEA, in turn, also has considerable changes to make if it is to play its part in supporting schools in the development of child-centred learning & encouraging processes of curriculum and staff development; gaining much deeper knowledge about schools and validating the work of the school as an institution.

This Authority is clear that the negotiation of the learning process is incomplete unless it includes both parents as individuals and the community as a whole in the dialogue. As one senior officer put it the new educational approach 'should be open, accessible and interpretable by parents and the public'. Schools and the Authority must be outward looking to parents, establishing a continual dialogue with them. It is an immediate form of accounting. Parents and governors need to know that what the school is saying has validity. Teachers need to promote the confidence of parents in the school because effective learning depends so much upon parental support:

> parents need to be perceived as complementary educators. Parents and the community are our most valuable resource. Without the support of parents our day-by-day contact with pupils is worthless.
>
> (Headteacher A)

> Teachers should be accountable. The mystique of all professions has been exploded . . . The curriculum is not God-given. The individual teacher must be more articulate and listen to the community. It leads to an agreement between the community (parents and politicians) and the teachers as to what we can achieve. People have had unreal expectations of us. We have to negotiate. We have to reach agreement about what we are to do. In the absence of agreement criteria are not helpful. With agreement there are some reasonable expectations of the purpose of education – what we should be teaching. Without this agreement any judgements about a school's performance are arbitrary.
>
> Adults knowledge of teaching is out of date. This is the problem for us. Unless we talk more to parents their criteria (of evaluation) will reside more in their own experience: especially at primary level. We need to get to the stage where parents can come in. Teachers are resistant to their own colleagues seeing them work, let alone parents. Teaching is a very private, isolated occupation. But we need to breakdown the barriers.
>
> (Headteacher C)

Effective learning depends upon home and school working together, reaching agreement about the values and purposes the school is trying to achieve. Much of this is already familiar but what is new and important in this statement is the growing realisation – as it is within the Authority – of the need to establish a contract of learning not only with parents individually but with the community as a whole. Working with parents to achieve a unity of purpose is seen as leading to broader discussions with the community as well as to shifting relations of power between profession and public accountability can lead to a discourse about the distribution of power within as well as the purposes of public services. This view is articulated most strongly by radical black leaders in the City. Summarising their position as he perceived it, a senior adviser commented:

> There must be negotiation, a shifting of control. The school must show interest in parents and the community, listen to them and accept them as having a stake in the institution.
>
> The bottom line is the openness of the school to be prepared to listen to the expressed need of the community which the school is trying to serve. The school must be receptive, develop understanding. Schools have a lot to do to understand the community and what makes the kids tick.
>
> This involves changing the power relations between the school and the community. It means understanding how the kids are treated by the power figures outside the school – like the police and magistrates – and understanding, as well as seeking to change, the attitudes they express. The school is a power institution also and if schools respond in the same way as these other (negative) institutions then the school will be perceived as unlistening and racist.
>
> Schools must give the black community confidence that the school is open and responding to expressed needs. This is leading to discussion of big issues.
>
> It is threatening to schools. What is the school opening itself up to? To attitudes, values, aspirations of parents which teachers may incompletely understand. Schools may have to think about the structure and organisation of the school as well as the curriculum it is offering. The school cannot assume that what is on offer is understood and valued by the community. The school may need to rethink the balance of what it is offering to gain the confidence of the local community. But it must be negotiated. This means a great deal of building of understanding of the outcomes of learning as well as the processes of learning.

As a result, the form and processes of accountability in Civitas City are beginning to undergo fundamental review. Public accountability is no longer to be conceived merely as a process of communicating with the public but rather as one of negotiation with the public about what the account (as purpose) should be, who should be taken into account as well as the accounting (explaining) of the conditions of educational effectiveness.

Conclusion: Education and the Polity

In each LEA the interpretive schema of accountability define an account of education – in terms of the purposes of education as well as the conditions which create effective educational achievement – and relations of accountability that define who is answerable to whom in education. Table 1 summarises the LEAs beliefs about accountability:

Table Accountability

LEA	Purpose	The Account Performance Conditions	Holding to Account Relations of accountability
OCEANA County	Public development	Reform of the learning process	Professional dominance (Self-evaluation)
MARKET Town	Exam passes (academic standards)	Competition of schools	Consumer sovereignty
CIVITAS City	Public Devlp. + Citizenship	Negotiating the learning contract	Community participation, Citizenship Public accountability

Each LEA presents very different policies and emerging practices that are designed to improve the accountability of schools and teachers in their authorities. And yet there was one assumption about accountability which they held in common: that effective schooling depended upon the partners to education – the teachers, the members and the parents – reaching agreement about the purposes and processes of learning:

> If you reflect upon what we are about, the curriculum we aim to achieve . . . then each community should decide what is socially useful knowledge and experience. This presupposes agreements: there must be a shared value system to create an effective school.
>
> (CEO, Oceana)

> Accountability is the Heads presentation of the school, the public view and the LEA view. A successful system is one in which these three dimensions are in phase with each other. Problems exist when the three images get separated from each other.
>
> (Senior officer, Market-Town)

> Teachers should be accountable . . . It leads to an agreement between the Community (parents and politicians) and the teachers about what it is reasonable for schools to achieve . . . We have to negotiate.
>
> (Headteacher Civitas)

The tacit agreement across these three very different local authorities is that effective schooling depends upon, presupposes, an agreed account of what is to count as learning. It presupposes the profession and the public reaching a shared understanding about the purposes and conditions of education (the practice of Habermas' 'communicative rationality' is clearly a precondition for developing accountable and effective schooling!) The partners of education may hold different accounts about educational purpose but for the accounting process to flourish it requires the negotiation of an agreed account.

We agree with this important principle informing the development of public accountability in education. Arguably, however, although each of the LEAs asserts the principle, only one Authority is developing policies and practices which are consistent with that principle. Professionalism in Oceana does not accord enough recognition or access to the public and although Market Town seeks to strengthen the active participation of the public, in fact chooses a method which fragments and destroys the public as community. Consumerism isolates people and, importantly, eschews the practice of reason between groups: the market does not conceive of accountable discourse.

Only the emerging policies and practices of Civitas City have the potential to develop the guiding principle of a public accountability which allows the partners in education to reach agreement about the purposes and conditions of effective learning. This authority, more than the others, also acknowledges and is articulating the political theory of consent which underlies public accountability. Authority in local democracy resides with the people whose consent needs actively and continually to be negotiated and legitimated. Civitas City is developing institutions of citizenship in education which would not only improve learning but create the conditions for an educated democracy.

Notes and References

1 This paper forms a developmental study for the ESRC research programme on Exams and Accountability at the Universities of Birmingham and Sheffield (Project: HR 8602). We are grateful to ESRC for their support.

2 *Education in Schools: A Consultative Document*, Cmnd. 6869, HMSO, July, 1977.

3 See Note 1 above.

4 Sockett H.T., 'Accountability: the Contemporary Issues', in Sockett H.T. (ed) *Accountability in the English School System*, Hodder and Stoughton, 1980.

5 Stewart J.D., 'The role of information in Public Accountability', in

Tomkins C. (ed), *Current Issues in Public Sector Accountability*, Phillip, Allan, London, 1984.

6   Lello J. (ed) *Accountability in education*, Ward Lock, 1979, p. 3.

7   Jones G.W., *Responsibility in Government*, London School of Economics, 1977.

8   Dunsire A., *Control in a Bureaucracy, The Execution Process* Vol. 2, Martin Robertson, 1978, p. 41.

9   Giddens A., *The Constitution of Society*, Polity, 1984, p. 30.

10   See Ranson S., Towards a Political Theory of Public Accountability in Education *Local Government Studies*, Vol. 12, Number 4, July/August 1986.

11   Habermas J., *The Theory of Communicative Action*, Heinemann, 1984.

12   Pateman T., 'Accountability, Values and Schooling', in Becher T. and Maclure S. (eds) *Accountability in Education*, NFER/Nelson, 1978, p. 61.

13   Kogan M., 'Different Definitions of Accountability in Education', in *ESRC Newsletter*, Number 53, Supplement, 1984, p. xiii.

14   See Sen A., *Choice, Welfare and Measurement*, Blackwell, 1982; Elster J., *Sour Grapes* Cambridge, 1983; Parfit D., *Reasons and Persons*, Oxford, 1984.

15   Sallis J., Beyond the Market Place: A Parent's View, in Lello J. (ed) *Accountability in Education*, Ward Lock, 1979, p. 116.

16   Kogan M. *Education Accountability: An Analytic Overview*, Hutchinson, 1986.

17   Ranson S., 'Government for a Learning Society', in Ranson S. and Tomlinson J. (eds) *The Changing Government of Education*, Allen and Unwin, 1986.

CHAPTER TWO

Teacher Motivation and the Conditions of Teaching: A Call for Ecological Reform

Rodman B. Webb and Patricia T. Ashton

(The research upon which this paper is based was conducted under contract number 400-79-1175 of The National Institute of Education, Washington, D.C. it does not necessarily reflect the views of that agency.)

From the beginning of educational research, the study of student motivation has been a prominent topic. In contrast, teacher motivation has received little attention. It has been assumed until recently that teachers are motivated and that the profession provides its members with the support needed to maintain dedication and carry out their duties effectively.

Two lines of research, one into the conditions of teaching and the other into teachers' efficacy attitudes, suggest that these assumptions are mistaken. The last National Education Association (1982) poll which investigated the status of public school teachers revealed that their motivation has been severely threatened in recent years. A national sample of teachers was asked, 'Suppose you could go back to your college days and start over again, in view of your present knowledge, would you become a teacher?' Only 25 percent of females and 16 percent of males indicated that they 'certainly would' choose teaching again. These numbers represent a significant erosion of teacher morale. When the same question was asked in 1961, 57 percent of females and 35 percent of males indicated that teaching 'certainly would' be their career choice.

Research into the conditions of teaching suggests that declining morale among educators is due to such interacting factors as the failure of salaries to keep up with inflation, the lack of a career ladder that rewards teacher competence, the loss of public confidence in the quality of American teachers and the education they offer, school violence, hostile or apathetic parents, and a lack of professional autonomy (Boyer, 1983; Sizer, 1984; Webb, 1982). Teachers further report that heavy work loads, lack of time, growing responsibilities, classroom interruptions, poor discipline, negative student attitudes, and incompetent administration have diminished their morale and hindered their efforts to teach competently (NEA, 1982, p. 78). These data suggest that the quality of education and the conditions of teaching are closely linked and that we are unlikely to significantly improve the former without first enhancing the latter.

'Sense of efficacy' refers to teachers' beliefs regarding their ability to teach and students ability to learn. The construct was introduced to educational research in two Rand Corporation studies that reported a strong association between teachers' sense of efficacy and student achievement (Armor, *et al.*, 1976; Berman *et al.*, 1977). In their evaluation of reading programs in Los Angeles schools, Armor *et al.* reported that teachers' sense of efficacy was 'strongly and significantly related to increases in reading' achievement (p. 23). In the second study, an evaluation of teachers' willingness to adopt educational innovations, Berman *et al.* found a 'strong positive relationship' between teachers' sense of efficacy and such dependent variables as the percentage of goals achieved during innovation projects, the degree to which teachers maintained project innovations over time, the amount of teacher change occurring during those projects, and student achievement (p. 137).

Past efforts to identify specific attitudes that are related to student achievement have been discouraging (Dunkin and Biddle, 1974; Getzels and Jackson, 1963). The findings of the Rand studies represent a significant break-through because of correlations they found between teachers' sense of efficacy and student achievement and because they suggest that efficacy attitudes are a component of teacher motivation. More recent studies have further established the link between teachers' sense of efficacy and student achievement (Gibson and Dembo, 1984; Ashton, Webb, and Doda, 1983; Ashton and Webb, 1986).

While we are encouraged by the findings of the 'efficacy research' and look forward to more work being done in the area, we are concerned about how the findings will be interpreted by policy makers. The path from research data to policy prescription is slick and steep and must be travelled with care. The current pressure to improve schooling in the United States encourages policy makers and researchers to run that path with reckless abandon. A purpose of this paper is to offer an interpretation of the teacher efficacy attitude studies so that a careful policy debate might begin.

At least two mutually exclusive assumptions appear to drive current interpretations of the teacher efficacy research. The first assumes that efficacy attitudes are akin to character traits and that low sense-of-efficacy teachers are somehow flawed and unable to carry out their duties effectively. The obvious policy implication to come from this assumption is that teachers should be screened in order to keep those with 'bad attitudes' out of the nation's classrooms. A shorter prescription, drawn from the same assumption, suggests that teachers with a low sense-of-efficacy must be helped to change their views so that they can become more productive workers. We refer to this set of policy prescriptions (screening and re-education) as having an 'individualistic' orientation.

The second assumption used to interpret the research is that efficacy attitudes are not personality traits, but rather responses to teachers' cultural, social, institutional, and personal environment. The policy implication that flows from this assumption is that efforts to improve teachers' efficacy attitudes must change the conditions of teaching rather than teachers. We refer to this prescription as an 'ecological' orientation because its intervention is directed at the school environment and not focused narrowly on the personalities and beliefs of individual teachers.

We believe it is more warranted to apply an ecological perspective rather than an individualistic orientation when interpreting the efficacy attitude research in education. The purpose of our paper is to document that belief.

Data and Method

The data for our analysis were drawn from in-depth interviews with 42 middle-school and high-school teachers working in five schools in a southeastern city and a rural town. Interviews lasted from a half hour to two hours, were taped, and then transcribed. In addition, more than 80 hours of observational data were collected in the classrooms of middle-school teachers. We searched the data asking 'What is going on here? What are teachers doing, and what meaning do their acts have for them? What do teachers make of the actions of others and the everyday events of their own professional lives?' To answer such questions we were attentive to the 'minute particulars' of everyday events and the reality constructs that teachers used to make sense of those events. We stayed close to the teachers, but at the same time we consciously detached ourselves so that we could view their social reality from the objective perspective of a sympathetic stranger (Schutz, 1971, p. 37). Thus our actions in gathering and analysing data were governed not solely by the rules of etiquette or the customs of the classroom, but by the pre-established rules of the scientific method.

The process of data analysis is complex and cannot be detailed here. It is enough to say that it is from the standpoint of a sympathetic but detached observer the subjective world of teachers can be made an object of analysis. Following Spradley (1980), data were analysed line by line for 'domains' or categories, and domains in turn were organised into broader themes. Thus we discovered patterns of thought and action, or what phenomenologists call 'typifications' (Schutz, 1971, pp. 59, 73, 281). The goal of ethnographic research is not simply to report the utterances and actions of teachers, but to find order in them and to place them in a wider social context.

It was our goal to render the social world of teachers intelligible. The aim of social science is to gain understanding by making the subjective objective, by making what is taken-for-granted in everyday life seeable and thus knowable. This is the point of the stanza from T. S. Eliot's 'Little Gidding':

> We shall not cease from exploration
> And the end of all our exploring
> Will be to arrive where we started
> And know the place for the first time.

Rendering the social world intelligible (making it knowable for the first time) is perhaps the greatest single contribution of social science. We have said elsewhere that

> It is only when others become intelligible to us that we can empathise with their situation and enlarge and enlighten our sense of community and common purpose. These elements (a warranted interpretation of the lives of teachers, a sense of community, and a commonality of purpose) are sadly lacking in education today. Their absence constitutes a significant impediment to school improvement
>
> (Ashton and Webb, 1986).

Certainly knowing something about how teachers interpret their world is essential if we hope to make policies that will improve teacher performance.

Teacher Efficacy Attitudes: A Situation Specific Variable

Bandura (1977) has noted that a person's sense of efficacy varies from one situation to another. One may feel quite competent at computer programming but utterly incompetent at interpreting poetry or carrying on lively dinnertable conversation. Teachers in our study made similar observations. They reported that their sense of competence was influenced by what they were being asked to do and, more specificially, by the conditions under which they were expected to work. Some teachers felt more able to teach high achieving students than low achieving students. Some felt they taught one subject quite well and another subject rather badly.

Teachers also reported general (what we call 'ecological') threats to their ability to teach and their sense of professional competence. We asked teachers to describe their work and to discuss the conditions that most helped or hindered their teaching. They reported that their sense of competence was threatened by one or more of seven factors, each of which we discuss below.

Seven Ecological Threats to Teacher Efficacy

(1) Excessive Role Demands.
Teachers mentioned that they felt overwhelmed by the sheer quantity of their workload and consequently were unable to perform effectively. One teacher explained:

> My objection is that I'm spread so thin. I can't do a good job. I've been about a C- teacher [this year], and I'm better than that. I'm not in a situation where I can succeed, and everybody likes to succeed. I can't do a good job. I not only [have to teach] different grade levels, I'm in four different classrooms. That really hurts. Unless you've taught, you don't understand how much you can do in those five minutes between classes [if] you don't have to run [to another classroom when the bell rings].

Another teacher explained that the amount of work he had to do was discouraging:

> I've gotten to the point where I've stopped making the superhuman effort. I still make the extra effort. I used to take a lot of work home with me, work nights and weekends, and I don't do that anymore. How much can you take? How long can you take it? You just reach the point where you've got other needs, and you have to meet them. And that's the problem that all teachers have.

Class size was a major contributor to teachers' perceptions that they were not as effective as they wanted to be and thought they were capable of being. One teacher said:

> I have a lot less learning going on [in my larger classes] than in my smaller classes, the larger being around 30, and the smaller being around 20.

A remedial reading teacher explained that in a large group she couldn't 'have much effect' on individual students. Another teacher contended that classes of '25 students and no more' would help teachers 'survive.'

Glass and Smith (1979) concluded from their meta-analysis of class size research that there is a relationship between the number of pupils in a class and student achievement. Although their research indicated that significant effects were not usually evident until class size decreased to approximately 15 students, the teachers we interviewed perceived positive benefits from more modest reductions. They believed they could get more done in smaller classes because they would have more control over their pupils and a more manageable workload.

Confrontations with students who were difficult to control diminished teachers' sense of efficacy. A first-year teacher described how the classroom environment deteriorated when she lost control of her students:

> God, the abuse you had to put up with. The first thing that happens [when I am challenged by students] is that I get a killing headache. I begin to feel physically bad. And then [I] kind of want to get back at them. That's especially true just before vacation time. I'll find myself almost going down to their level. Rather than sending them out or telling them that this has to stop, I'll come back at them. And that's when it gets bad. You get physically exhausted and you say, 'I'm not going to let you do this to me anymore,' and you try and get back at them. And that's a mistake because things just get worse. They get defensive and they come back at you again. It's a vicious circle.

(2) Inadequate Salaries and Low Status
Teachers might be able to bear the burden of large classes, excessive expectations, and difficult students if they felt that they received fair remuneration and respect for their efforts, but they receive neither, and many spoke with bitterness about it:

> Teachers are not recognized the way they should be. I feel that with my ability in mathematics I could have easily become an engineer, any kind of scientist, a medical doctor, anything like that. I'm not sure I'd necessarily have been happier doing that, but I would have had more recognition in society. I would have had more financial rewards.

Another teacher asserted:

> I'm getting out of teaching. It's not so much that I don't like teaching. It's because I'm not making any money. I think I do too many things too well to sit around here and make ten or twelve thousand dollars a year. It's the money. It's a real problem. I think we're just above the poverty level right now. We're just not doing well at all.

Webb (1983) explained that the problem of low pay goes beyond economics and strikes at the heart of teachers' professional self-esteem:

> Teachers come to their work with aspirations of vertical mobility, but today they find little opportunity for advancement in their chosen

profession. They come with the hope that they will earn an adequate income, but they find that their salaries are not keeping pace with inflation and that the pay of many blue-collar workers equals or exceeds their own. They come with the expectation that white-collar work will afford them respectably high status in the community, but they find that their prestige is damaged by the decline of public confidence in education. It would appear that teachers are suffering what C. Wright Mills [1959, pp. 254– 259] once called 'status panic.' Such anxiety is damaging to their professional self-esteem and has diminished their commitment to education (pp. 41–42).

(3) Lack of Recognition and Professional Isolation
Teachers are further demoralised by lack of recognition and support from their administrators and colleagues. One discouraged teacher admitted:

> I think this year I have suffered from what they call 'teacher burnout'. There is very, very little recognition here. Even a dog needs to be patted on the head, but we don't get that here. It makes you question whether it's worth it.

Another teacher said:

> My general complaint is how quickly administrators forget what it's actually like to be working in classrooms. They forget some of the problems and frustrating times that you go through. They forget that you need some support and understanding, and it's very seldom that you have someone who's genuinely interested [in what you're doing] and willing to lend you an ear and listen to your problems.

The isolation of teachers described by Lortie (1975) continues to be the norm in the schools we studied. One teacher described her need for collegial support:

> Anybody's input would [have been] a help. If they would just share some of the things they have tried. But you know, teachers get hold of a good idea and instead of sharing it, they hoard it. A lot of teachers are that way. They get some material and hoard it and won't let you see it. But I need some ideas and materials. I'm dying for information.

Another teacher described feeling abandoned by her colleagues and supervisor:

> At the beginning of the school year I was faced with no books, no materials and a class to teach. I essentially received no help from the people I thought should have helped. I walked in and [was told], here, you're teaching this.

(4) Uncertainty
Isolation from peers deprives teachers of the opportunity to see others at work and develop a shared technical culture (Dreeben,

1970; Lortie, 1975). An apparent absence of professionally-sanc-
tioned goals and the paucity of scientifically-verified instructional
techniques force teachers to make their own classroom decisions and
ultimately to calculate their own professional competence. Yet
teaching provides few day to day (or year to year) assurances that
one's decisions have been wise and effective and that students are
making progress academically, socially, or psychologically. As a
consequence, teachers are perpetually vulnerable to self-doubt. The
teachers we interviewed expressed their uncertainties in many ways:

> I don't know that what I'm teaching will make any difference. [Teaching
> the basic skills] doesn't do my students a whole lot of good. It makes me
> sad to see some of my students leave. I think, 'Oh, boy, what's going to
> happen to you?' I feel they need the basics. But I wish I had something else
> to offer them. The problem is that we're not teaching them anything they
> can use later on.

A first-year teacher contemplated leaving the profession because, as
she put it,

> I don't think I've done a great deal of good. When they had to take a test
> [at the end of the semester] they didn't do much better than they did at the
> beginning. That was when it really hit me. I tried to give a review assign-
> ment that would get them ready for the semester test. But they acted as if
> they had never seen the material before. And I just sat there and thought,
> 'There has got to be a better way to teach.'

We asked an enrichment teacher how he could tell if he had met his
objectives at the end of the year. He shook his head slowly and
answered, 'I don't know. I really don't. In fact, I really don't know.
I suppose I use my own subjective judgment.'
  Teachers usually hold at bay their doubts about their competence,
but they cannot completely push them from their minds. They find it
difficult to convince themselves and their several audiences that, in
fact, they are as competent as they think they can and should be.
Questions that can never be conclusively answered keep returning.
Why did so many students fail the mid-term exam? Am I doing
enough? Do I know enough? Should I be teaching in another way?
How can I be sure that students are learning, and, if they are, how
can I be sure that what they are learning will help them later on? Such
questions are worrisome and make teaching an uncertain profession.
If uncertainty becomes too pronounced, teaching becomes unre-
warding, and teachers' efficacy attitudes plummet.

(5) A Sense of Powerlessness
Teachers were frustrated because they were unable to influence
important decisions that affected their work. For example, one

teacher explained that the inability to influence decision making had a detrimental impact on her sense of efficacy:

> Sometimes I think we're not treated very professionally. I mean all the teachers. I might be asked to give my opinion, but it really doesn't matter, and I know it doesn't. So it's hard not to say, 'Well, why bother.' So issues that are very important, like teaching assignments, are messed up and that makes a difference. People are assigned all kinds of classes, and it makes a difference in how effective you are and how much you can get done.

(6) Alienation

At least for some teachers, the combination of excessive demands, inadequate salary and status panic, lack of recognition and support, uncertainty, and powerlessness engendered attitudes of quiet conformity and unreflective acceptance of the status quo. In their eagerness to find security in an uncertain profession, many teachers took care not to rock the boat or offend colleagues, parents, or supervisors. Minds so set on survival were unlikely to entertain suggestions for change or to instigate reforms. Thus, when we asked teachers to suggest changes that might improve their morale and classroom performance, many were stymied by the question. When pushed, they suggested that teachers should work harder and that administrators should 'get tough with incompetent faculty members.' No teacher suggested changes in the organisational structure of the school, and only a few recommended that teachers work together to solve common problems.

Though dissatisfied with teaching, many of the teachers we interviewed traced the causes of their dissatisfaction to the individual failures of 'dumb students,' 'incompetent teaching,' 'ineffective administration,' and flaws in themselves. Few teachers attributed their dissatisfaction to structural problems within the school itself. They were unable to achieve what Mills (1959) called a 'lucid summation of what is going on in the world and what may be happening within themselves' (p. 5). They had reified what they called 'the system' and did not see it to be within their power (individually or collectively) to fully comprehend, let alone change, that system. As the German sociologist Arnold Gehlen (1980) has pointed out, 'reified . . . operations . . . resist criticism and are immune to objections' (p. 154). Within reified systems, most criticism is self-criticism or is leveled at specified functionaries or policies. There is no Promethean vision that change is possible, but only a creeping resignation that, in the end, 'the system' will triumph over the human spirit.

A teacher described her feelings of resignation:

> I still have the capacity for [effective teaching]. But in some instances, I'm

not sure that I care. But other times, I care a great deal. Sometimes I feel, what's the use? Teaching can be [a] very frustrating, very frustrating experience. I'm not going to mince words about it. That's the way I feel. I feel threatened too.

Yet even as this teacher gave herself over to the system, she criticised younger teachers who are going through the same process:

It bothers me that a lot of teachers come into . . . the system and after a short while are just as jaded as the rest of us. I'd think that at least their enthusiasm would stick with them for a good three or four years. But it doesn't.

The conditions of teaching promote the loss of a meaningful relationship with one's work – a form of alienation that social psychologists have called 'self-estrangement.' Blauner (1964) explained, 'When an individual lacks control over the work process and a sense of purposeful connection to the work enterprise, he may experience a kind of depersonalised detachment rather than an immediate involvement in the job task' (p. 27).

Many of the teachers we interviewed confessed sadly that teaching provided them with only a weak sense of accomplishment. They did not feel fulfilled through their work and were frustrated because teaching did not tap their potential. Blauner (1964) described how the loss of connection with one's work reinforces a negative professional self image:

Self-estranging work compounds and intensifies [the] problem of negative occupational identity. When work provides opportunities for control, creativity, and challenge – when in a word, it is self-expressive and enhances an individual's unique potentialities – then it contributes to the worker's sense of self-respect and dignity and at least partially overcomes the stigma of low status. Alienated work – without control, freedom, or responsibility – on the other hand, simply confirms and deepens the feeling that societal estimates of low status and little worth are valid (p. 31).

(7) The Decline in Teacher Morale
The morale of teachers is declining at an alarming rate. In a national survey of teachers (NEA, 1982), only half of the respondents indicated that they definitely planned to stay in teaching until retirement. Twenty-seven percent of teachers surveyed by the Metropolitan Life Insurance Company (1985) said it was likely that they would leave their profession within the next five years (p. 26). The reasons they gave for their dissatisfaction centered on the conditions of their work. Sixty-two percent said low pay was a major reason for considering another occupation. Forty-one percent identified excessive paperwork, long working hours, and overcrowded classrooms as

primary causes of dissatisfaction (pp. 3–5). Thirty-four percent
said that they experienced 'great stress' at least once a week; twenty
percent experienced great stress 'several days a week;' and another
sixteen percent experienced great stress 'nearly every day' (p. 34).
The degree of teacher dissatisfaction was directly related to the
inadequacy of the work environment, the frequency of felt stress,
the hours teachers worked, and the relative poverty of the school
district (pp. 51–52).

Teacher dissatisfaction and attrition, high levels of stress and
eventual 'burnout', and declining efficacy attitudes are indications
that the teaching profession is in a state of crisis. Drawn to teaching
because they saw it as an exalted profession (Doda, 1982), many
educators have come instead to view teaching as a precarious
occupation. A sixth-grade teacher told us:

> I haven't handled [stress] too well. I've been breaking into perspiration
> lately [and] I think it's nerves. Yesterday, I told you I felt like I [was suff-
> ering] from the D. T.'s. I was really trembling and that, I know, [is caused
> by] stress. Unfortunately, I want students to learn, and I can't cope with
> the idea that they don't want to learn.

The Individualisation of Reform

What can be done to help teachers who suffer from a sense of
occupational futility? How we answer that question depends on
where we think the problem is located. The staff-development and
teacher-burnout literature often locates the problem of teacher stress
where its symptoms are most evident, in individual teachers. Thus
remedies are designed to train 'stress-prone' professionals to cope
with the pressures of school life, not to make teachers' work less
stressful. One expert (Cedoline, 1982) acknowledged that negative
work settings contribute to job stress, but he went on to describe
burned-out professionals as cynical, negative, inflexible, resistant to
change, subtly paranoid, helpless, emotionally fatigued, dehum-
anised, non-empathic, irritable, game-playing, accident-prone individuals who have not learned to cope adequately with realities of
everyday life. He suggested that administrators help teachers 'learn
to cope with stress' (p. 164) by offering programs in meditation,
progressive relaxation, thought-intrusion exercises, focused brea-
thing, desensitisation, yoga, biofeedback, and more. He advised
teachers to learn to control their griping, be more effective discipl-
inarians, improve their communication skills, develop attitudes of
'detached concern' for students, and 'look for something pleasant
in their encounters with students, colleagues, and administrators'
(p. 151).

At a time when so many educators suffer from the effects of teaching, it is difficult to oppose programs that may bring some relief, no matter how superficial it may be. Yet, our interviews with teachers suggest that their dissatisfactions are not often caused by their own 'maladaptive responses' to their work, but rather by the circumstances in which they are expected to perform their duties. The sheer number of teachers who report that they are unhappy with their work suggests that 'burnout' is a structural rather than a personal problem (see Mills, 1963). If we focus remedies for teacher 'burnout' on the behavior of individual teachers, we not only mistake a symptom for a cause, but we subtly shift the responsibility for 'burnout' from a 'maladaptive' school system to its victims.

The individualisation of issues in education blinds professionals to the system in which they work and invites them to see school problems as a series of unconnected case studies. Each case has its own story, but these tales are never woven together into a larger plot with explanatory power. Problems are defined in terms of the individuals who express them, and those individuals are encouraged to take responsibility for solving their own troubles. This is a cruel hoax for three reasons: (1) Individualised reforms have little or no effect on organisational problems and social issues; (2) they erroneously trace the causes of organisational and social problems to victims of those problems; and (3) they divert attention from teachers' shared experiences and an analysis of their work environment. Though the stated goal of individualised reform is always to improve the quality of schools by improving teachers, the result of such reform at best is to maintain the status quo and, at worst, to further demoralise the teaching profession.

Teachers' Sense of Efficacy and the Individualisation of Reform

In a qualitative study of basic-skills, high school classrooms, Ashton and Webb (1986) found significant and positive correlations between teachers' sense of efficacy[1], teacher behavior[2], and student achievement[3]. Such findings are grist for the mill of the individualisers of educational reform. If they ignore the fact that correlations do not prove causality, 'individualisers' can make the claim that student achievement will be raised if teachers go through an in-service programme of motivational training. The aim of such training would not be to help teachers analyse the conditions that erode their motivation and alienate them from their profession. Instead, teachers would be asked to reflect on their own 'shortcomings' and to take responsibility for improving their own 'bad attitudes'. When such programs fail, as they inevitably will, the same logic that tempted the 'individualisers' to call for motivational training will tempt them to blame the failure of that training on the recalcitrance of teachers rather than on the futility of their own plan.

Ecological Reform

Our interviews with teachers and observations in their classrooms suggested that the logic of individualised reform is flawed at its root. Teachers' efficacy attitudes are not simply mistaken ideas to be corrected. Rather, we agree with Goodlad's (1984) contention that greater attention must be paid to the quality of work life within the school. It is neither fair nor prudent to expect educators to alter their negative attitudes toward teaching without attending to the workplace circumstances that fostered those attitudes.

An alternative to the individualisation of reform and the engineering mentality it implies (Callahan, 1962; Tesconi and Morris, 1972) is ecological reform designed to democratise the workplace. The aim of ecological reform is to transform schools so that they no longer alienate teachers, administrators, and students. It is to free the intelligence of those who work in schools so that they might better analyse school problems, invent solutions, and improve the quality of education. Rather than 'de-skilling' teachers (Apple, 1981) by lessening their autonomy and subjecting them to prepackaged solutions to 'individualised' problems, the goal of ecological reform is to empower teachers to take greater control of, and responsibility for, their professional lives. John Dewey (1950) observed in 1903 that effective schools are those that provide opportunities for the 'free and full play of vigour and intelligence' (p. 65). Such schools permit everyone, 'from the first grade teacher to the principal of the high school some share in the exercise of educational power' (p. 65).

An ecological approach to the problem of low-efficacy attitudes would begin by addressing the causes of teacher dissatisfaction and alienation. The elements of satisfying and productive work are not mysterious. We are likely to be satisfied in our work when we value what we do, when it challenges and extends us, when we do it well, and when we have ample evidence confirming our success. In order for our work to be fulfilling, significant others on the job and in the community must appreciate the importance of our task and acknowledge the quality of our performance. We must have opportunities to take part in decisions that affect our work lives and to help solve work-related problems. We must understand clearly how our efforts contribute to the mission of the institution for which we work.

(Goodlad, 1984; Herzberg, Mauser, Paterson, and Capwell, 1975; Locke, 1976; Maslach, 1976; Rawls, 1971; Rush, Hershauer and Wright, 1976.)

Teachers become alienated because, at almost every level, they are deprived of the knowledge necessary to sustain job satisfaction and professional self-respect. Ecological reform will bring teachers into new relationships with their work and with their colleagues. Such relationships cannot be mandated by management fiat or engineered by outside consultants; they must be fashioned by all members of the school community. As Dewey (1950) put it:

> The remedy [for our educational ills] is not to have . . . expert[s] dictating educational methods . . . to a body of passive, recipient teachers, but the adoption of intellectual initiative, discussion, and decision throughout the entire school corps. The remedy . . . is an appeal to a more thorough-going democracy (p. 65).

Rather than tighten management controls, ecological reform looks for ways to liberate teachers' problem solving capacities.

It will surprise no one that ecological reform is difficult. Norbert Weiner (1954) pointed out thirty years ago that 'It is easier to set in motion [institutions] in which human beings [use only] a minor part of their capacities . . . rather than create a world in which human beings fully develop' (p. 524). The logic of ecological reform is deeply rooted in the pragmatic tradition. It is now finding support among critical theorists, for example, Stanley Aronowitz and Henry Giroux (1985), who contend:

> Teachers must take active responsibility for raising serious questions about what they teach, how they teach it, and what the larger goals are for which they are striving. This means they must take a responsible role in shaping the purposes and conditions of schooling (p. 31).

Like Dewey, however, Aronowitz and Giroux understand that teachers cannot simply take responsibility as one might pluck an apple from a tree. In most schools, responsibility is not there for the taking. Responsibility is not a label we give to an act of will; it is the name given to a specific kind of relationship individuals have within their social and intellectual environment. Thus teachers cannot become responsible and act as intelligent professionals until and unless a democratic work environment allows them to develop these skills.

Democracy means a sharing of power and purpose. It entails, as Dewey (1950) said, 'the emancipation of the mind . . . to do its work' (p. 62). Dewey explained the role the work environment plays in helping teachers develop intellectual skill and social responsibility:

Only by sharing in some responsible task does there come a fitness to share in it. The argument that we must wait until men and women are fully ready to assume intellectual and social responsibilities would have defeated every step in the democratic direction that has ever been taken (p. 67).

A dependence on external authority disempowers teachers and perpetuates the very deficits that are used by administrators to legitimate a centralisation of power and justify what Dewey called their 'regime of authority' (p. 67).

Education will not free itself from the 'regime of authority' or the individualisation of reform until greater attention is paid to the interactional nature of individual and organisational development. This is the promise of ecological reform. It provides an opportunity for teachers to define school problems, design strategies of inquiry, pool expertise and intelligence, develop community and responsibility, and decide upon a common course of action. As they take a greater role in school decisions, teachers fashion small reforms that encourage still greater participation. As individuals are empowered and schools are improved, opportunities for further improvements present themselves.

A growing body of literature exists that relates how ecological reforms and the democratisation of the workplace have been accomplished in industry (Carnoy and Shearer, 1980; Cooley, 1980; Emery and Thorsrud, 1976; Emery and Trist, 1973; Herbst, 1974, 1976; Maccoby, 1979; Zwerdling, 1978). Similar work is being developed in education (Joyce, Hersh, and McKibbin, 1983; Stenhouse, 1975; Wirth, 1983). Ecological reform is at once modest and ambitious. The process begins by focusing on small, manageable problems that concern teachers and moves by gradual steps toward the democratisation of teachers' work lives. The aim is to transform schools in to self-analysing, self-reforming institutions.

We are not so naive to believe that ecological reform will gain instant popularity, and that probably is just as well. There is much to be learned about democratising the workplace and improving the conditions of teaching. Researchers must carefully study both the reform process and its attendant outcomes (Bronfenbrenner, 1976; Schaefer, 1967). As Wirth (1983) noted:

It would be a salutary exercise in honesty and humility to admit we don't know many of the answers and to permit groups of teachers to design a variety of programs to which they are professionally committed. Then study them in collaboration with researchers to see what can be learned and reported . . . (p. 124).

No greater problem faces education today than the demoralisation of its professional workforce. Most teachers enter the profession with great expectations and a high sense of efficacy. Our research indicates that the experience of teaching lowers the expectations teachers have for themselves and their students. Not all teachers entirely lose faith in their ability to teach, or their students' ability to learn, or in the efficacy of public schooling. However, all teachers must struggle against environmental forces that work to alienate them. No quick fix will solve the problems teachers face today. Some of those problems, such as low pay and declining status, lie outside teachers' collective control. However, other problems (isolation, uncertainty, powerlessness, alienation, low motivation, and an eroding sense-of-efficacy) can be addressed through collective work. Ecological reform is one way to begin that work.

Conclusion

In a recent article on staff development, Goodlad (1983) pointed out that schools with more satisfied teachers differed from schools with less satisfied teachers in the conditions of teaching, especially in the collegial relationships among teachers and administrators. The schools did not differ in instructional strategies. Goodlad concluded that teachers' instructional strategies are highly resistant to change and tackling this sensitive area of teacher autonomy, before addressing the more pressing problems of the conditions of teaching, will result in 'unmitigated disaster' (p. 10). Our efficacy research supports Goodlad's conclusion and emphasises the urgency of the need to address the deteriorating conditions of teaching, not by focusing on changing individual teachers, but rather by fostering efficacy attitudes through democratising the workplace.

Notes

1   As measured by two Likert scale items borrowed from the Rand studies (Armor *et al.*, 1976; Berman *et al.*, 1977).
2   As measured by the Florida Climate and Control System, developed by Robert and Ruth Soar (in Coker, Medley, and Soar, 1984) and the Teacher Practices Observational Record (Brown, 1968).
3   As measured by scores on appropriate portions of the Metropolitan – Achievement Tests ($r = .78, < .003$ in basic skills mathematics classes, and $r = .83, < .02$ in basic skills communication classes).

References

Apple, M. (1981). 'Curriculum Form and the Logic of Technical Control.' *Economic and Industrial Democracy*, 2 (3).

Aronowitz, S., Giroux, H. (1985). *Education Under Siege: The Conservative, Liberal and Radical Debate Over Schooling*. Amherst, MA: Bergin & Garvey Publishers.

Ashton, P.T., Webb, R.B., & Doda, N. (1983). *A Study of Teachers' Sense of Efficacy*. (Contract No. 400-79-0075). Washington, DC: National Institute of Education.

Ashton, P.T. & Webb, R.B. (1986). *Making A Difference: Teachers' Sense of Efficacy and Student Achievement*. New York: Longman, Paperback edition.

Armor, D., Conry-Oseguera, P., Cox, M., King, N., McDonnell, L., Pascal, A., Pauly, E., & Zellman, G. (1976). *Analysis of the School Preferred Reading Program in Selected Los Angeles Minority Schools*. (Report No. R-2007-LAUD). Santa Monica, CA: The Rand Corporation. (ERIC Document Reproduction Service No. ED 130 243).

Bandura, A. (1977). 'Self-efficacy: Toward a Unifying Theory of Behavior Change.' *Psychological Review*, 84, 191–215.

Berman, P., McLaughlin, M., Bass, G., Pauly, E., & Zellman, G. (1977). *Federal Programs Supporting Educational Change*. Vol. 7: *Factors Affecting Implementation and Continuation*. Santa Monica, CA: The Rand Corporation. (ERIC Document Reproduction Service No. ED 140 432).

Blauner, R. (1964). *Alienation and Freedom*. Chicago: University of Chicago Press.

Bronfenbrenner, U. (1976). The Experimental Ecology of Education. *Educational Researcher*, 5, 5–15.

Brown, B.B. (1968) *The Experimental Mind in Education*. New York: Harper & Row.

Callahan, R. (1962). *Education and the Cult of Efficiency*. Chicago: The University of Chicago Press.

Carnoy, M., & Shearer, D. (1980). *Economic Democracy: The Challenge of the 1980s*. New York: M.E. Sharpe.

Cedoline, A. (1982). *Job Burnout in Public Education: Symptoms, Causes, and Survival Skills*. New York: Teachers College Press.

Cooley, M. (1981). *Architect or Bee*? Boston: South End Press.

Dewey, J. (1950). *Education Today*, Westport, CT: Greenwood Press Publishers.

Doda, N. (March, 1982). *Middle School Organization and Teacher World View*. Paper presented at the meeting of the American Educational Research Association, New York.

Dreeben, R. (1970). *The Nature of Teaching*. Glenview, IL: Scott, Foresman.

Dunkin, M. J., & Biddle, B. J. (1974). *The Study of Teaching*. New York: Holt: Rinehart & Winston.

Emery, F., & Thorsrud, E. (1976). *Democracy at Work*. Leiden: Martinus Nijhoff Social Sciences Division.

Emery, R., & Trist, F. (1973). *Towards a Social Ecology*. New York: Plenum/Rosetta.

Freire, P. (1973). *Education for Critical Consciousness*. New York: The Seabury Press.

Gehlen, A. (1980). *Man in an Age of Technology*. New York: Columbia University Press.

Getzels, J.W., & Jackson, P.W. (1963). 'The Teacher's Personality and Characteristics'. In N.L. Gage (Ed.) *Handbook of Research on Teaching* (pp. 506–582). Chicago: Rand McNally.

Gibson, S., & Dembo, M. (1984). Teacher Efficacy: A Construct Validation. *Journal of Educational Psychology. 76* (4), 569–582.

Glass, G., & Smith, M. (1979). 'Meta-analysis of Research on Class Size and Achievement.' *Educational Evaluation and Policy Analysis, 1* (1), 2–16.

Glickman, C., & Tamashiro, R. (1982). 'A Comparison of First-year, Fifth-year, and Former Teachers on Efficacy, Ego Development, and Problem Solving. *Psychology in the Schools, 19*, 558–552.

Goodlad, J. (1983). 'The School as Workplace. In G. A. Griffin (Ed.) *Staff development. The eighty-second yearbook of the National Society for the Study of Education. Part II*. Chicago: The University of Chicago Press.

Goodlad, J. (1984). *A Place Called School*. New York: McGraw-Hill.

Herbst, P. (1974). *Socio-technical Design*. London: Tavistock.

Herbst, P. (1976). *Alternatives to Hierarchies*. Leiden: Martinus Nijhoff Social Sciences Division.

Herzberg, F., Mauser, B., Peterson, R., & Capwell, D. (1957). *Job attitudes: Review of Research and Opinion*. Pittsburgh: Psychology Service.

Jackson, P.W. (1968). *Life in Classrooms*. New York: Holt. Rinehart, & Winston.

Joyce, B.R., Hersh, R. H., & McKibbin, M. (1983). *The Structure of School Improvement*. New York: Longman.

Locke, E. (1976). 'The Nature and Causes of Job Satisfaction.' In M. Dunnette (Ed.), *Handbook of Industrial and Organizational Psychology*. Chicago: Rand McNally.

Lortie, D.C. (1975). *Schoolteacher: A Sociological Study*. Chicago: University of Chicago Press.

Maccoby, M. (1979). *What is productivity*? Cambridge: Harvard Project on Technology, Work, and Character.

McGuire, W. (1979). 'Teacher Burnout.' *Today's Education, 68*, 5.

Maslach, C. (1976). 'Burned-out.' *Human Behavior, 5*, 16–22.

Medley, D., Coker, H., and Soar, R. S. (1984) *Measurement-based Evaluation of Teacher Performance: An Empirical Approach*. New York: Longman.

Metropolitan Life (1985). *The American Teacher 1985: Strengthening The Profession*. Metropolitan Life and Affiliated Companies.

Mills, C.W. (1959). *White-Collar: The American Middle Class*. New York: Oxford University Press.

Mills, C.W. (1963). 'The Big City: Private Troubles and Public Issues.' In I.L. Horowitz (Ed.), *Power, Politics and People*. New York: Oxford University Press.

National Education Association (1982) *Status of the American Public School Teacher: 1980—81*. Washington, DC: National Education Association Research Division.

Rawls, J. (1971). *A Theory of Justice*. Cambridge, MA: Harvard University Press.

Ruch, W., Hershauer, J., & Wright, R. (1976). 'Toward Solving the Productivity Puzzle: Workers Correlates to Performance.' *Human Resource Management, 15*, 2—6.

Schaefer, R. (1967). *The School as a Center of Inquiry*. New York: Harper & Row.

Schutz, A. (1971). *Collected papers, Vol. 1: The Problem of Social Reality*. (M. Natanson Ed.). The Hague: Martinus Nijhoff.

Spencer, D. A. (1984). 'The Home and School Lives of Women Teachers: Implications for Staff Development.' *The Elementary School Journal, 84* (3), 299—314.

Spradley, J. (1980). *The Ethnographic Interview*. New York: Holt, Rinehart, & Winston.

Stenhouse, L.A. (1975). *An Introduction to Curriculum Research and Development*. London: Heinemann Educational Books.

Tesconi, C. A. Jr., & Morris, V.C. (1972). *The Anti-man Culture: Bureau-Technocracy and the Schools*. Urbana, IL: University of Illinois Press.

Webb, R. B. (1983). 'Teacher Status Panic: Moving up the Down Escalator.' *Journal of Thought, 18* (4), 39—48.

Weiner, R. (1954). *The Human Use of Human Beings*. New York: Doubleday.

Writh, A.G. (1983). *Productive Work — in Industry and Schools: Becoming Person Again*. New York: University Press of American.

Wise, A. (1979). *Legislated Learning: The Bureaucratization of the American Classroom*. Berkeley, CA: University of California Press.

Zwerdling, D. (1978). *Democracy at Work*. Washington, DC: Association for Management.

CHAPTER THREE

Burntout or Beached: Weeding Women Out of Woman's True Profession

Sara Freedman

Between 1979 and 1983, hundreds of thousands of teachers were laid off from the public schools of the United States of America. In 1981, the state of Massachusetts alone lost 8000 teachers. (*Boston Globe*, November 21, 1982) Cities such as Boston, Massachusetts and Madison, Wisconsin laid off teachers with experience of up to 12 years in their school systems. The cuts in the teaching force were accompanied by other blows to public school systems, particularly but not exclusively to those serving the poor. Thousands of school buildings were closed – as though to insure that there would be no possibility of recalling the laid off teachers because no school would remain in which they could teach. The buildings they and their students formerly had occupied were quickly converted to private condominiums, housing for the elderly, or office parks. Compensatory educational programmes, enrichment activities, transportation for students, budgets for school supplies, curriculum innovation, in-service training, and reductions in class size were all halted or severely limited.

How did this come about? And how did it happen so suddenly, or so it seemed to the teachers who were left like beached fish gasping upon the shores of a dried up pool of resources? This paper will examine how the public, and more importantly many teachers themselves, came to accept these lay-offs, viewing them as a chance to renew the teaching profession and salvage the lives of individual teachers. The paper will first compare the situation faced by teachers to other public servants faced with massive layoffs. It will then trace the ideological campaign, symbolised by the creation of the psychological category of 'burnout', that supported the lay-offs and its effects on teachers' morale. The paper will conclude with a critique of current policy initiatives now being considered and/or enacted to restructure teaching.

At the time of the cuts, the reasons usually cited were a combination of fiscal and ideological factors, part of a general taxpayers' revolt. On the federal level, the Reagan administration upon its inauguration immediately retreated from the commitment of the national government to promote social welfare policies, particularly in the field of education. Even before he was elected, Candidate Reagan had vowed to close down the Department of Education, which had been established as a separate level cabinet post in the last years of the Carter administration. Although Reagan retreated from that position, he was successful in excising or greatly reducing federal education funds and programmes which state and local governments had come to rely on as the motor force and pump primer for many new programmes and capital improvements over the past 20 years.

On the local level, explanations can be sought in the system of raising funds for municipal services. These services, at the minimum, usually include maintaining a city or town's road system, policing its neighborhoods, putting out its fires, collecting the trash, maintaining its water supply and sewerage system, and educating its children. Money for these services comes from local property taxes, which have risen dramatically over the past decade. The dependence on property taxes to raise a town's revenues was seen as crushing the middle class, who are taxed heavily on the only toehold they have in the capitalist world – the family home. Laws like *Proposition 2½* which was passed in Massachusetts placed a cap on the percentage of the assessed value of a town's property that could be used to calculate an individual homeowner's tax. Since most towns had levied taxes considerably greater than 2½ percent, the result was an immediate and severe loss in municipal revenues, particularly in the poorer communities.

Within weeks of the 'taxpayers' revolt' in Massachusetts heavy cuts in all public services were announced. Police, firefighters, and teachers all lost significant numbers of their workforce. When the public recognised how drastic the cuts would be, many citizens took action. They camped out in police and fire stations, and petitioned city hall, protesting the consequences of a tax cut they recently had approved enthusiastically.

Politicians responded to these demonstrations and restored many of the cuts they had made. Police returned to their beats and firefighters again risked their lives in sufficient numbers to quell public protests. The one group of employees who by and large were not rehired were teachers – particularly elementary school teachers who had suffered the deepest cuts. Where there had been an immediate sense of deprivation at the thought of reductions in the ranks of police and firefighters, no such movement arose when hundreds of thousands of teachers cleared out their desks and left years of experience behind them. No group of parents or students stood at the school house door, vowing to occupy a school in order to keep it open and fully staffed. Although fears of a breakdown in public safety had driven many citizens to demand the return of the police and firefighters, the breakdown in the care and attention of children did not seem to have a similar, immediate impact on the 'public' at large.

The media often cited 'declining enrollment' for the pronounced difference in the public's attitude toward the closing of police stations versus schools. Fewer pupils lined up each year to enter schools. The baby boom was over, and not reproducing itself nearly as avidly as their own parents had done. A great number of the taxpayers who paid the property taxes no longer shared their homes with children. They were far more concerned with rising health costs and retirement security.

But curiously, it was not only the 'empty nesters' that seemed indifferent to an almost overnight decimation of the teaching workforce, but many of the parents of the children now attending public schools appeared to display a similar acquiesence, if not indifference to the cuts. These cuts were absorbed primarily by women, as are most daily and long-term crises that affect children. To call attention to their own needs as workers would be to break the only legitimate claim teachers have to public support – the belief that teachers teach best when they sacrifice most – that the 'dedicated' teacher is modelled after the ideal mother/wife, who sacrifices her own interests to support the interests of those bound to her by duty and love. She does this best with a minimum of public attention and acclaim. Indeed the better the teacher, the more she is able to keep her own concerns, and those dependent upon her, 'private.'

Teachers – both those surviving the cuts and those laid off felt invisible – best kept behind closed doors and therefore not soon missed when the work they did was no longer performed.

Teaching is such a compartmentalised kind of thing. You are in your room and you close the door and you sort of don't mingle with the rest of the school community. There are some things about it, if things aren't going too well, you feel terribly alone. Terribly responsible for every single thing that goes on. There is fairly limited contact professionally with your peers and, of course, it's true for the children too. We're pretty much confined in here, we go to the music room, we go to the cafeteria, we go to recess but the contact is pretty limited. When you read newspaper articles about education, you feel like a ghost really. You feel like you're not really there. That people aren't seeing you. I think a lot of my

colleagues share this feeling of alienation – that you feel you don't belong, that somehow you're not there, everything you do is for nothing.
(Freedman, 1982)

And while teachers were frightened and depressed at the thought of losing their jobs, many who themselves were facing lay-offs seemed to embrace the prospect of leaving teaching.

When I was a kid in the fifties I went to a strict, traditional school. The teachers were thirty and forty year veterans. They never varied from plans written many years ago. In September the same pictures were posted on the blackboard. The construction paper borders were replaced each year but the paper faced early in November and was a dull sheen by March. I loved those teachers. They conformed to many of the stereotypes of long-time women schoolmarms – stern, swift in justice, unimaginative, inflexible, sure of their methods. They praised the docile, hard-working, quick-to-grasp pupil and were alternately punishing or neglectful of the silent majority. The wicked were quickly subdued.

In fifth grade a spate of male teachers arrived, returning GI's straight out of college, who had a fertile field in the burgeoning school industry. They were different – young, creative, with lots of energy. They introduced SCIENCE!, giant paper-mache animals, and new seating patterns. We all wanted to be in their classrooms. Most of them soon moved to other positions in the quickly expanding system – principal, science co-ordinator, creative arts department. The children were left with the old women teachers – and with a disdain of old women teachers.

When I began teaching ten years ago, I had a clear image of the kind of teacher I wanted to be – Mr. Williams, the fifth grade teacher who had introduced the most daring educational experiments and who worked tirelessly, coming to school on Saturday. And I managed. I worked tirelessly, tried all kinds of experiments, came in on Saturdays. It was exhilarating – for the first few years. But as the years wore on I began to notice that the drive was being replaced by myriad frustrations. Many teachers who arrived with me on the crest of the sixties' wave, felt tethered in place. We became less experimental, angrier, more isolated. In my voice, and face and walk I was watching a metamorphosis. I was turning into my present perception of one of them – those female teachers of long ago who worked year after year in a closed space, each class merging into the next, stale ideas, frayed construction paper.
(Freedman, 1979)

'Burnout' is the term now popular to describe the phenomenon. In the middle seventies, the term began to appear regularly in the popular press and in journals addressed to teachers, as a means of explaining widespread feelings among teachers of inadequacy, listlessness and decreased dedication to teaching. 'Burnout' implies that at some point a finite amount of energy has been consumed. It is understood that the institution will deaden those who work in it if they do not have new infusions of energy from some outside source, preferably from younger teachers who inevitably will face the same pressures.

The coining of the term 'burnout' at the same time that teachers were threatened with the loss of their jobs served to direct the focus of each teacher's growing anger away from a critical analysis of schools as institutions to a preoccupation with her own failure. Curiously the preoccupation in describing teachers as burned out or deadwood became a way of using these terms of deviance to represent the 'true identity' of all teachers by which every dedicated teacher will eventually be defined. It encompassed even those who hadn't burned out because if 'burnout' is the natural end of a dedicated teacher, those who had managed to survive were seen as callous, self-serving.

The two labels of 'burnout' and 'deadwood' further divided the teaching workforce. Younger teachers or those still with other career options were told they had worked too hard and had therefore 'burned out.' Older teachers were told they weren't working hard enough and had become 'deadwood.' The fact that both were demoralised pointed to similar concerns, but the labels obscured the commonalities.

The teacher could either accept the label of 'burnout' and leave, or retreat even further emotionally and physically. Experts on 'burnout' and teacher effectiveness, by zeroing in on the individual teacher and her classroom to explain education's increasingly documented failures, have chosen repeatedly to scrutinise the most vulnerable member of the school system's hierarchy – the classroom teacher, 87 percent of whom are women on the elementary school level. (NEA 1978) Those teachers are the people least critical of the investigators' findings because they confirm the teacher's own lack of self-esteem. Documentation of teachers' failures without linking individual problems to institutional roadblocks does not spur the teacher to re-dedicate herself to the profession. She was now convinced of her own worthlessness and was sure she would simply continue to fail.

The concept of 'burnout' was further encouraged by the ideology of professionalism which encouraged teachers, and parents, to see teachers as more powerful than they actually were and, therefore, more responsible alone to correct complex societal and institutional dilemmas.

The funny thing is that I'm a good teacher and a good teacher can teach in almost intolerable situations. . . . I see so many not bad teachers, just people who should not be teaching and it's important to me that if I thought I wasn't doing a good job of it, I wasn't helping the kids, I would get out of it right away. I guess the term is 'burned out'. The ideas, the spontaneity wasn't coming. I wasn't feeling fresh or excited when I was coming into the classroom. I guess the term is 'burned out'.

(Freedman, 1982)

Once the teacher was convinced that she had 'burned out' she had admitted that she had used up her inner resources, that she was personally deficient, and that she must leave the occupation for her own good and that of her pupils.

For many of us, the isolation which allowed us to embrace 'burnout' as an explanation for our feelings of dissatisfaction and anger did not come only from the media or lack of public support. It was also based on a model we used in analysing and improving our own school experiences as teachers. This model, influenced by a number of books written in the late 1960s, emphasised the individual contribution by caring teachers whose dedication could significantly alter and improve schools. These books had been an inspiration as we entered teaching and provided a standard by which we had been judging ourselves and our fellow-teachers. Nothing in those books mentioned the powerful influence of the structure of schools on the relationship between the teacher and the child, principal, parent, or specialist.

Several years later, the publication of many articles on teacher 'burnout' reinforced this essentially individualistic point of view. Thus, the teacher literature that we read – the books that had influenced our decisions to enter the profession, and the articles suggesting that we leave – refrained from investigating the areas most painful to many teachers – a growing sense of isolation and alienation from all with whom they came into daily contact: the students, their parents, fellow teachers, and administrators.

The media, the general public, and commissions on 'excellence' now complete the very closed circle of recrimination by agreeing with the teacher's analysis of her failures. Educational problems are defined as an aggregate of disaffected or incapable teachers whose deficiencies are seen as personal rather than as a reflection of the failure of the educational system to grapple with and confront the contradictory demands made of teachers.

In an article in the *Boston Globe* (August 1, 1981) entitled 'Choose the Best Teachers' Peter R. Greer states:

While the national debate rages over public school, it is increasingly clear that our students will continue to suffer if educational leaders cannot find the courage and good sense to keep only the best and qualified teachers in the nation's classroom: teachers who know their subjects, love children, are versatile, and from whom children are able to learn things that matter . . .

Of course teachers who are falling in their responsibilities should be told so, worked with and given opportunities for improvement. But at the time of a reduction in staff, the primary question must be: 'Who is the best teacher?'

Unless we are willing to accept the responsibility for selecting and rewarding only the very best teachers, we can sit back and watch the inevitable destruction of the American system of public-school education and with it, the decline of public support and sympathy.

And now, an array of Presidential commissions and/or blue ribbon commissions-on-excellence have given added force to this kind of analysis. Within the past few years, a number of them have reported their findings on the current state of the American educational system. They have influenced legislatures throughout the country to revamp the public school system. One common stance of all the reports is, again, that the right people are not teaching, and as a consequence, the American educational system has seriously deteriorated. The chief of these reports, titled 'A Nation at Risk', issued by the National Commission on Excellence in Education, perceives a 'rising tide of mediocrity' within education, a tide they believe to be so strong that it has brought America to the shores of economic ruin and decay. The seriousness of the problem is emphasised by the terminology used – apocalyptic and, not incidentally, militaristic.

> If an unfriendly foreign power had attempted to impose on America the mediocre educational performance that exists today, we might well have viewed it as an act of war.

> (NCEE, 1984).

The impression conveyed is that anyone responsible for this decline has committed an act of treason and is part of a fifth column that is destroying America from within. 'We have, in effect, been committing an act of unthinking, unilateral educational disarmament.'

By using terms currently popular in the controversy concerning the arms race, the reports neatly connect those who advocate the position of nuclear disarmament and those who work in schools. It is helpful to remember that in both of these groups women outnumber men. The gender of those targeted for criticism in these reports is never mentioned, but it is naive to ignore the unstated belief – women are undermining America's economic and military strength. The reports thus continue the attacks begun by the New Right on the achievements of individual women and the increased influence of the women's movement as a whole. As we shall see, the solution offered for the deterioriation in education is to remodel teaching, and the goals of teachers, along the lines traditionally employed in male-dominated professions – perhaps in the hope that turning teaching into 'men's work' will stem the flow of this 'rising tide of mediocrity.'

The first question to be asked is, 'Why is the economic crisis of American monopoly capital depicted as primarily the result of what goes on in elementary and high school classrooms?' Norm Fruchter, in an article published in *In These Times* on July 27, 1983 makes the point that 'These reports attack the wrong problems because the reverse the direction of casuality; the economy affects education far more than education affects the economy. To blame schooling for the national economic decline is an entertaining but finally trivial diversion from the knotty structural problems plaguing our schools.'

The commissions on education also divert attention from the connections between an increasingly out-of-work and/or routinised workforce and the structural problems of the American economy and world capitalism in general. The business leaders whose mentality strongly dominates these reports may be convinced that America's serious economic problems cannot possibly be the result of their own mistakes; or intrinsic to capitalism in general. Or perhaps they have simply found a convenient scapegoat. There is no concrete evidence presented in any of these reports that a miraculous rise in test scores of school children across America would in anyway insure the return to America of the post World War II economic miracle and world wide political domination.

The reports chastise the American educational system, singling out parents and teachers for not producing a workforce of sufficient quality to keep the American system competitive. They do not mention, however, that the 'healthier' economies they cite depend on a massive workforce that is unskilled and unorganised, directed by a smaller proportion of highly trained technocrats and personnel and business managers.

The reports' horror at the 'rising tide of mediocrity' thus becomes an argument for changing the pattern of educational funding established in the 1960's. Since that time, compensatory programmes have shifted some amount of money to poorer sections of the community, although it has often been argued that much of this money was spent on elaborate rote learning systems that answered the needs of employers rather than the demands of the communities who had pushed for needed reforms. The use of the word 'skill' in education illustrates this point. The emphasis on 'skill learning' embodied in the minimum competency testing and 'back to basics' movement, replaced the positive definition of the word 'skill' to reflect the type of work today's students can expect to find when they enter the job market. Its metamorphosis demonstrates the transformation of a community demand for quality education for previously neglected segments of students to a fixation on measuring those students according to easily quantifiable criteria devoid of political or cultural content.

'Skilled labor' had traditionally been used to describe a type of worker with the necessary expertise to evaluate a situation, devise an overall plan to correct a problem or improve upon an existing method of operation, and carry out all the phases of the operation to its completion. In education, 'skill' has come to mean choosing among extremely narrow, pre-determined isolated pieces of information. At best it is characterised by great attention to the mechanics of information gathering rather than the selection of information or examination of its critical content. 'Skill work' in elementary grades means sounding out 'pin' and 'pan' when flash cards are held up. In high school, it means handing in an essay with no obvious grammatical or spelling errors. Students who are thus 'skilled' in basic school subjects are therefore not being prepared to enter the 'skilled trades' if indeed these trades will still exist upon their graduation, but are equipped only for those positions which limit the scope of intelligence and creativity necessary to complete the assigned tasks effectively.

It appears the employers in large corporations such as those represented on the boards of these commissions have come to believe that they can no longer afford even the illusion of this type of equal opportunity embodied in 'skill learning'. According to these reports, sufficient amounts of money are not going into programs which would train the kinds of workers corporations need in order to maintain or create a competitive edge – highly skilled technocrats and managers. Yet even if these companies succeeded in channeling large amounts of money into educational systems which support creative, self-directed programs for the few and rote sessions for the many, they may not be able to stem the process of deskilling that their dual systems of job classifications – a few highly trained managers versus a large pool of unskilled labor – inevitably create.

'Deskilling' is a term recently coined to explain a new type of work situation. From its traditional base in factories and filing pools, this process of deskilling or 'proletarianisation' has been observed spreading to the professions, particularly ones that are female-saturated or are now more hospitable to women joining their ranks. In all of these professions we now see women and minorities 'ghettoised' into the less lucrative, lower paying and routinized areas while white men continue to dominate the remunerative and powerful sectors.

In addition, new positions within these fields are being created. Even though all nurses, lawyers, engineers and social workers share the same title, a portion of them now manage the others. In female-saturated occupations some are recruited into those professions with the express purpose of having them fill those new positions. The two key proposals of the Commissions on Excellence – the creation of a 'master teacher' slot and the allocation of merit pay – reflect attempts to restructure teaching along similar lines in the belief that these incentives will recruit and retain better teachers.

It is important to note that the deskilling of the labor force isn't just happening to workers 'out there', or to the students in the classrooms. A part of the workforce also labors in schools, and the deskilling of that labor force – teachers – is occurring in ways that affect that particular group of workers as well as those they train.

Two stories that appeared back to back on Wednesday, August 24, 1983, in the *Boston Globe* provide concrete examples of what is happening within teaching. On the front page of the *Globe* was a report by the Carnegie Foundation for the Advancement of Teaching. This report is an exception to the majority of reports which emphasise the culpability of the individual teacher. This report concluded, 'What is wrong with American public schools cannot be fixed without the help of those teachers already in the nation's classrooms. Most of them will be there for years to come . . . To talk about recruiting better students into teaching without examining the current circumstances that discourage teachers is simply a diversion'. The story goes on to report that one of the major issues for teachers is the inability of teachers to exercise control over issues outside their classrooms which directly affect their jobs within the classroom. The example cited is textbook selection. There are numerous others.

Directly following that story, on page two, is a long feature article on Rosemary Rosen. Rosemary Rosen was a sixth grade teacher a few years ago. At the time, she was financial manager for the Boston Public Schools, righthand person to Superintendent Spillane and by all accounts an extremely bright and effective administrator. Her story provides a case history of what will undoubtedly happen to many teachers who are tapped to become master teachers, and who will be taken out of the classroom for a portion of the day to direct the work of other teachers, those left to work with children, on a workbook by workbook – or computer stroke by computer stroke – basis.

Rosen states that she became a teacher because 'It was one of the normal options for me.' After one year she discovered, 'I think the skills that the teacher has the least opportunity to develop are decision-making skills in an organisational sense'. She concluded that 'I learned I didn't want to teach, because one has very little control of one's environment. And I was not content to just close my door and confine myself to the classroom. The kids were great but I also didn't think that my emotional energy would hold out for the next 10 years.' So she took a job as a financial manager in the New York State Department of Education in the budget office.

For some reason, unreported in the story, and despite enormous success in her new field, Rosemary returned to teaching after three years with a fifty percent cut in salary. Teaching had somehow lured her back. 'I loved it. I got involved in curriculum and ended up being union representative in my building'. At that point the story abruptly shifts to being chosen Superintendent Spillane's financial expert for the Boston Public Schools. The writer of the article doesn't divulge, or doesn't pursue, if Rosemary's old feelings of isolation prompted this new career change, but numerous studies suggest that this isolation, and its companion, powerlessness, were the real reasons she left teaching, not a pay incentive. Awareness of the lack of recognition and powerlessness of teachers was not carried over to her new role of administrator, however. Instead of advocating an expansion in the role and clout of teachers as a whole, 'Rosen's current determination [is] to reduce their [teachers'] authority through collective bargaining'.

Rosemary Rosen may also have wanted to leave teaching before she became too identified as competent and effective with children. With the departure of aides and curriculum specialists, and with the threatened pull-out of 'master teachers', general classroom teachers are forced to spend more and more time in the classroom. Their situation is analagous to mothers whose time spent exclusively with children is seen as disqualifying them for more rewarding and prestigious jobs. 'In our isolated families the mother is the person who is supposed to introduce the world to the child, and communicate to it its cultural heritage, when she is herself sealed off from participating in the world outside the home and in sharing creatively in the culture.' (Kitzinger, 1978) The isolation of the classroom creates the illusion of the 'powerful female' who is alone responsible for the major ills of society. Isolated in her classroom, she is assumed to wield total control, and is of course responsible for the total failure of her charges, and by extrapolation, American industry as a whole. Thus concentrating on 'the most important job', taking care of children, ironically creates a barrier for being seriously considered for any other kind of position.

Another barrier to choosing such teachers for removal from the classroom, even on a partial basis, is the dissatisfaction it would cause for powerful sets of parents who have successfully placed their children in that teacher's classroom and want to keep her there. Principals are unwilling to incur the displeasure of such parents. Such teachers are also generally quite effective at classroom management, and removing them from the classroom and replacing them with others might create discipline problems principals are loath to handle. The identification of good teaching with nurturing, coupled with the assumption that such traits are inherent or best developed

by increased classroom contact, therefore results in a lack of promotion for those teachers who are identified as the most understanding and willing to attend to the mundane and personal concerns of their students. This trend is similar to that recorded for other female-identified occupations. As one career secretary noted, 'The more efficient she became and the more indispensable she is to him in a secretarial capacity the less likely he will be to run the risk of crippling or inconveniencing himself by recommending her promotion to an independent position in the business world'. (Kessler-Harris, 1982)

In contrast, those who exhibit managerial, i.e. distant, 'objective' relationships with colleagues and students would have the edge in being chosen master teacher, much as they now have the edge on being chosen principal.

> You have to make yourself very well known to get any recognition in this system. I've decided that. You have to belong to the teachers' union and the negotiating team and negotiate with these people. Then I think they get a feeling for your strengths and weaknesses and get to know you . . . I was just thinking the other day, 'Who are the busy little bees that do all the dirty work, put together minimum competency standards and tests, do all the background work for curriculum development? Women. Who's on the negotiating committee? Men.' And I think if you don't do those things there is no other way they get to know you because they certainly don't go in classrooms. No one would ever recognise you for that. And that's what I've done all my life and I don't think they know me from a hole in the wall. Or if they did, it doesn't really count.
>
> (Freedman, 1982)

The reward offered to master teachers – removal from the classroom and a chance to participate in curriculum development, supervision, and decision making on institutional concerns – confirms the true confinement of being inside the classroom and the dearth of possibilities for classroom teachers to influence the more content and structurally oriented areas. As feminist critiques have often pointed out, in order to succeed women are forced to choose between concentrating on nurturing children and cooperation among peers, or a more individualistic, competitive position that has traditionally been modeled on a male notion of strict role separation. Being smart and being a woman are seen as contradictory for the teacher as for the business executive.

These reports also deplore the level of intelligence of teachers, particularly those presently entering the field. They do not investigate the absence within teaching of opportunities for exhibiting this characteristic. This critique of teachers is not new, despite the nostalgic assertion of the majority of these reports that teachers just aren't what they used to be. It may be that intelligent women were lured

into teaching as these reports content, but it wasn't their intelligence
and the promise of being able to use it that was seen as an effective
hook. To the teachers themselves, their now much vaunted intelligence was never mentioned. What was emphasised was their
'natural' ability for working with children, a trait that earned teaching the label 'women's true profession'. The emphasis on the nurturing qualities of good teaching – empathy, patience – made irrelevant
any discussion of the intellectual abilities of teachers. In *Life in
Classrooms*, Philip Jackson describes a group of teachers he has
chosen to interview on the basis of their ability to work effectively
with children. He states,

> If teachers sought a more thorough understanding of their world, insisted
> on a greater rationality in their actions, were completely open-minded in
> their consideration of pedagogical choices, and profound in their view of
> the human condition, they might well receive greater applause from
> intelleciuals, but it is doubtful that they would perform with greater effi-
> ciency in the classroom. On the contrary, it is quite possible that such
> paragons of virtue, if they could be found to exist, would actually have a
> deuce of a time coping in any sustained way with a class of third graders in
> a play-yard full of nursery tots.
>
> (Jackson, 1968)

The book was written in 1968, and at that time it appears the experts
were asserting that intelligence was a detriment to sound teaching.
That is not to suggest that these women were not intelligent. Rather,
Jackson's analysis reveals his lack of awareness and/or appreciation
of the need for intelligence in working effectively with children. Pre-
ferring to assume that those working 'in the trenches' are there
because they are less intelligent, albeit perhaps more intuitive than
principals such as himself, he would have been unlikely to encourage, or unable to notice, a more intellectual response offered by any
of the teachers he had selected to interview.

Intelligence is only the latest in a string of attributes reputed to be
lacking in each attribute having been seen at the time of its exposure
as part of the essential make-up of a good teacher. Rather than investigating how the system often deadens teachers, these reports concentrate on the individual, who alone in her classroom creates the
soft pockets of civilization. Focussing criticism on the individual
person, who – for different reasons at different moments in history
– 'just shouldn't teach' or is not of master teacher quality, perpetuates the idea that it is the individual alone who must make a difference, or that by being the right kind of person a teacher will be
exempt from the failures others have experienced. There is no recognition within these reports of the structural barriers to enhancing
educational potential for either student or teacher and no incentive
to look at how the institutional framework of schools frequently

creates stagnation while punishing attempts to challenge and improve bad school practices. The two major suggestions offered by these reports for upgrading the quality of the teaching staff – the creation of the post of master teacher and the doling out of merit pay – do little to seriously address why teaching itself limits the possibilities for the personal and professional growth of teachers.

Thus promoting the policy of merit pay in no way insures that teaching will in fact permit the expression of ingenuity, resourcefulness, compassion and intelligence on the part of teachers who will remain working with children. In fact there appears to be an inverse ratio between the level of education now demanded to retain the job of teacher and the level of education needed to work well at the job. Ironically, as teachers' own education has increased, the disparity between their professional attainment and personal commitment, and the inability to translate these qualities into a strong position within the school, has exacerabated teacher alienation. The much publicised issue of 'burnout', a supposed depletion of finite resources of patience and dedication, has been conjured up to explain this widespread alienation.

What has been labelled 'burnout' is, in fact, anger and frustration not easily or without fear of censure expressed in schools. It is particularly suited to a woman's profession, as it capitalises on a woman's readiness, and that of the public, to accept her own, personal failings for the real problems that she senses all around her in the school. 'Burnout', however, does not come from overtaxing one's intellectual and mental capacities. 'Burnout' comes from not being able to use those abilities to handle difficult emotional and managerial problems. These problems are often the result of administrators' analysis of a situation far removed from their personal and immediate responsibility. The establishment of the master teacher position which would remove teachers from classroom to oversee other teachers would add another level of managers who are separated from the rank and file.

Precisely when intellectual challenge and opportunities for nurturing are being curtailed even more than in the past, the panacea of merit pay is introduced as a way of defusing or obscuring the true roots of that alienation. The overriding concern of the authors of these reports – reversing a declining rate of profits – explains their solution to the problem of teacher alienation – merit pay for the few, luckily also a neat justification for maintaining the rest of the teaching staff at present or lower levels of salaries. Their recommendation of merit pay is gambling that teachers will accept the replacement of a cash reward for the goal of helping individual children and society as a whole. Merit pay quite baldly tells teachers they should recognise that that goal is a old-fashioned, a pipe dream, a mirage used to lure them into teaching. Now provided with the diagnosis of 'burnout', they have depleted their resources of patience and empathy and should either leave teaching or discard the diagnosis of 'burnout' as an out-of-date vestige from a bygone era. They should now recognise that the few will always be used to downgrade the work of the many.

Rewarding the work of the few while downgrading the contributions of the many is actually quite a well-worn combination. The father of scientific management, Frederick Winslow Taylor, connected these two administrative tactics when he chose his 'high-priced man' as the worker who would best follow Taylor's newly laid guidelines which required strict adherence to pre-determined tasks. In answer to the worker's question as to what Taylor meant by a 'high-priced man', Taylor answered, 'A high-priced man does just what he's told to do, and no back talk. Do you understand that? When this man tells you to walk, you walk; when he tells you to sit down, you sit down, and you don't talk back to him'. Salaries increased for a short period of time for such 'high-priced men' and then rapidly declined as larger numbers of workers lost control over various crafts, and thus their ability to negotiate for a decent wage.

Myra Strober and David Tyack have noted a similar phenomenon occurring in teaching at the time Taylor was investigating scientific management. The large number of teachers required by the common school movement resulted in a new type of teacher and a new type of master teacher – the principal – to oversee those teachers.

> By structuring jobs to take advantage of sex-role stereotypes about women's responsiveness to rules and male authority, and men's presumed ability to manage women, urban school boards were able to enhance their ability to control the curriculum, students, and personnel. Male managers in the 19th century urban schools regulated the core activities of instruction through standardised promotional examinations on the content of the prescribed curriculum and strict supervision to ensure that teachers were following mandated techniques.
>
> (Strober, 1980)

The system of raising one teacher above the others promotes competition for scarce resources while increasing the alienation among the majority of teachers. Furthermore, it degrades any of the cooperative, if unrecognised and often discredited, examples of teacher affiliation and cooperation. The types of evaluation that have recently been introduced into schools illustrate the lack of regard for cooperation among teachers in ways that support the staff as a whole rather than creating dissension. These evaluations take great pains to code and enumerate the type, number, and direction of the interactions of the teacher with her pupils within the classroom. Teachers are not evaluated outside the classroom because presumably these contributions to the school in general, enhancing the sense of community of the schools, are not properly considered her responsibility or, more strongly, not really 'her business'. Such instances of support would be further problematic in these new schemata because the teacher could not be evaluated as an individual but rather as a member of a community. A group of teachers playing with children during recess or investigating pond life on a field trip with several classes working together – one now soothing a child, one now asking questions while another watches to see if the children understand or appear confused – are not viewing their expertise as private property but as a community resource. It would be a distortion of their roles, and interject a competitive element that would effectively end their working together, if any of these teachers were evaluated by this new 'objective' method in order to be chosen master teacher.

To argue that creating a level of master teacher would enhance cooperation among teachers and improve the teaching of all teachers is disingenuous and sadly inaccurate. Certainly it is an attack on the strategies and philosophy of the feminist movement with its emphasis on sisterhood and its use of consciousness-raising techniques. These techniques helped women recognise that individual dilemmas are shared experiences created by the interaction of diverse personalities operating within a rigid, standardised institution.

Merit pay deflects attention away from the job of teacher as normally defined, raising some teachers above others, a solution which will leave untouched the basic problems of the average, online teacher. It will simply add a new refinement within teaching itself to the deskilling taking place in the rest of the workforce. Furthermore there is nothing to insure that all merit pay would not go to mathematics and science teachers (a large percentage of whom are men) whose efforts these reports assume are most closely linked to improving the nation's competitive edge, or to those teaching the 'gifted and talented', or to those who teach to the test. These directions would do little to spur on other teachers who work in less easily quantifiable areas, and whose subject areas do not yield a ready market value.

Merit pay/master teacher will appease the few by co-opting their anger and frustration. It will standardise the work of every teacher anxious to follow the method of the present master teacher and eager to discern what teaching style would best fit in with the principal's present conception of a good teacher. Thus, merit pay can easily increase mediocrity, as teachers hold on to a sure thing or seek to emulate other 'sure things' practiced by favoured teachers.

The end result will be that those who seek a creative outlet, whether or not they receive merit pay, will leave teaching. They will be greatly lamented by concerned parents who may well turn their anger on the remaining teachers. The dual career mother/professional woman moving into banking, law, or computer programming may not understand why an intelligent woman is willing to spend her day with children. The rising corporate woman, thrilled with her new career but mindful of her children's needs, explains to herself that she needs a fulfilling job in an important area. She would like to be convinced that being with children and finding such a job are incompatible.

Paradoxically, for the working class woman the teacher represents the powerful professional woman who the media has suggested is secure in a demanding position. Both sets of mothers will not understand that their desire to secure the excellent teacher for their child – with their varying conceptions of what that means – often ends up in the departure of some of those same teachers and the demoralisation of the others who will teach their remaining children. As the teacher packs her homemade games, her aquarium and rock collection, and carts them off, the teacher herself now wonders about her own future and her ability to adjust to the world outside and its reflection in the interior world of the classroom. She may also wonder about the further adjustments to be made by the pupils and teachers who remain in schools.

Bibliography

Freedman S. *Personal Journal*, 1979.

Freedman S., Jackson J. and Boles K. *The Effects of the Institutional Structure of Schools on Teachers*, National Institute of Education Grant G-81-0031, 1982.

Kessler-Harris A. *Out to Work*, Oxford University Press. (Oxford, 1982)

Jackson P. *Life in Classrooms*. (Holt, Rinehart and Winston, New York, 1968).

Kitzinger S. *Woman as Mother* (Fontana, London, 1978).

Strober M. and Tyack D. 'Why Do Women Teach and Men Manage?' *Signs*, University of Chicago Press, Chicago, Spring, 1980.

CHAPTER FOUR

Are Teachers Being Proletarianised? Some Theoretical, Empirical and Policy Issues

Hugh Lauder and Beverley Yee

Recent work in the sociology of education has claimed that teachers are being proletarianised (Wright, 1979; Ozga & Lawn, 1981a; Lawn & Ozga, 1981b; Apple, 1983; Harris, 1982). Underlying this claim are certain assumptions about the relationships between the captialist mode of production (CMP), the state, state professional workers and the latter's position within the class structure. For example, Ozga and Lawn, and Harris, subscribe to Marx's view that:

> Society as a whole is more and more splitting up into the two great hostile camps, into two great classes directly facing each other; Bourgeoisie and Proletariat.[1]

For these authors the catalyst for the polarisation of society is proletarianisation, which in turn is a result of capital's drive to accumulation. According to this view, capital breaks down the tasks of the skilled craftsperson and turns them into the routine and repetitive operations of the machine minder. This aids the accumulation process because it is cheaper to use machines to produce than it is skilled human beings and, of course, capital has control over machines in a way it does not over labour. But the consequence for labour is that the autonomy associated with skilled craftwork is replaced by the tyranny of the conveyor belt. For the above authors this process applies as much to state workers and in particular teachers, as it does to others. In making this claim it is assumed explicitly by Harris and implicitly by Ozga and Lawn[2] that the state acts as a servant of capital and thereby controls education to ensure it fulfils the requirements of capital as cheaply as possible.

In the case of Apple and Wright, the wider context in which

teacher proletarianisation takes place is not discussed, although the former suggests it is a function of economic crisis. Both, however, agree proletarianisation has the effect of cutting state expenditure while increasing political control over teachers. There are a number of ways in which this can be done: Wright, Apple and Harris cite loss of control over the content and processes of teaching through the advent of the new technologies of curriculum packaging. Wright, Ozga and Lawn, and Harris also identify deteriorating conditions of employment, citing, for example, loss of teacher autonomy through increasing accountability to the state, and loss of job security and income.

The question we want to raise in this paper is whether these processes of teacher proletarianisation are as inevitable as the literature tends to suggest. In our view the literature provides a deterministic account of teacher proletarianisation because it has, for the most part, been discussed within the framework of the structuralist problematic. This is particularly so of Harris who adopts an Althusserian view of the state as servant of capital and relies heavily on Carchedi's (1977) theory of class. However, recent empirical and theoretical developments suggest an alternative model which allows far greater space for political action to influence the work situation and class position of teachers. The empirical developments concern the case of New Zealand post primary teachers about whom we shall present data which indicates they are not being proletarianised at a time of economic crisis. As such they represent an anomaly for the claim that teachers in capitalist societies are being proletarianised. In order to develop an alternative model for which the New Zealand case is not an anomaly we have turned to recent work on class and its relationship to the state. The literature we have in mind constitutes an alternative to the structuralist tradition. This alternative can be constructed from the work of Giddens (1973), Giddens and McKenzie (1982), Lee (1982), Cohen (1982), Abercrombie and Urry (1983) and Offe (1984). In our view, this tradition is potentially more empirically sensitive, than the structuralist has proved to be, to the relationships between work practices, work organisations, class and state. And, in contrast to the structuralist tradition, it can allow the possibility for effective political intervention. According to this alternative view class relations are mediated by the labour market and the power of work organisations to socially construct skills. In addition, it is acknowledged that, in Cohen's words, the state 'is a source of stratification and power rather than merely a reflection of socio-economic inequalities'.[3] Diagramatically we can represent this alternative view as follows:

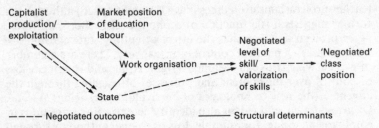

In the above diagram the demands of capital accumulation and production relations set constraints upon the state and determine the nature of the labour market. As Offe has suggested:

> there is a dual determination of the political power of the capitalist state: the institutional form of this state is determined through the rules of democratic and representative government, while the material content of state power is conditioned by the continuous requirement of the accumulation process.[4]

This means that the state is constrained to legitimate its activities to its electors while not disrupting the process of capital accumulation. But within these broad constraints the state has considerable room for manoeuvre. As such, rather than being the servant of capital, as Harris and other structuralists have suggested, the state's relationship to capital can be seen as one which allows for negotiation and political initiative.

As regards the labour market, production relations determine, in a general sense, the type of labour required. For example, corporate capitalism requires a large army of educated labour to fill its managerial and administrative positions, whereas, early capitalism had no such requirement for educated labour. In turn the labour market determines the nature of the work organisation, for example, trade union, professional association and so on. But in the case of a state monopsony the strength of labour organisation will be, in part, dependent on the stance taken by the state to it. For example, in the case of teachers, where the state retains a high level of commitment to education, teachers' work organisations are likely to be stronger than where the state has little commitment to education. Relatedly, the strength of teachers' work organisations will be reflected in the degree to which teachers' skills are valorized.

However, a strong ideological element enters with respect to the state's stance toward education and the valorization of teachers' skills. The state's position will be largely determined by the role played by education in the legitimation of state policy. While, for teachers, the valorization of their skills is necessarily a reflection of their social (i.e., ideological) construction. This is because teachers' skills aren't measurable in any unproblematic sense and their valorization then becomes a matter of persuasion, and where necessary industrial struggle.[5]

In the context of this model, therefore, teachers' class position will be the outcome of politically and ideologically determined negotiations and struggle. But there are limits to this process. While many kinds of deterioration in teachers' work conditions can be reversed; salaries which have been eroded can be increased, career paths that have been torn up re-laid and staff-student ratios improved, history teaches us that the process of proletarianisation cannot be reversed when technology replaces the skills of individuals. In the case of teachers we can imagine an education system in which students are instructed by computer packages and teachers' only function will be that of 'child minding'. In this scenario teachers, like many craftspeople before them, would find themselves unskilled labourers, firmly situated in the working class.

The replacement of teachers by technology may be considered the paradigmatic sense of proletarianisation because it will permanently strip them of their skills and autonomy. But in the alternative model we have sketched this is not a necessary fate for all teachers in all capitalist societies. Rather, teachers work conditions in any specific social formation will be dependent on a conjuncture of ideological and political factors. With this latter point in mind we now present two case studies concerning recent conflicts between New Zealand secondary school teachers and the state. And in the following section we put flesh on the bones of the model we have just elucidated in order to explain the nature and outcomes of the conflicts described in the two case studies.

Teacher Proletarianisation? Two Case Studies

The two case studies we have chosen are concerned with conflict between the New Zealand Post Primary Teachers Association (PPTA) and the state. As studies in crisis they reveal the nature of the power relations underlying the daily teaching round. The first is concerned with the so-called 'day of protest' in 1978 when New Zealand secondary school teachers went on strike for the first time in their history. The second concerns the running battle in 1983–84 between the PPTA and the state over the abolition of the University Entrance (UE) examination.

The 'Day of Protest'
The PPTA gave two reasons for strike action. The first was related to the introduction of new salary scales in 1971. The restructuring of the scales according to qualification groups meant that translation

anomalies between old and new scales arose affecting sizeable proportions of non-graduate teachers.[6] For example, technical teachers with superior trade qualifications and with an equivalent time spent in training to university graduates had been on an equivalent scale to them. But with the introduction of the new scales they were downgraded. Further negotiation in 1972 failed to resolve the translation anomalies.

The second reason related to the protracted nature of salary claims and negotiations. In 1975 the PPTA lodged a salary claim for pay increases at the same time as primary scales were being negotiated with the NZEI.[7] The salary increases gained by the NZEI meant that margins enjoyed by secondary school teachers over their primary counterparts since 1971 effectively disappeared. In 1976 the PPTA lodged another claim which amounted to an estimated annual increase of $40M. It was subsequently revised downward to $29.5M, still well above the $1.5–2M thought by the government to be an acceptable claim.[8]

The PPTA justified its salary claims on the basis of three criteria: retention, recruitment and relativity. The qualifications possessed by teachers, argued the PPTA, must be seen as a marketable commodity and if people wanted well qualified and trained people as teachers, higher salaries were seen as the only solution to ensure an adequate supply. If their salary claims were not met, then secondary teachers, their pupils and the whole of the nation would suffer.[9]

However, these claims submitted by the PPTA were not upheld and the question of salaries remained unresolved. Finally, in 1978, in an attempt to break the impasse in negotiations the PPTA recommended to its members, a day of protest. Rather than break the deadlock, the action taken by teachers achieved the opposite effect with the government breaking off all negotiations in retaliation. While strained relations continued, the PPTA at a special conference decided that its absolute priority was to press for a correction of the 1971 translation anomaly.

On June 13, 1978 a settlement was agreed upon. The 'serious injustices' which arose out of the translation anomalies were resolved. Other gains made by the PPTA included pay increases for teachers holding positions of responsibility and basic adjustments to the lower end of the scale to ensure that these rates were not lower than the primary scales.[10]

In terms of the public debate over this issue it seemed straightforwardly one concerned with income and pay differentials. However, the publicly stated grounds for conflict do not always tell the complete story. For example, while teachers' grievances were expressed as a demand for increased income, we wanted to safeguard against the possibility that this demand was not an expression of displaced anxiety caused by a loss of autonomy in the classroom.

Unlike the craftsperson who can see quite clearly the process by which he/she is replaced by machines, teacher proletarianisation can be a creeping process. For example, the Taylorisation of pedagogy through packaged management behaviour programmes can be presented as a technological breakthrough which can 'prove an indispensable aid' (sic) to teachers. The problem is in getting what may be a sharply felt but difficult to articulate grievance accepted in a public arena in which debate is so much shaped by the demand for statistical quantification. And, in which a case for higher wages can be put far more easily than one couched in such imprecise terms as those of grievance and alienation.[11]

Therefore in order to test whether the 'day of protest' was about more than income and pay differentials we first calculated teachers' real income for the decade 1971–1981 to see to what extent teachers had suffered erosion, either as a consequence of changing pay scales or inflation. By charting the levels of real income across this decade we were able to assess both the decline in real income up to the 'day of protest' and whether the strike had been effective in restoring teachers' purchasing power. In addition, we also administered a questionnaire to teachers (N = 92) in three Christchurch, N.Z. high schools to see whether they felt that prior to 1978 they had suffered proletarianisation and other forms of intensification and erosion. The questionnaires were administered in June 1985 and we further asked teachers to comment on the period between 1978 and 1985. This is because the economic depression in New Zealand began to bite in the mid-seventies and has continued ever since (Freeman-Moir, 1985). As such, if the claim that economic crisis necessarily acts as a catalyst to teacher proletarianisation is correct, we could expect the latter to be an ongoing process.

The erosion of income:
To calculate teachers' changing level of real income (adjusting for rates of inflation and income tax) for the decade 1971–81 we took three groups of teachers chosen on the basis of the qualifications they held and their length of service. The three groups representing lower, middle and upper positions on the salary scale are as follows:

G2 – S1: non graduate first year teachers
G3 – S5: graduate fifth year teachers
G4 – S7: graduate seventh year teachers.

Their changing levels of real income are depicted in Figure 1 below. It can be seen that all three groups of teachers suffered a relatively substantial degree of income erosion up to the 1978 strike, thereafter they all experienced an increase in purchasing power suggesting that the strike had, in fact, been effective in remedying this grievance. In real terms it was the G3 teachers who suffered the greatest loss in income relative to G2 and G4 teachers but it was G2 teachers who

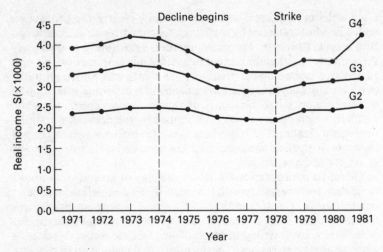

Figure 1 *Trends in real income for teachers over a 10 year period 1971 – 1981*

were most vocal in pushing for strike action, in part because this group had been economically disadvantaged by the introduction of the new salary scales in 1971, and in part because, in absolute terms, their decline in real income would be more acutely felt since they were close to the bottom of the salary scale. But the fact that all teachers suffered income erosion must have contributed to the solidarity in taking what was, after all, an unprecedented step.

The Loss of Autonomy

In order to gain data on teachers' work conditions we devised questionnaire items which addressed the central issues of loss of control over the content and process of teaching. The questionnaire was administered to three types of school: working class inner city (N = 40), middle class suburban (N = 29), and ruling class 'up market' suburban (N = 23). The results appear to be emphatic. In response to the question, 'has your power to determine what subject matter is taught to students diminished?', only 2 per cent said it had prior to 1978, while 4 per cent said it had post-1978 to the present. Similarly, in response to the question, 'in your classroom, has your control over how students are taught decreased?', 2 per cen said it had prior to 1978, while 5 per cent said it had post-1978. Moreover, teachers indicated that their power had increased in terms of what and how they taught. Prior to 1978 28 per cent reported their power had increased in both these areas, while post-1978 59 per cent thought their power to determine curriculum content had increased and 51 per cent thought their power over how they taught had increased.

These figures do not suggest proletarianisation was or is taking place. But we wondered whether it was taking place surreptitiously through the increasing use of curriculum packages. We therefore asked teachers, 'what percentage of curriculum material used by you is created independently by you?' Prior to 1978 they responded that sixty nine per cent of materials had been self-created, while post-1978 sixty seven per cent of materials had. In other words, creeping proletarianisation through the introduction of packaged materials was not strongly in evidence.

There were no significant differences between the data from the three schools and what it suggests is that loss of autonomy was not a reason for teachers striking. Of course, teachers may be mistaken or may mis-report what is really the case. And, we are aware that the questionnaire method does not always accurately reflect the complex nature of individuals' perceptions. However, when these results are placed within the context of the data on income erosion and the following case study we believe that they do provide strong evidence against the claim that teachers in New Zealand are being proletarianised.[12]

The Struggle over the Abolition of University Entrance

Since 1977 the PPTA has been in favour of moving UE out of the 6th form and into the 7th form leaving Sixth Form Certificate (SFC)[13] as the only award for the 6th form. UE as it now stands, the PPTA argued, was irrelevant for eighty–ninety per cent of the students in the 6th form because it was geared to academic (university) work while SFC was seen as more widely relevant and acceptable to students and those who wished to employ them.

Frustrated by the lack of movement in the area with the Education Minister's 'final and fixed' decision that UE would remain in the 6th form, the PPTA had two options, it could retreat or take action. It chose the latter.

The 1983 Annual Conference recommended to its members not to participate in the administration procedures of the 1984 UE examination.

Administration procedures included the setting and marking of UE scripts and papers, passing out of entry forms and the collection of fees. If progress was not forthcoming the PPTA threatened further action.

Over protests made by the Minister that the 'threatened embargo' by the PPTA was 'the worst expression of trade unionism on the shop floor',[14] and replies by teachers that there would be no personal economic gains made by teachers and that the motivation behind such actions were purely professional and entirely in the best interests of students,[15] a war of words was fought over the issue.

The situation thawed when teachers called off their ban on administering UE in June 1984 in order to get 'sensible discussion' under way again.

While the threatened action may have been motivated out of professional concern for students, a more important issue arose out of the debate, that of teacher autonomy and control over determining the school curriculum. The proposed PPTA policy was to have an internally assessed sixth form certificate with a board of studies, to oversee the whole field of curriculum and assessment in the senior school. The only external examination with a syllabus strongly influenced by university requirements would be UE in the seventh form. Overall this proposal would have arrogated considerably more autonomy to New Zealand teachers in the areas of curriculum and assessment than they had previously enjoyed.

In the end the struggle between the PPTA and the National Minister of Education was terminated by a Labour victory in the June 1984 elections. Since coming to office, Labour has accepted the PPTA case, it has also given notice of its intention to abolish the externally examined fifth form school certificate and it most likely will be replaced by a system of moderated internal assessment, which will also serve to increase teacher autonomy. In addition, close on a thousand new teaching positions have been created as part of a long-term Labour policy of reducing class numbers to a ratio of one to twenty.

According to the proletarianisation thesis conflict between teachers and the state will be the outcome of a *defensive* response by teachers to the threat of proletarianisation. But what is interesting about this case is that the PPTA took the *offensive* and it did so against, arguably, one of the most dogmatically conservative administrations in the history of New Zealand education. An added point of significance about this episode is that the PPTA was prepared to withdraw its labour over what may centrally be considered a 'professional' issue (i.e., one concerned with curriculum and assessment). What this suggests is that the model implicitly espoused in the literature on the proletarianisation thesis is inappropriate in this case.

According to this model, as teachers are proletarianised their work organisations shed their professional strategies in favour of those of trade unions. Initially trade union strategies are applied to work conditions and professional tactics are reserved for issues which are seen as being concerned with 'professional' skills. But as these are eroded teachers progressively turn to union tactics to defend their skills and expertise. In this view teacher organisations are seen as inherently unstable being in the process of transition from professional body to trade union. However, this particular case study implies a different view, one which sees the PPTA as a relatively stable 'professional union' in which the combination of professional and union strategies do not indicate a body in transition but rather one which is *sui generis*. And which uses both sets of strategies pragmatically to achieve its ends, whether they be defensive or offensive. The conflict over UE shows a professional union organisation strong enough to take the offensive and successful in winning greater autonomy for its members. A corollary of seeing the PPTA as a stable and quite powerful work organisation, is that teachers can be considered, in the New Zealand context, as part of a subaltern class to the ruling class instrumental in forging educational policy.[16]

Explaining Teachers' Work Situation

To understand teachers' work situation, the strength of their work organisations and their class position we need first to look at the relationships between the education system, the state and the various fractions of the ruling class. In New Zealand the state has, since the 1860s, played a leading role in the development and maintenance of capital. This is particularly so with the advent of the Labour Government in 1936. Through a policy of import substitution they set in place the machinery which has until recently forged a consensus between the various factions of capital and labour (Fougere, 1981). Import substitution created trade barriers behind which a nascent New Zealand industry could grow while also ensuring a high rate of employment. Industrial conflict has been regulated and controlled by strong state intervention within the spheres of accumulation, exchange and production (Martin, 1984). At the same time various state policies with respect to agriculture, including minimum price guarantees, state controlled marketing of agricultural produce, generous tax allowances and more recently large government subsidies have meant that the big landowners have been maintained in considerable comfort.

Within this context education has played a central legitimating role because the 'bargain' the state has struck with the working class is that in return for the unequal structures the state is instrumental in maintaining the working class has the opportunity through education of 'making it' into a position of power and privilege. In New Zealand this liberal ideology is part of a more encompassing dominant ideology – what has been called the myth of the New Jerusalem (Smart & Lauder, 1984). This myth gives the ideology of equality of opportunity an added potency because integral to it is a view of New Zealand as a classless society, in explicit contrast to England which is viewed as the exemplar of a class society.

Educational opportunity is central to the manufacture of consensus and those within the ruling class who have sought, in recent years, to emulate Thatcherite educational policies have made little progress. The former National party Minister of Education was promptly demoted by his party as soon as it left office and it was openly acknowledged that his handling of the education portfolio had contributed to National's loss in the 1984 election. Similarly, although the incoming Labour Government has adopted the right wing economic policies advocated by the Treasury, it has not implemented these policies in the education area, despite the Treasury's urging to the contrary.[17]

While it has been suggested that economic crisis is a catalyst to the proletarianisation of state 'professional' employees the present Labour party's policies suggest that the state doesn't have to mimic capital in this respect; that a degree of insulation is possible. In New Zealand this has occurred because of the weakness of the capital class and in particular the divisions within it between urban and rural areas. And in the divisions within the rural fraction. The latter are divided between those who farm to produce commodities and those who hold land for speculative purposes (amongst whom there's a growing number of urban corporate capitalist owners (Simpson, 1984). These divisions have been fully exploited by a Labour government which has stripped away agricultural subsidies and other traditional forms of state support. For farmers who live on what they produce, these policies have caused hardship, but for the corporate framing sector who can write their losses off, there are also compensations in Labour's policies designed to increase the wealth of urban capital. Hence these divisions within the landowning fraction have allowed Labour to mount a severe assault on the traditional privileges of rural capital. At the same time as reducing state expenditure on agriculture it has increased it on education.

For Labour support for education as a mechanism for forging consensus has become all the more important because, while it draws a large share of its electoral support from the urban working class, its policies are quite deliberately designed to increase the gap between rich and poor by, for example, reducing the incidence of personal income tax for the rich. Under these circumstances Labour is dependent, in part, on the promise of equality of opportunity through education to maintain its working class electoral support.

Set alongside state support for education is the strength of the PPTA. Unlike their English counterparts, New Zealand secondary teachers only have one union to represent them. Confronted by the abrasive policies and style of the National Minister of Education the PPTA demonstrated a unity and strength which enabled it to go on the offensive. Underlying this organisational strength is a common ideology dubbed by the former National Minister of Education as a 'liberal conspiracy': a liberal world-view which reflects the relatively strong work situation and consequently class position of New Zealand teachers.[18]

In summary, it can be seen how, in terms of the model we have developed, the state in New Zealand does not serve the unified interests of capital. Rather it has balanced the twin demands of maintaining the accumulation process while legitimating its policies to the electorate by exploiting divisions within the capital class. By increasing support for urban capital and reducing support for rural capital it has been able to increase the finance to education necessary to legitimate its policies. As a result teachers have been insulated from the proletarianisation process during a time of economic crisis. However, while the model we have developed can explain the anomaly of why teachers in New Zealand are not being proletarianised, the question we raise in conclusion is whether the anomaly of the New Zealand case can be, in any way, instructive for teachers in other capitalist societies. The positive conclusion is that it is possible for the state to insulate education from the vicissitudes of capitalism. Potentially it can create a space for the development of socialist educational policies.[19] But this conclusion has to be tempered with caution because it may be a fairly unique set of power relations, within capitalism, which can produce such a consequence.

Notes

1 Quoted from Ozga & Lawn (1981), p. 124.
2 See Harris (1982), p. 76 and following. Ozga and Lawn (1981) Ch 4.
3 Cohen (1982), p. 197.
4 Offe (1984), p. 121.
5 At present, in the U.K., that struggle is, in part, taking the form of a 'debate' about accountability or 'appraisal'. For an historical analysis of the issues involved here, see Grace (1985).
6 For a discussion of the pay scales created in 1971 and the anomalies they produced, see the PPTA magazine *The Journal*, September 1977.
7 New Zealand Educational Institute – the organisation which represents primary school teachers.
8 See *The Press* (Christchurch, N.Z.) February 22, 1978, p. 6.
9 This argument is elaborated in *The Journal*, April 1978.
10 See *The Journal*, July 1978 for documentation of the settlements reached.
11 Ian Hacking (1981) has an excellent short article on the historical development of statistics and the use made of them by the state. He

concludes the article by saying, 'the bureaucracy of statistics imposes not just by creating administrative rulings but by determining classifications within which people must think of themselves and of those actions which are open to them'.

12   This finding is consistent with the view taken by a number of commentators who have suggested that white collar workers, including teachers, have been prepared to take industrial action as a result of a loss in income through inflation rather than as a consequence of proletarianisation. See Coates (1972), Parkin (1979), Kelly (1980).

13   A certificated internally assessed, externally moderated course in the sixth form which the PPTA considered appropriate for the development of a non- 'academic' curriculum.

14   See the *New Zealand Times* March 18, 1984. The Minister of Education also (perhaps acutely!) saw this struggle with the PPTA 'as another attempt to secure teacher domination in education . . . what is at stake in this issue is who controls New Zealand education.' Quoted from *The Press*, May 5, 1984.

15   Against the PPTA's claim of professional disinterest it was argued that by shifting UE to the 7th form students would be forced to stay on an extra year to gain a qualification recognised by employers. The increase in the 7th form rolls would mean more senior teachers would be required at higher rates of pay. In other words, teachers did have a financial interest in the proposed changes.

16   The term subaltern class is used by Halsey *et al.* (1980) to describe those administrators and technicians who form the lower ranks of the service (what we have called the ruling) class, that group who make fundamental policy decisions. In so far as teachers are instrumental in helping to forge educational policy we would suggest they form part of this subaltern class.

17   See *Economic Management*, a New Zealand Treasury publication, July 1984.

18   We are assuming here that the Liberal ideology of equality of opportunity is essentially *the* ideology of the educated subaltern class. It is also interesting to note in this context that the PPTA rejected in 1982 affiliation with the central trade union organisation in New Zealand, the Federation of Labour.

19   The sort of policies we have in mind are those of workplace democracy. See White (1983) for a discussion of workplace democracy in schools. In a New Zealand context the space that has been created is, from a socialist perspective, problematic. Precisely because teachers in New Zealand are in a strong position (the subaltern class) does this preclude solidarity with the working class in the development of socialist educational policies?

References

Abercrombie, N. & Urry, J. (1983) *Capital, Labour and the Middle Classes*. (London, Allen & Unwin).

Apple, M. (1983) Work, Gender and Teaching, in *Teachers College Record*, Spring 1983.

Barton, L. & Walker, S. (1981) *Schools, Teachers & Teaching*. Lewes, The Falmer Press.

Carchedi, G. (1977) *On the Economic Identification of Social Classes* (London, Routledge & Kegan Paul).

Coates, R. (1972) *The Teacher Unions and Interest Group Politics* (Cambridge, Cambridge University Press).

Cohen, J. (1982) *Class and Civil Society* (Oxford, Martin Robertson).

Fougere, G. (1981) The last 50 years: paradoxes of import substituting industrialisation and the remaking of the New Zealand state. Mimeo, Sociology Department, University of Canterbury, New Zealand.

Freeman-Moir, D. F. (1985) Capitalist Crisis and Education in New Zealand. In R. Sharp (1985).

Giddens, A. (1973) *The Class Structure of the Advanced Societies*. (London, Hutchinson).

Giddens, A. & Mackenzie, G. (1982) *Social Class and the Division of Labour*. (Cambridge, Cambridge University Press).

Grace, G. (1985) Judging Teachers: the social and political contexts of teacher evaluation. *British Journal of Sociology of Education*, 6:1.

Hacking, I. (1981) The Taming of Change by an Army of Statistics, *Times Higher Educational Supplement*, 30 October.

Halsey, A., Heath, A. & Ridge, J. (1980) *Origins and Destinations*. (Oxford, Clarendon Press).

Harris, K. (1982) *Teachers and Classes*. (London, Routledge & Kegan Paul).

Kelly, M. (1980) *White-collar Proletariat*. (London, Routledge & Kegan Paul).

Lawn, M. & Ozga, J. (1981) 'The Educational Worker? A Re-Assessment of Teachers' in Barton & Walker (1981).

Lee, D. (1982) Beyond deskilling: skill, craft and class. In Wood (1982).

Martin, J. (1984) Rural and Industrial Labour and the State. In Wilkes & Shirley (1984).

Offe, C. (1984) *Contradictions of the Welfare State* (London, Hutchinson).

Ozga, J. & Lawn, M. (1981) Teachers, Professionalism and Class (Lewes, The Falmer Press).

Parkin, F. (1979) *Marxism and Class Theory*. (London, Tavistock Publications).

Sharp, R. (1985) *Capitalist Crisis, the State and Schooling*. (Melbourne, Routledge & Kegan Paul).

Simpson, T. (1984) *A Vision Betrayed*. (Hodder and Stoughton, Auckland).

Smart, J. & Lauder, H. (1985) Ideology and Political Art in New Zealand: A Radical View. In *Landfall*, March (Christchurch, Caxton Press).

Walker, P. (1979) *Between Capital and Labour* (Boston, South End Press).

White, P. (1983) *Beyond Domination* (London, Routledge & Kegan Paul).

Wilkes, C. & Shirley, I. (1984) *In the Public Interest: Health, Work and Housing in New Zealand*. (Auckland, Benton Ross).

Wood, S. (Ed.) (1982) *The Degradation of Work?* (London, Hutchinson).

Wright, E.O. (1979) 'Intellectuals and the Class Structure of Capitalist Society' in Walker, P. (1979).

PART 2

New Initiatives for Schooling?

Introduction

At the centre of the new initiatives for schooling being developed in the 1980s as part of the broader reforms being pressed by the political administrators of the New Right, is the drive to force the world of education into a much closer relationship with the world of work and the push to increase the emphasis in schooling upon vocational, technological and economic affairs. The direct consequence for teachers, as discussion in this section indicates, of the programmes like TVEI, TRIST and YTS which implement these policy goals are both traumatic and contradictory (Evans and Davies; Sikes). As more and more schools and colleges become involved in these programmes then, certainly, some new, creative opportunities are created for some teachers to develop fresh teaching packages and different career structures and a new instrument is provided with which teachers can motivate some disaffected pupils. These programmes also bring with them, however, as the first three papers in this section evidence, increased competition amongst teachers as the successful bids for the scarce resources of time, money and status are increasingly those related to vocational initiatives, increased differentiation within schools between academic and vocational pathways and pupil careers and increased pressure on teachers to defend the appropriateness of their own skills and experiences when measured against industrial criteria.

Vocational initiatives, however, also bring a more subtle pressure on teachers. In linking education more directly with the world of work, especially – as Apple argues in this section, through the increased use of technology in schools and classrooms, then there is a strong risk that the changes taking place in the labour process *outside* of education will infiltrate schools. In these conditions, teachers are likely to face new kinds of de-skilling and de-powering and even a challenge to the kind of questions given priority in educational encounters as technical concerns become the new rationality base for the curriculum and for classroom discourse.

Of course, de-skilling and de-powering teachers is not necessarily the *specific* intention of either all or some policy-makers. In the final paper in this section (Ozga), it is suggested that our ability to respond to the problems and pressures created by policy-makers will be enhanced by an appreciation of the contradictions and inconsistencies within the administrative culture itself and the paper suggests a programme for such study.

CHAPTER FIVE

Mandating Computers: The Impact of the New Technology on the Labour Process, Students and Teachers

Michael W. Apple

The Politics of Technology

In our society, technology is seen as an autonomous process. It is set apart and viewed as if it had a life of its own, independent of social intentions, power, and privilege. We examine technology as if it was something constantly changing and as something that is constantly changing our lives in schools and elsewhere. This is partly true, of course, and is fine as far as it goes. However, by focusing on what is changing and being changed, we may neglect to ask what relationships are remaining the same. Among the most important of these are the sets of cultural and economic inequalities that dominate even societies like our own.[1]

By thinking of technology in this way, by closely examining whether the changes associated with 'technological progress' are really changes in certain relationships after all, we can begin to ask political questions about their causes and especially their multitudinous effects. Whose idea of progress? Progress for what? And fundamentally, who benefits?[2] These questions may seem rather weighty ones to be asking about schools and the curricular and teaching practices that now go on in them or are being proposed. Yet, we are in the midst of one of those many educational bandwagons that governments, industry, and others so like to ride. This wagon is pulled in the direction of a technological workplace, and carries a heavy load of computers as its cargo.

The growth of the new technology in schools is definitely not what one would call a slow movement. In one recent year, there was a fifty-six per cent reported increase in the use of computers in schools

75

in the United States and even this may be a conservative estimate. Of the 25,642 schools surveyed, over 15,000 schools reported some computer usage.[3] In the United States alone, it is estimated that over 350,000 microcomputers have been introduced into the public schools in the past four years.[4] In a number of states, as well, there are moves to mandate 'computer competencies' as requirements for graduation from secondary school. This is a trend that shows no sign of abating. Nor is this phenomenon only limited to the United States. France, Canada, England, Australia, and many other countries have 'recognised the future'. At its centre seems to sit a machine with a keyboard and a screen.

I say 'at its centre', since in both governmental agencies and in schools themselves the computer and the new technology have been seen as something of a saviour economically and pedagogically. 'High tech' will save declining economies and will save our students and teachers in schools. In the latter, it is truly remarkable how wide a path the computer is now cutting.

The expansion of its use, the tendency to see all areas of education as a unified terrain for the growth in use of new technologies, can be seen in a two day workshop on integrating the microcomputer into the classroom held at my own university. Among the topics covered were computer applications in writing instruction, in music education, in secondary science and mathematics, in primary language arts, for the handicapped, for teacher record keeping and management, in business education, in health occupation training programs, in art, and in social studies. To this is added a series of sessions on the 'electronic office', how technology and automation are helping industry, and how we all can 'transcend the terror' of technology.[5]

Two things are evident from this list. First, vast areas of school life are now seen to be within the legitimate purview of technological restructuring. Second, there is a partly hidden but exceptionally close linkage between computers in schools and the needs of management for automated industries, electronic offices, and 'skilled' personnel. Thus, recognising both what is happening inside and outside of schools and the connections between these areas is critical to any understanding of what is likely to happen with the new technologies, especially the computer, in education.

As I have argued elsewhere, all too often educational debates are increasingly limited to technical issues. Questions of 'how to' have replaced questions of 'why'.[6] In this paper, I shall want to reverse this tendency. Rather than dealing with what the best way might be to establish closer ties between the technological requirements of the larger society and our formal institutions of education, I want to step back and raise a different set of questions. I want us to consider a number of rather difficult political, economic, and ethical issues about some of the tendencies in schools and the larger society that may make us want to be very cautious about the current technological bandwagon in education. In so doing, a range of areas will need to be examined: Behind the slogans of technological progress and high tech industry, what are some of real effects of the new technology on the future labour market? What may happen to teaching and curriculum if we do not think carefully about the new technology's place in the classroom? Will the growing focus on technological expertise, particularly computer literacy, equalise or further exacerbate the lack of social opportunities for our most disadvantaged students?

Of course, there are many more issues that need to be raised. Given limited space, however, I shall devote the bulk of my attention to those noted above. I am certain that many of you can and will have many more that you could add to the list.

At root, my claim will be that the debate about the role of the new technology in society and in schools is not and must not be just about the technical correctness of what computers can and cannot do. These may be the least important kinds of questions in fact. At the very core of the debate instead are the ideological and ethical issues concerning what schools should be about and whose interests they should serve.[7] The question of interests is very important currently since, because of the severe problems currently besetting economies like our own, a restructuring of what schools are for has reached a rather advanced stage.

Thus, while there has always been a relatively close connection between the two, there is now an even closer relationship between the curriculum in our schools and corporate needs.[8] In a number of countries, educational officials and policy makers, legislators, curriculum workers, and others have been subject to immense pressure to make the 'needs' of business and industry the primary goals of the school system. Economic and ideological pressures have become rather intense and often very overt. The language of efficiency, production, standards, cost effectiveness, job skills, work discipline, and so on – all defined by powerful groups and always threatening to become the dominant way we think about schooling[9] – has begun to push aside concerns for a democratic curriculum, teacher autonomy, and class, gender, and race inequality. Yet, we cannot fully understand the implications of the new technology in this restructuring unless we gain a more complete idea of what industry is now doing not only in the schools but in the economy as well.

Technological Myths and Economic Realities

Let us look at the larger society first. It is claimed that the technological needs of the economy are such that unless we have a technologically literate labour force we will ultimately become outmoded economically. But what will this labour force actually look like?

A helpful way of thinking about this is to use the concepts of increasing *proletarianisation* and *deskilling* of jobs. These concepts signify a complex historical process in which the control of labour has altered, one in which the skills workers have developed over many years are broken down and reduced to their atomistic units, automated, and redefined by management to enhance profit levels, efficiency and control. In the process, the employee's control of timing, over defining the most appropriate way to do a task, and over criteria that establish acceptable performance are slowly taken over as the prerogatives of management personnel who are usually divorced from the place where the actual labour is carried out. Loss of control by the worker is almost always the result. Pay is often lowered. And the job itself becomes routinised, boring, and alienating as conception is separated from execution and more and more aspects of jobs are rationalised to bring them into line with management's need for a tighter economic and ideological ship.[10] Finally, and very importantly, many of these jobs may simply disappear.

There is no doubt that the rapid developments in, say, micro-electronics, genetic engineering and associated 'biological technologies', and other high-tech areas are in fact partly transforming work in a large number of sectors in the economy. This may lead to economic prosperity in certain sections of our population, but its other effects may be devastating.

Thus, as the authors of a recent study that examined the impact of new technologies on the future labour market demonstrate:

> This transformation . . . may stimulate economic growth and competition in the world marketplace, but it will displace thousands of workers and could sustain high unemployment for many years. It may provide increased job opportunities for engineers, computer operators, and robot technicians, but it also promises to generate an even greater number of low level, service jobs such as those of janitors, cashiers, clericals, and food service workers. And while many more workers will be using computers, automated office equipment, and other sophisticated technical devices in their jobs, the increased use of technology may actually reduce the skills and discretion required to perform many jobs.[11]

Let us examine this scenario in greater detail.

Rumberger and Levin make a distinction that is very useful to this discussion. They differentiate between high-tech industries and high-tech occupations, in essence between what is made and the kinds of jobs these goods require. High tech industries that manufacture technical devices such as computers, electronic components and the like currently employ less than fifteen percent of the paid work force in the United States and other industrialised nations. Just as importantly, a substantial knowledge of technology is required by less than one fourth of all occupations within these industries. On the contrary, the largest share of jobs created by high-tech industries are in areas such as clerical and office work or in production and assembly. These actually pay below average wages.[12] Yet this is not all. High-tech occupations that do require considerable skill – such as computer specialists and engineers – may indeed expand. However, most of these occupations actually 'employ relatively few workers compared to many traditional clerical and service fields'.[13] Rumberger and Levin summarise a number of these points by stating that 'although the percentage growth rate of occupational employment in such high technology fields as engineering and computer programming was higher than the overall growth rate of jobs, far more jobs would be created in low-skilled clerical and service occupations than in high technology ones'.[14]

Some of these claims are supported by the following data. It is estimated that even being generous in one's projections, only seventeen percent of new jobs that will be created between now and 1995 will be in high tech industries. (Less generous and more restrictive projections argue that only three to eight percent of future jobs will be in such industries).[15] As I noted though, such jobs will not be all equal. Clerical, secretaries, assemblers, warehouse personnel, etc., these will be the largest occupations within the industry. If we take the electronic components industry as an example here, this is made much clearer. Engineering, science, and computing occupations constituted approximately fifteen percent of all workers in this industry. The majority of the rest of the workers were engaged in low wage assembly work. Thus, in the late 1970's, nearly two thirds of all workers in the electronic components industry took home hourly wages 'that placed them in the bottom third of the national distribution'.[16] If we take the archetypical high tech industry – computer and data processing – and decompose its labour market, we get similar results. In 1980, technologically oriented and skilled jobs accounted for only twenty-six percent of the total.[17]

These figures have considerable weight, but they are made even more significant by the fact that many of that twenty-six percent may themselves experience a deskilling process in the near future. That is, the reduction of jobs down into simpler and atomistic components, the separation of conception from execution, and so on – processes that have had such a major impact on the labour process of blue, pink, and white collar workers in so many other areas – are now advancing into high technology jobs as well. Computer programming provides an excellent example. New developments in software packages and machine language and design have meant that a considerable portion of the job of programming now requires little more than performing 'standard, routine, machine-like tasks that require little in-depth knowledge'.[18]

What does this mean for the schooling process and the seemingly widespread belief that the future world of work will require increasing technical competence on the part of all students? Consider the occupations that will contribute the most number of jobs not just in high tech industries but throughout the society by 1995. Economic forecasts indicate that these will include building custodians, cashiers, secretaries, office clerks, nurses, waiters and waitresses, elementary school teachers, truck drivers, and other health workers such as nurses-aides and orderlies.[19] None of these are directly related to high technology. Excluding teachers and nurses, none of them require any post secondary education. (Their earnings will be approximately thirty percent below the current average earnings of workers, as well).[20] If we go further than this and examine an even larger segment of expected new jobs by including the forty job categories that will probably account for about one half of all the jobs that will be created, it is estimated that only about twenty-five percent will require people with a college degree.[21]

In many ways, this is strongly related to the effects of the new technology on the job market and the labour process in general. Skill levels will be raised in some areas, but will decline in many others, as will jobs themselves decline. For instance, 'a recent study of robotics in the United States suggests that robots will eliminate 100,000 to 200,000 jobs by 1990, while creating 32,000 to 64,000 jobs'.[22] My point about declining skill requirements is made nicely by Rumberger and Levin. As they suggest, while it is usually assumed that workers will need computer programming and other sophisticated skills because of the greater use of technology such as computers in their jobs, the ultimate effect of such technology may be somewhat different. 'A variety of evidence suggests just the opposite: as machines become more sophisticated, with expanded memories, more computational ability, and sensory capabilities, the knowledge required to use the devices declines'.[23] The effect of these trends on the division of labour will be felt for decades. But it will be in the sexual division of labour where it will be even more extreme. Since historically *women's work* has been subject to these processes in very powerful ways, we shall see increased proletarianisation and deskilling of women's labour and, undoubtedly, a further increase in the feminisation of poverty.[24]

These points clearly have implications for our educational programmes. We need to think much more rigorously about what they mean for our transition from school to work programmes, especially since many of the 'skills' that schools are currently teaching are transitory because the jobs themselves are being transformed (or lost) by new technological developments and new management offensives.

Take office work, for example. In offices, the bulk of the new technology has not been designed to enhance the quality of the job for the largest portion of the employees (usually women clerical workers). Rather it has usually been designed and implemented in such a way that exactly the opposite will result. Instead of accomodating stimulating and satisfying work, the technology is there to make managers' jobs 'easier', to eliminate jobs and cut costs, to divide work into routine and atomised tasks, and to make administrative control more easily accomplished.[25] The vision of the future society seen in the microcosm of the office is inherently undemocratic and perhaps increasingly authoritarian. Is this what we wish to prepare our students for? Surely, our task as educators is neither to accept such a future labour market and labour process uncritically nor to have our students accept such practices uncritically as well. To do so is simply to allow the values of a limited but powerful segment of the population to work through us. It may be good business but I have my doubts about whether it is ethically correct educational policy.

In summary, then, what we will witness is the creation of enhanced jobs for a relative few and deskilled and boring work for the majority. Furthermore, even those boring and deskilled jobs will be increasingly hard to find. Take office work, again, an area that is rapidly being transformed by the new technology. It is estimated that between one and five jobs will be lost for every new computer terminal that is introduced.[26] Yet this situation will not be limited to office work. Even those low paying assembly positions noted earlier will not necessarily be found in the industrialised nations with their increasingly service oriented economies. Given the international division of labour, and what is called 'capital flight', a large portion of these jobs will be moved to countries such as the Phillipines and Indonesia.[27]

This is exacerbated considerably by the fact that many governments now find 'acceptable' those levels of unemployment that would have been considered a crisis a decade ago. 'Full employment' in the United States is now often seen as between seven-eight percent measured unemployment. (The actual figures are much higher, of course, especially among minority groups and workers who can only get part time jobs.) This is a figure that is double that of previous economic periods. Even higher rates are now seen as 'normal' in other countries. The trend is clear. The future will see fewer jobs. Most of those that are created will not necessarily be fulfilling, nor will they pay well. Finally, the level of technical skill will continue to be lowered for a large portion of them.[28]

Because of this, we need convincing answers to some very important questions about our future society and the economy before we turn our schools into the 'production plants' for creating new workers. *Where* will these new jobs be? *How many* will be created. Will they *equal* the number of positions lost in offices, factories, and service jobs in retailing, banks, telecommunications, and elsewhere? Are the bulk of the jobs that will be created relatively unskilled, less than meaningful, and themselves subject to the inexorable logics of management so that they too will be likely to be automated out of existence?[29]

These are not inconsequential questions. Before we give the schools over to the requirements of the new technology and the corporation, we must be very certain that it will benefit all of us, not mostly those who already possess economic and cultural power. This requires continued democratic discussion, not a quick decision based on the economic and political pressure now being placed on schools.

Much more could be said about the future labour market. I urge the interested reader to pursue it in greater depth since it will have a profound impact on our school policies and programmes, especially in vocational areas, in working class schools, and among programmes for young women. The difficulties with the high-tech vision that permeates the beliefs of the proponents of a technological solution will not remain outside the school door, however. Similar disproportionate benefits and dangers await us inside our educational institutions as well and it is to this that we shall now turn.

Inequality and the Technological Classroom

Once we go inside the school, a set of questions concerning 'who benefits?' also arises. We shall need to ask about what may be happening to teachers and students given the emphasis now being placed on computers in schools. I shall not talk about the individual teacher or student here. Obviously, some teachers will find their jobs enriched by the new technology and some students will find hidden talents and will excell in a computer oriented classroom. What we need to ask instead (or at least before we deal with the individual) is what may happen to classrooms, teachers, and students differentially. Once again, I shall seek to raise a set of issues that may not be

easy to solve, but cannot be ignored if we are to have a truly democratic educational system in more than name only.

While I have dealt with this in greater detail in *Ideology and Curriculum* and *Education and Power*,[30] let me briefly situate the growth
of the technologised classroom into what seems to be occurring
to teaching and curriculum in general. Currently, considerable
pressure is building to have teaching and school curricula be totally
pre-specified and tightly controlled for the purposes of 'efficiency',
'cost effectiveness', and 'accountability'. In many ways, the deskilling that is affecting jobs in general is now having an impact on
teachers as more and more decisions are moving out of their hands
and as their jobs become even more difficult to do. This is more
advanced in some countries than others, but it is clear that the movement to rationalise and control the act of teaching and the content
and evaluation of the curriculum is very real.[31] Even in those countries that have made strides away from centralised examination
systems, powerful inspectorates and supervisors, and tightly controlled curricula, there is an identifiable tendency to move back
toward state control. Many reforms have only a very tenuous hold
currently. This is in part due to economic difficulties and partly due
as well to the importing of American styles and techniques of educational management, styles and techniques that have their roots in
industrial bureaucracies and have almost never had democratic
aims.[32] Even though a number of teachers may support computer
oriented curricula, an emphasis on the new technology needs to be
seen in this context of the rationalisation of teaching and curricula in
general.

Given these pressures, what will happen to teachers if the new
technology is accepted uncritically? One of the major effects of the
current (over) emphasis on computers in the classroom may be the
deskilling and depowering of a considerable number of teachers.
Given the already heavy work load of planning, teaching, meetings,
and paperwork for most teachers, and given the expense, it is
probably wise to assume that the largest portion of teachers will not
be given more than a very small amount of training in computers,
their social effects, programming, and so on. This will be especially
the case at the primary and elementary school level where most
teachers are already teaching a wide array of subject areas. Research
indicates, in fact, that few teachers in any district are actually given
substantial information before computer curricula are implemented. Often only one or two teachers are the 'resident experts.'[33]
Because of this, most teachers have to rely on prepackaged sets of
material, existing software, and especially purchased material from
any of the scores of software manufacturing firms that are springing
up in a largely unregulated way.

The impact of this can be striking. What is happening is the exacerbation of trends we have begun to see in a number of nations. Rather then teachers having the time and the skill to do their own curriculum planning and deliberation, they become isolated executors of someone else's plans, procedures, and evaluative mechanisms. In industrial terms, this is very close to what I noted in my previous discussion of the labour process, the separation of conception from execution.[34]

The reliance on prepackaged software can have a number of long term effects. First, it can cause a decided loss of important skills and dispositions on the part of teachers. When the skills of local curriculum planning, individual evaluation, and so on are not used, they atrophy. The tendency to look outside of one's own or one's colleagues' historical experience about curriculum and teaching is lessened as considerably more of the curriculum, and the teaching and evaluative practices that surround it, is viewed as something one purchases. In the process – and this is very important – the school itself is transformed into a lucrative market. The industrialisation of the school I talked of previously is complemented, then, by further opening up the classroom to the mass produced commodities of industry. In many ways, it will be a publisher's and salesperson's delight. Whether students' educational experiences will markedly improve is open to question.

The issue of the relationship of purchased software and hardware to the possible deskilling and depowering of teachers does not end here though. The problem is made even more difficult by the rapidity with which software developers have constructed and marketed their products. There is no guarantee that the mass of such material has any major educational value. Exactly the opposite is often the case. One of the most knowledgeable government officials has put it this way. 'High quality educational software is almost non-existent in our elementary and secondary schools'.[35] While perhaps overstating his case to emphasize his points, the director of software evaluation for one of the largest school systems in the United State has concluded that of the more than 10,000 programmes currently available, approximately 200 are educationally significant.[36]

To their credit, the fact that this is a serious problem is recognised by most computer enthusiasts, and reviews and journals have attempted to deal with it. However, the sheer volume of material, the massive amounts of money spent on advertising software in professional publications, at teachers' and administrators' meetings, and so on, the utter 'puffery' of the claims made about much of this material, and the constant pressure by industry, government, parents, some school personnel, and others to institute computer programmes in schools immediately, all of this makes it nearly impossible to do more than make a small dent in the problem. As one educator put it, 'There's a lot of junk out there'.[37] The situation is not made any easier by the fact that teachers simply do not now have the time to thoroughly evaluate the educational strengths and weaknesses of a considerable portion of the existing curricular material and texts before they are used. Adding one more element, and a sizeable one at that, to be evaluated only increases the load. Teachers' work is increasingly becoming what students of the labour process call intensified. More and more needs to be done; less and less time is available to do it.[38] Thus, one has little choice but to simply buy ready-made material, in this way continuing a trend in which all of the important curricular elements are not locally produced but purchased from commercial sources whose major aim may be profit, not necessarily educational merit.[39]

A significant consideration here, besides the loss of skill and control, is expense. This is at least a three-pronged issue. First, we must recognise that we may be dealing with something of a 'zero-sum game'. While dropping, the cost of computers is still comparatively high, though some manufacturers may keep purchase costs relatively low, knowing that a good deal of their profits may come from the purchase of software later on or through a home/school connection, something I shall discuss shortly. This money for the new technology must come from some where. This is an obvious point but one that is very consequential. In a time of fiscal crisis, where funds are already spread too thinly and necessary programmes are being starved in many areas, the addition of computer curricula most often means that money must be drained from one area and given to another. What will be sacrificed? If history is any indication, it may be programmes that have benefitted the least advantaged. Little serious attention has been paid to this, but it will become an increasingly serious dilemma.

A second issue of expense concerns staffing patterns, for it is not just the content of teachers' work and the growth of purchased materials that are at stake. Teachers' jobs themselves are on the line here. At a secondary school level in many nations, for example, lay-offs of teachers have not been unusual as funding for education is cut. Declining enrollment in some regions has meant a loss of positions as well. This has caused intense competition over students within the school itself. Social studies, art, music, and other subjects must fight it out with newer, more 'glamorous' subject areas. To lose the student numbers game for too long is to lose a job. The effect of the computer in this situation has been to increase competitiveness among staff, often to replace substance with both gloss and attractive packaging of courses, and to threaten many teachers with the loss of their livelihood.[40] Is it really an educationally or socially wise decision to tacitly eliminate a good deal of the choices in these other fields so that we can support the 'glamour' of a computer future? These are not only financial decisions, but are ethical decisions about teachers' lives and about what our students are to be educated in. Given the future labour market, do we really want to claim that computers will be more important than further work in humanities and social sciences or, perhaps even more significantly in working class and ethnically diverse areas, in the students' own cultural, historical, and political heritage and struggles? Such decisions must not be made by only looking at the accountant's bottom line. These too need to be arrived at by the lengthy democratic deliberation of all parties, including the teachers who will be most affected.

Third, given the expense of microcomputers and software in schools, the pressure to introduce such technology may increase the already wide social imbalances that now exist. Private schools to which the affluent send their children and publicly funded schools in more affluent areas will have more ready access to the technology itself.[41] Schools in inner city, rural, and poor areas will be largely priced out of the market, even if the cost of 'hardware' continues to decline. After all, in these poorer areas and in many public school systems in general in a number of countries it is already difficult to generate enough money to purchase new textbooks and to cover the costs of teachers' salaries. Thus, the computer and literacy over it will 'naturally' generate further inequalities. Since, by and large, it will be the top twenty percent of the population that will have computers in their homes[43] and many of the jobs and institutions of higher education their children will be applying for will either ask for or assume 'computer skills' as keys of entry or advancement, the impact can be enormous in the long run.

The role of the relatively affluent parent in this situation does not go unrecognised by computer manufacturers.

> Computer companies . . . gear much of their advertising to the educational possibilities of computers. The drive to link particular computers to schools is a frantic competition. Apple, for example, in a highly touted scheme proposed to 'donate' an Apple to every school in America. Issues of philanthropy and intent aside, the clear market strategy is to couple particular computer usages to schools where parents – especially middle class parents with the economic wherewithal and keen motivation (to insure mobility – purchase machines compatible with those in schools. The potentially most lucrative part of such a scheme, however, is not in the purchase of hardware (although this is also substantial) but in the sale of proprietary software.[43]

This very coupling of school and home markets, then, cannot fail to further disadvantage large groups of students. Those students who already have computer backgrounds – be it because of their schools or their homes or both – will proceed more rapidly. The social stratification of life chances will increase. These students' original advantage – one not due to 'natural ability', but to wealth – will be heightened.[44]

We should not be surprised by this, nor should we think it odd that many parents, especially middle class parents, will pursue a computer future. Computer skills and 'literacy' is partly a strategy for the maintenance of middle class mobility patterns.[45] Having such expertise, in a time of fiscal and economic crisis, is like having an insurance policy. It partly guarantees that certain doors remain open in a rapidly changing labour market. In a time of credential inflation, more credentials mean less closed doors.[46]

The credential factor here is of considerable moment. In the past, as gains were made by ethnically different people, working class groups, women, and others in schooling, one of the latent effects was to raise the credentials required by entire sectors of jobs. Thus, class, race, and gender barriers were partly maintained by an ever increasing credential inflation. Though this was more of a structural than a conscious process, the effect over time has often been to again disqualify entire segments of a population from jobs, resources and power. This too may be a latent outcome of the computerisation of the school curriculum. Even though, as I have shown, the bulk of new jobs will not require 'computer literacy', the establishment of computer requirements and mandated programmes in schools will condemn many people to even greater economic disenfranchisement. Since the requirements are in many ways artificial – computer knowledge will not be so very necessary and the number of jobs requiring high levels of expertise will be relatively small – we will simply be affixing one more label to these students. 'Functional illiteracy' will simply be broadened to include computers.[47]

Thus, rather than blaming an unequal economy and a situation in which meaningful and fulfilling work is not made available, rather than seeing how the new technology for all its benefits is 'creating a growing underclass of displaced and marginal workers', the lack is personalised. It becomes the students' or workers' fault for not being computer literate. One significant social and ideological outcome of computer requirements in schools, then, is that they can serve as a means 'to justify those lost lives by a process of mass disqualification, which throws the blame for disenfranchisement in education and employment back on the victims themselves'.[48]

Of course, this process may not be visible to many parents of individual children. However, the point does not revolve around the question of individual mobility, but large scale effects. Parents may see such programmes as offering important paths to advancement and some will be correct. However, in a time of severe economic problems, parents tend to overestimate what schools can do for their children.[49] As I documented earlier, there simply will not be sufficient jobs and competition will be intense. The uncritical introduction of and investment in hardware and software will by and large hide the reality of the transformation of the labour market and will support those who are already advantaged unless thought is given to these implications now.

Let us suppose, however, that it was important that everyone become computer literate and that these large investments in time, money, and personnel were indeed so necessary for our economic and educational future. Given all this, what is currently happening in schools? Is inequality in access and outcome now being produced? While many educators are continually struggling against these effects, we are already seeing signs of this disadvantagement being created.

There is evidence of class, race, and gender based differences in computer use. In middle class schools, for example, the number of computers is considerably more than in working class or inner city schools populated by children of colour. The ratio of computers to children is also much higher. This in itself is an unfortunate finding. However, something else must be added here. These more economically advantaged schools not only have more contact hours and more technical and teacher support, but the very manner in which the computer is used is often different than what would be generally found in schools in less advantaged areas. Programming skills, generalisability, a sense of the multitudinous things one can do with computers both within and across academic areas, these tend to be stressed more[50] (though simply drill and practice uses are still widespread even here).[51] Compare this to the rote, mechanistic, and relatively low level uses that tend to dominate the working class school.[52] These differences are not unimportant, for they signify a ratification of class divisions.

Further evidence to support these claims is now becoming more readily available as researchers dig beneath the glowing claims of a computer future for all children. The differential impact is made clearer in the following figures. In the United States, while over two thirds of the schools in affluent areas have computers, only approximately forty-one percent of the poorer public schools have them. What one does with the machine is just as important as having one, of course, and here the differences are again very real. One study of poorer elementary schools found that white children were four times more likely than black children to use computers for programming. Another found that the children of professionals employed computers for programming and for other 'creative' uses. Non-professional children were more apt to use them for drill and practice in mathematics and reading, and for 'vocational' work. In general, in fact, 'programming has been seen as the purview of the gifted and talented' and of those students who are more affluent. Less affluent students seem to find that the computer is only a tool for drill and practice sessions.[53]

Gender differences are also very visible. Two out of every three students currently learning about computers are boys. Even here these data are deceptive since girls 'tend to be clustered in the general introductory courses', not the more advanced level ones.[54] One current analyst summarises the situation in a very clear manner.

> While stories abound about students who will do just about anything to increase their access to computers, most youngsters working with school computers are (economically advantaged), white and male. The ever-growing number of private computer camps, after-school and weekend programs serve middle-class white boys. Most minority (and poor) parents just can't afford to send their children to participate in these programmes.[55]

This class, race, and gendered impact will also occur because of traditional school practices such as tracking or streaming. Thus, vocational and business tracks will learn operating skills for word processing and will be primarily filled with (working class) young women.[56] Academic tracks will stress more general programming abilities and uses and will be disproportionately male.[57] Since computer programmes usually have their home bases in mathematics and science in most schools, gender differences can be heightened even more given the often differential treatment of girls in these classes and the ways in which mathematics and science curricula already fulfill 'the selective function of the school and contribute to the reproduction of gender differences'.[58] While many teachers and curriculum workers have devoted considerable time and effort to equalise both the opportunities and outcomes of female students in mathematics and science (and such efforts are important), the problem still remains a substantive one. It can be worsened by the computerisation of these subjects.

Towards Social Literacy

We have seen some of the possible negative consequences of the new technology in education, including the deskilling and depowering of teachers and the creation of inequalities through expense, credential inflation, and limitations on access. Yet it is important to realise that the issues surrounding the deskilling process are not limited to teachers. They include the very ways students themselves are taught to think about their education, their future roles in society, and the place of technology in that society. Let me explain what I mean by this.

The new technology is not just an assemblage of machines and their accompanying software. It embodies a form of thinking that orients a person to approach the world in a particular way. Computers involve ways of thinking that are primarily technical.[59] The more the new technology transforms the classroom into its own image, the more a technical logic will replace critical political and ethical understanding. The discourse of the classroom will centre on technique, and less on substance. Once again 'how to' will replace 'why', but this time at the level of the student. This situation requires what I shall call social, not technical, literacy for all students.

Even if computers make sense technically in all curricular areas and even if all students, not mainly affluent white males, become technically proficient in their use, critical questions of politics and ethics remain to be dealt with in the curriculum. Thus, it is crucial that whenever the new technology is introduced into schools students have a serious understanding of the issues surrounding their larger social effects, many of which I raised earlier.

Unfortunately, this is not often the case. When the social and ethical impacts of computers are dealt with, they are usually addressed in a manner that is less than powerful. One example is provided by a recent proposal for a statewide computer curriculum in one of the larger states in the United States. The objectives that dealt with social questions in the curriculum centered around one particular set of issues. The curriculum states that 'the student will be aware of some of the major uses of computers in modern society . . . and the student will be aware of career opportunities related to computers'.[60] In most curricula the technical components of the new technology are stressed. Brief glances are given to the history of computers (occasionally mentioning the role of women in their development, which is at least one positive sign). Yet in this history, the close relationship between military use and computer development is largely absent. 'Benign' uses are pointed to, coupled with a less than realistic description of the content and possibility of computer careers and what Douglas Noble has called 'a gee-whiz glance at the marvels of the future'. What is nearly never mentioned is job loss or social disenfranchisement. The very real destruction of the lives of unemployed autoworkers, assemblers or clerical workers is marginalised.[61] The ethical dilemmas involved when we choose between, say, 'efficiency' and the quality of the work people experience, between profit and someone's job, these too are made invisible.

How would we counterbalance this? By making it clear from the outset that knowledge about the new technology that is necessary for students to know goes well beyond what we now too easily take for granted. A considerable portion of the curriculum would be organised around questions concerned with social literacy. 'Where are computers used? What are they used to do? What do people actually need to know in order to use them? Does the computer enhance anyone's life? Whose? Does it hurt anyone's life? Whose? Who decides when and where computers will be used?'[62] Unless these are fully integrated in a school program at all levels, I would hesitate advocating the use of the new technology in the curriculum. To do less makes it much more difficult for students to think critically and independently about the place the new technology does and should have in the lives of the majority of people in our society. Our job as educators involves skilling, not deskilling. Unless students are able to deal honestly and critically with these complex ethical and social issues, only those now with the power to control technology's uses will have the capacity to act. We cannot afford to let this happen.

Conclusion

I realise that a number of my points may prove to be rather contentious in this essay. But stressing the negative side can serve to highlight many of the critical issues that are too easy to put off given the immense amount of work that school personnel are already responsible for. Decisions often get made too quickly, only to be regretted later on when forces are set in motion that could have been avoided if the implications of one's actions had been thought through more fully.

As I noted at the outset of this discussion, there is now something of a mad scramble to employ the computer in every content area. In fact, it is nearly impossible to find a subject that is not being 'computerised'. Though mathematics and science (and some parts of vocational education) remain the home base for a large portion of proposed computer curricula, other areas are not far behind. If it can be packaged to fit computerised instruction, it will be, even if it is inappropriate, less effective than the methods that teachers have developed after years of hard practical work, or less than sound educationally or economically. Rather than the machine fitting the educational needs and visions of the teacher, students, and community, all too often these needs and visions are made to fit the technology itself.

Yet, as I have shown, the new technology does not stand alone. It is linked to transformations in real groups of people's lives, jobs, hopes, and dreams. For some of these groups, those lives will be enhanced. For others, the dreams will be shattered. Wise choices about the appropriate place of the new technology in education, then, are not only educational decisions. They are fundamentally choices about the kind of society we shall have, about the social and ethical responsiveness of our institutions to the majority of our future citizens.

My discussion here has not been aimed at making us all neo-Luddites, people who go out and smash the machines that threaten our jobs or our children. The new technology is here. It will not go away. Our task as educators is to make sure that when it enters the classroom it is there for politically, economically, and educationally wise reasons, not because powerful groups may be redefining our major educational goals in their own image. We should be very clear about whether or not the future it promises to our students is real, not ficticious. We need to be certain that it is a future all of our students can share in, not just a select few. After all, the new technology is expensive and will take up a good deal of our time and that of our teachers, administrators, and students. It is more than a little important that we question whether the wagon we have been asked to ride on is going in the right direction. It's a long walk back.

Notes

This chapter is based on a more extensive analysis in Michael W. Apple, *Teachers and Texts: A Political Economy of Class and Gender Relations in Education* (Boston and London: Routledge and Kegan Paul, in press).

1   Noble D., *Forces of Production: A Social History of Industrial Automation* (New York: Alfred A. Knopf, 1984), pp. xi–xii. For a more general argument about the relationship between technology and human progress, see Nicholas Rescher, *Unpopular Essays on Technological Progress* (Pittsburgh: University of Pittsburgh Press, 1980).
2   Ibid, p. xv.
3   Olson P., 'Who Computes? The Politics of Literacy,' unpublished paper, Ontario Institute for Studies in Education, Toronto, 1985, p. 6.
4   Campbell B., 'The Computer Revolution: Guess Who's Left Out?,' *Interracial Books for Children Bulletin* 15 (no. 3 1984), 3.
5   'Instructional Strategies for Integrating the Microcomputer Into the Classroom,' The Vocational Studies Center, University of Wisconsin, Madison, 1985.
6   Apple M.W., *Ideology and Curriculum* (Boston: Routledge and Kegan Paul, 1979).
7   Olson, 'Who Computes?,' p. 5.
8   See Apple W., *Education and Power* (Boston: Routledge and Kegan Paul, 1982).
9   For further discussion of this, see Apple, *Ideology and Curriculum*, Apple, *Education and Power*, and Shor I., *Culture Wars* (Boston: Routledge and Kegan Paul, 1986).
10 This is treated in greater detail in Edwards R. *Contested Terrain*

(New York: Basic Books, 1979). See also the more extensive discussion of the effect these tendencies are having in education in Apple, *Education and Power*.

11 Rumberger E. and Levin H.M., 'Forcasting the Impact of New Technologies on the Future Job Market,' Project Report No. 84–A4, Institute for Research on Educational Finance and Government, School of Education, Stanford University, February, 1984, p. 1.
12 Ibid, p. 2.
13 Ibid, p. 3.
14 Ibid, p. 4.
15 Ibid, p. 18.
16 Ibid.
17 Ibid, p. 19.
18 Ibid, pp. 19–20.
19 Ibid, p. 31.
20 Ibid, p. 21.
21 Ibid.
22 Ibid, p. 25.
23 Ibid.
24 The effects of proletarianization and deskilling on women's labour is analysed in more detail in Apple M.W.,'Work, Gender and Teaching,' *Teachers College Record* 84 (Spring 1983), 611–628 and Apple M.W. 'Teaching and 'Woman's Work': A Comparative Historical and Ideological Analysis,' *Teachers College Record* 86 (Spring 1985). On the history of women's struggles against proletarianisation, see Kessler-Harris A. *Out to Work* New York: Oxford University Press, 1982.
25 Reinecke I., *Electronic Illusions* (New York: Penquin Books, 1984), p. 156.
26 See the further discussion of the loss of office jobs and the deskilling of many of those that remain in Ibid, pp. 136–158. The very same process could be a threat to middle and low level management positions as well. After all, if control is further automated, why does one need as many supervisory positions? The implications of this latter point need to be given much more consideration by many middle-class proponents of technology since their jobs may soon be at risk too.
27 Dwyer P., Wilson B., and Woock R., *Confronting School and Work* (Boston: George Allen and Unwin, 1984), pp. 105–106.
28 The paradigm case is given by the fact that three times as many people now work in low paying positions for MacDonalds as for U.S. Steel. See Carnoy M., Shearer D., and Rumberger R., *A New Social Contract* (New York: Harper and Row, 1983), p. 71. As I have argued at greater length eslewhere, however, it may not be important to our economy if all students and workers are made technically knowledgeable by schools. What is just as important is the production of economically useful knowledge (technical/administrative knowledge) that can be used by corporations to enhance profits, control labour, and increase efficiency. See Apple, *Education and Power*, especially Chapter 2.
29 Reinecke, *Electronic Illusions*, p. 234. For further analysis of the economic data and the effects on education, see Norton Grubb W. 'The Bandwagon Once More: Vocational Preparation for High-Tech

Occupations,' *Harvard Educational Review* 54 (November 1984), 429–451.

30   Apple, *Ideology and Curriculum* and Apple, *Education and Power*. See also Apple M.W. and Weis L., eds. *Ideology and Practice in Schooling* (Philadelphia: Temple University Press, 1983).

31   Ibid. See also Wise A., *Legislated Learning: The Bureaucratisation of the American Classroom* (Berkeley: University of California Press, 1979).

32   Apple, *Ideology and Curriculum* and Apple, *Education and Power*. On the general history of the growth of management techniques, see Edwards R., *Contested Terrain*.

33   Noble D., 'The Underside of Computer Literacy,' *Raritan* 3 (Spring 1984), 45.

34   See the discussion of this in Apple, *Education and Power*, especially Chapter 5.

35   Noble D., 'Jumping Off the Computer Bandwagon,' *Education Week*, October 3, 1984, 24.

36   Ibid.

37   Ibid. See also, Noble, 'The Underside of Computer Literacy,' 45.

38   For further discussion of the intensification of teachers' work, see Apple, 'Work, Gender and Teaching.'

39   Apple, *Education and Power*. For further analysis of the textbook publishing industry, see Apple M.W., 'The Culture and Commerce of the Textbook,' *Journal of Curriculum Studies* 17 (number 1 1985).

40   I am endebted to Susan Jungck for this point. See her excellent dissertation, 'Doing Computer Literacy,' unpublished Ph.D. dissertation, University of Wisconsin, Madison, 1985.

41   Reinecke, *Electronic Illusions*, p. 176.

42   Ibid, p. 169.

43   Olson, 'Who Computes?,' p. 23.

44   Ibid, p. 31. Thus, students' familiarity and comfort with computers becomes a form of what has been called the 'cultural capital' of advantaged groups. For further analysis of the dynamics of cultural capital, see Apple, *Education and Power* and Bourdieu P. and Passeron J-C., *Reproduction in Education, Society and Culture* (Beverly Hills: Sage, 1977).

45   Ibid, p. 23.

46   Once again, I am endebted to Susan Jungck for this argument.

47   Noble, 'The Underside of Computer Literacy,' 54.

48   Noble D., 'Computer Literacy and Ideology,' *Teachers College Record* 85 (Summer 1984), 611. This process of 'blaming the victim' has a long history in education. See Apple, *Ideology and Curriculum*, especially Chapter 7.

49   Connell R.W., *Teachers' Work* (Boston: George Allen and Unwin, 1985), p. 142.

50   Olson, 'Who Computes?,' p. 22.

51   For an analysis of the emphasis on and pedagogic problems with such limited uses of computers, see Streibel M., 'A Critical Analysis of the Use of Computers in Education,' unpublished paper, University of Wisconsin, Madison, 1984.

52 Olson, 'Who Computes?,' p. 22.
53 Campbell, 'The Computer Revolution: Guess Who's Left Out?,' 3. Many computer experts, however, are highly critical of the fact that students are primarily taught to program in BASIC, a less than appropriate language for later advanced computer work. Michael Streibel, personal communication.
54 Ibid.
55 Ibid.
56 An interesting analysis of what happens to young women in such business programs and how they respond to both the curricula and their later work experiences can be found in Valli L., 'Becoming Clerical Workers: Business Education and the Culture of Feminiity,' in Apple and Weis, ed. *Ideology and Practice in Schooling*, pp. 213–234. See also her forthcoming more extensive treatment in Valli L., *Becoming Clerical Workers* (Boston: Routledge and Kegan Paul, 1986).
57 Gaskell J. in Olson, 'Who Computes?,' p. 33.
58 Fomin F., 'The Best and the Brightest: The Selective Function of Mathematics in the School Curriculum,' in Johnson L. and Tyler D., eds. *Cultural Politics: Papers in Contemporary Australian Education, Culture and Politics* (Melbourne: University of Melbourne, Sociology Research Group in Cultural and Educational Studies, 1984), p. 220.
59 Michael Streibel's work on the models of thinking usually incorporated within computers in education is helpful in this regard. See Striebel, 'A Critical Analysis of the Use of Computers in Education.' The more general issue of the relationship between technology and the control of culture is important here. A useful overview of this can be found in Kathleen Woodward, ed. *The Myths of Information: Technology and Postindustrial Culture* (Madison: Coda Press, 1980).
60 Quoted in Noble, 'The Underside of Computer Literacy,' 56.
61 Ibid, 57.
62 Ibid, 40. For students in vocational curricula especially, these questions would be given more power if they were developed within a larger program that would seek to provide these young men and women with extensive experience in and understanding of *all* aspects of operating an entire industry or enterprise, not simply those 'skills' that reproduce workplace stratification. See Center for Law and Education, 'Key Provision in New Law Reforms Vocational Education: Focus is on Broader Knowledge and Experience for Students/Workers,' *Center for Law and Education, Inc. D. C. Report*, December 28, 1984, 1–6.

CHAPTER SIX

Fixing the Mix in Vocational Initiatives?

John Evans and Brian Davies

Introduction: Making the Bid

Our interest in this paper lies with the relationships between educational policy (in this case Technical and Vocational Educational Initiatives, TVEI), the perspectives of teachers and the school systems in which they operate. More broadly we are concerned with the relationship between schools and society (state and economy), with the degree and nature of autonomy or 'determination' experienced by teachers in schools of one sort or another. Our assertion is that educational policies, particularly those which originate outside of the school system, are always and inevitably subject to distortion, 'resistances' and contradiction as they are mediated by a complex interplay of organisational factors (such as time, resource, both human and physical) and the interpretive frameworks of teachers which together constitute the social and cultural worlds of schools.

The content of this paper is largely empirical. It is under-theorised though not atheoretical. We make no apologies for any of these conditions. Like Hargreaves (1982, 1985 and Hammersley *et al*, 1985) we feel that empirical research has an immensely important part to play in the development, testing and refinement of theory and we are conscious that to date much of the literature on the 'new vocationalism' has barely been so informed. Theoretically our research (as in our earlier work, see Davies and Evans 1984, Evans 1985) is guided by the work of both Bernstein (1977) and Lundgren (1977, 1983) and we have drawn on the concepts of classification and frame for the business of analysing our data. Here we use the concept frame to examine the nature of educational opportunities as they are organised and made available in the option systems of the four secondary schools involved in the study. We are interested in the

96

degree of control children have over their choice of options and in the range of options made available to them. We use the concept of classification to explore the relationships between educational categories such as the practical and the academic, the able and the less able child, and not, as intended by Bernstein (1971), to consider the boundaries between components of educational knowledge.

The research is focused on four large comprehensive schools within a TVEI consortium whose scheme failed in the competition within the LEA to become the scheme put forward for MSC funding. We would stress at the outset that this study has been limited in both its scope and penetration and that this is a report only upon the early stage of the data collection. The research began in January 1985 and has involved a series of interviews and casual conversation with TVEI coordinators and with teachers involved in vocational options in each of these schools. We have also observed lessons and engaged routinely in conversations with 'TVEI' pupils though most of the data is not yet ready for systematic use. Moreover, we have not yet had either the time or the opportunity to broaden the focus of research to include teachers not involved in TVEI, so the 'accounts' which follows are those of the missionaries rather than the unconverted. Nor are our concepts and categories at a stage of having reached a point of theoretical saturation (Glaser 1978). We hope, therefore, to avoid making any extravagant claims about TVEI. Our thoughts are largely speculative though they may illumine some of the currently neglected side effects of much researched 'official' schemes or even presage the day not too far ahead when the money runs out. Methodologically our guiding principles have been ethnographic rather than evaluative. We have set out to describe and explain the process of educational change in four secondary schools. The research is 'unsponsored' and our motivations for doing this work, as in our earlier work, largely reside in a mixture of ignorance and curiosity (a stimulating ethnographic cocktail). At base we have posed ourselves the question what is vocational education on this small patch? We are intrigued by a state scheme which bypasses all traditional funding channels the principles of which not only proclaim but prescribe equal opportunity of access to vocational curricula for all pupils irrespective of their 'ability', sex or class.

Technical and Vocational Education Initiative (TVEI) was announced in the House of Commons, by the Prime Minister, in November 1982. Four months later a National Steering Group constituted by representatives from industry, trade unions, educational organisations, local authorities and institutions of further and higher education had chosen the first fourteen projects to commence in September 1983. A year later, in September 1984 the number of

Authorities involved in the scheme had grown to 62. By September 1986 it was anticipated that eighty percent of all LEA's would be involved in the scheme (Pickard 1985). The pace of change has been nothing short of remarkable. Unsurprisingly, the noisy political and educational debate surrounding this policy innovation has sounded much like the noises of a wrestle between official false clarity and liberal teacher panic. While nearly all educational authorities are now involved in TVEI schemes, it might also be argued still that only a small number of schools and pupils are actually involved in MSC funded vocational initiatives. As Pickard (1985) points out, 'so far the scheme includes 3 percent of all 14 year olds, over eight percent of secondary schools', still a very tiny proportion of the secondary school population. But, we want to suggest that the expansion of vocationalism in the present British secondary school system may be a little more widespread than this brief chronology and description at first suggest. The process of TVEI and related innovation within and between schools is a bit more complex and problematic than is often suggested in the existing literature on the subject both by proponents and opponents alike.

The response to the range of in and post school vocational and training initiatives (YTS, YOPS, social and life skills courses, CPVE and TVEI) within the sociological and educational literature has been varied, interesting and not altogether unpredictable. For some, often those involved with it, TVEI has been seen, quite euphorically, to represent 'the most important opportunity for curriculum change for 14–18 year olds since the 1944 Education Act' (Wallace 1984, p. 3). It is a major national initiative, the means of re-directing the emphasis in the upper school curriculum away from the 'abstract and the theoretical' in the direction of 'practical experience and useful knowledge' (loc cit.). Even amongst more cautious academics TVEI has been seen to have a potential for 'radical change'. For Pring (1985) for example, TVEI is likely to 'force schools and teachers to re-examine the educational aims embodied in their curriculum organisation, teaching style and subject content' and 'reconceptualise (the) processes through which we educate young people' (p. 17). But perhaps the most powerful, provocative and challenging view of the 'new vocationalism' has come from those (see Bates *et al* 1984, Gleeson 1983, Clarke and Willis 1984, Moore 1983, 1984) who have seen recent and particularly post school training initiatives in a much less favourable light (and TVEI would be easily accommodated within this critique though it hasn't been specifically referred to). For these (see Bates *et al* 1984 in particular) the new vocationalism represents amongst other things, the culmination of a slow but inexorable (since the mid 1970's) process of political intervention into the school and college curriculum. This intervention is seen as likely to resurrect or harden existing curriculum and con-comitant social divisions within schools and colleges (see Gleeson 1983, 1985) along the lines of the 'old tripartism'. This critique has undoubtedly gone straight to the heart of the rationales which have accompanied many of the vocational initiatives; to attack the rhe-toric which has claimed that the educational system not only could, but also should, solve Britains' social and economic problems; and that teachers are to blame for failing to equip pupils with the nece-ssary basic skills and 'positive' attitude essential to enter work, at a time of unprecedentedly high adult and youth unemployment. Official agency and 'market oriented' media and academia press the notion of the 'anti-industry bias' of the educational system. At another pole, Moore (1984) views vocational initiatives and the justi-ficatory notions of relevance which they contain as merely hiding the fact that schools are primarily concerned with 'pragmatic adjust-ments in their practices in response to control problems in the class-room'. (p. 73) We know that these problems are not unconnected with the collapse of traditional levels and forms of training and employment themselves as well as the curricular inertia of a contra-cting school system.

Now our intention here is not to embark on a detailed critique of such positions/perspectives though we will have something to say about them later. The point here is that little of this literature (whether of a supportive or oppositional kind) really engages with the world of schools, organisational and institutional life as it is experienced by teachers and pupils as workers. In using this term, we wish to focus upon the active work of curricular production in which all teachers in all classrooms engage. Whether they have devised it personally or locally or not, all teachers 'provide' pupils with a world of classroom work, they embody or transmit content in specific modes. The central reality of a teacher's occupational life is the shaping, provision and controlling of such activity, just as a pupil's dominant experience is of classroom work (or energy expended in its avoidance, subversion etc.) contexts made available. Only a clear formulation of the organisational nature of these contexts is likely to help teachers towards the formulation of policy and an under-standing of how they might best achieve or avoid the kind of curri-cular or pedagogical conditions which this literature so interestingly skirts around but has not yet got in balanced focus. Perhaps this criticism is especially true of the view from the left. The fundamental aim of Bates *et al* (1984), for example, 'is to keep in mind the material experience and *cultures of the pupils* (our emphasis) and to see how teachers can respond to these problems' (Clarke & Willis 1984 p. 12). There is still an over-identification with the pupils of the working class who are portrayed as a group cleverly resisting the alien values of an oppressive school system (see Moore 1984). Empirically, as ethnographers (see Hargreaves 1982) and teachers will tell us, this comes close to being nonsense. Children who have successfully failed (and no more is it the case that all failures are working class than that all working class pupils are failures) for four or more years are often neither sophisticated in their thinking nor homogeneous in their motivations for action. And while they may be adequately trained in the family, community and local labour force, they may also not be educated; and this is the quest of most teachers. The cultural world of teachers, their histories, institutional life and actions as workers, are sadly overlooked and neglected. We understand little of teachers' difficulties, their culture, their resistances (though the promise to try and do so is there in Apple 1985), of the pressures which they work under and the material conditions of their organisational life.

Coming Second and The Second Coming

In September 1983 David Young wrote to all LEAs in England and Wales with the news that TVEI was to be extended and that the Commission was

> 'now inviting LEA's not already receiving financial support under TVEI to submit proposals in accordance with the criteria and guidelines for schemes to begin in September 1984'.
>
> (see MSC 1984)

Project applications were to reach the MSC by 12 noon on Monday December 12 (a bare eleven weeks after this announcement). The response of the LEA's to this invitation was understandably hurried and idiosyncratic (see Dale 1985). At Broxford (in which the research was located) the reaction of the LEA was to devolve responsibility for constructing TVEI schemes to schools and colleges within its educational divisions. The initiative was to lie with the motivations and interests of local schools and colleges. By mid October the Western regional consortium within which our four schools lay, had been established. A meeting was convened by the Principal of one of the division's sixth form colleges and invitations extended to the heads of its 'feeder' secondary schools and a neighbouring FE college. It sets out its goals '(i) to make preparations so as to be in a position to be considered for Broxford funding for TVEI 1984/85 and (ii) to prepare a cogent case to submit to the LEA for the sum of £12,000 still available in the current year budget for special projects' (Consortium Document). It is tempting to portray this phase of the innovation as both unproblematic and tension free, but this was hardly the case. The time-scales involved and the absence of central (LEA or Government) directives on the mechanisms of change ensured that schools and colleges within and between regions were placed in a position of competing with each other in the construction of schemes which they hoped would be accepted by LEAs for submission to the MSC. At the Western consortium's first meeting for example, it was noted that there was 'disquiet in other secondary schools (which weren't feeder schools) which had been unaware of the TVEI scheme' (Document). Within a month of the consortium having been formed it also learned that the Northeast regional consortium's scheme had been recommended as the County's submission to the MSC, and that, as one member of the Western consortium put it, 'Northeast division had been beavering away at a submission for over a year'. The actions of the County Education officers thus seemed both arbitrary and unfair particularly to those teachers who remained unaware of the conditions or the criteria which had secured the adoption and success of the Northeast submission. However, the Western consortium were now left in a position of having a great deal more on their hands than an educational idea which could be easily dissipated or dissolved in the absense of central (MSC) funding. The amount of time, energy, resource which had been invested in the formation of the consortium and its submission, along with the elaborate management structure which had been constituted to make concrete and support the initiative, meant that, unsurprisingly, teachers were rather unwilling to dismantle their efforts. Thus despite the fact that they had come second in the TVEI stakes (the Northeast division going on to receive MSC support) the consortium worked on in the hope that there would be a second coming, another later round of MSC handouts in which they would be financially favoured. In the meantime the LEA made available a relatively small sum of money to support and provide 'supply' teacher cover while teachers from each of the schools met together to design and develop their vocational initiatives.

Motivational Matters

It would be all too easy to portray and explain the attempted involvement of these schools and colleges in TVEI as the product of the incentive of financial inducement. This however would be a gross misrepresentation of the motivations of teachers and a severe reduction of the complexity of their actions. It would also tell us little of the conditions which so limit the possibilities for educational change in British secondary schools today. In order to emphasise and illustrate this point we will try, as briefly as possible, to provide some vignettes of four secondary schools, concentrating on their motivations for involvement. We would stress that the accounts given are largely those of the TVEI co-ordinators, the gatekeepers through whose perspectives and actions TVEI as an educational policy cum idea was initially mediated in each school. We also stress that although it is perfectly proper to talk about these schools planning for TVEI, their consortium bid was an initial failure and they worked not on MSC funds but limited LEA pump-priming. Despite this, they saw themselves as still in the 'TVEI business' though we will now refer to 'N(New)VEI' in these schools to indicate that they are not of the official sponsored kind.

Maindene

Maindene is a large, co-educational comprehensive school on the outskirts of a city. It is plagued by falling rolls and a pupil intake skewed towards the middle to lower end of the ability spectrum. Here, the school's senior management/Head and Deputy (the latter who was the NVEI co-ordinator) displayed early support for the idea of vocational education. Prior to the formation of the consortium the Head and Deputy had been 'following the debate with some interest' and they had made a deliberate effort to inform the staff of all vocational developments.

For this school, involvement in TVEI offered a great deal more than just the possibilities of financial sponsorship. As the NVEI co-ordinator put it . . .

'we could see a sharing of resources, a division of labour, a sharing of expertise. We could see a horizontal development across the secondary schools. Liaison has always been vertical as you know, but the horizontal liaison produces the division of labour we spoke of, the sharing of expertise and the sharing of material goods'.

He goes on to say . . . 'So there was a logic behind it all, as well as a bit of greed.'

This 'logic' has to be located within the specific conditions of schooling in which Maindene (as schools elsewhere) operated. As all other schools in the consortium, Maindene was in the business of trying to protect and improve its ability intake by working on its public image. It was seriously concerned with the implications of falling rolls upon levels of human and physical resource. As such it was competing with all other schools in the consortium for a limited supply of pupil talent, a task made all the more problematic because of the social and ability mix of its immediate client population.

In the increasingly 'marketised' conditions of this competition, Maindene's senior teachers greeted TVEI in language of collaboration and co-operation, assuming a willingness on the part of other schools and teachers to enter into a mutual exchange.

'This is part of what TVEI is all about, not only an interchange of ideas but an interchange of physical resources . . .'

(NVEI co-ordinator Maindene)

Such motivations for involvement were essentially managerial and pragmatic. They resided in concerns for the improvement of organisational life for both teachers and pupils. They revolved around considerations of levels of resource, staffing and the range of curricular options which could be made available to children. It was also felt that TVEI might help towards the management of the school's disinterested pupils and so indirectly improve its public image. As one NVEI teacher commented, TVEI is seen by senior management as a 'safety valve', though he was at pains to point out that this was not the reason for his own involvement and commitment to its' development.

Rainford

At Rainford, Maindene's neighbouring co-educational school, both the Head and Deputy (the latter again appointed as the NVEI co-ordinator) took up the initiative with some considerable enthusiasm. The school too was plagued by the problem of falling rolls and was seriously concerned to try and achieve a better social and ability mix of pupils at intake. The Head was appointed Chairman of the consortium's Management Group and was seen by some as the mainstay of the innovation, as a person without whom the consortium would sadly falter, even collapse. It was he who outlined the aims of the consortium and determined the mechanism by which the innovation should be introduced and disseminated within the school system. His prescriptions assumed a management structure conducive to open, participatory democracy through staff and departmental meetings and so on. In the perspective of his NVEI co-ordinator 'the climate was right for curriculum change, we were well down the road of curriculum development'. The school was working towards a 'broad curriculum for all its pupils, irrespective of age, ability etc.' for approximately seventy percent of the time, even in the 4th and 5th years. Consequently NVEI was seen as something which could fit fairly comfortably into the area of the options, in other words, twenty five or thirty percent of the pupil's time. Like other teachers within the school involved in NVEI, senior management rejected 'any implication that we were training kids for jobs'. And other teachers echoed these sentiments even more forceably.

However, as at Maindene, NVEI was also seen as the means of better managing a disaffected and disinterested majority of middle ability pupils.

> 'The more able we felt were able to cope, to cater for themselves in that they were much better motivated because they had much more success. But the middle lot we were thinking good grief, you know, lots of courses offered to them are just not relevant to what they want, they are not particularly well motivated, they are not very interested in what they are doing and we were looking for other things in many cases for them to do'.
>
> (NVEI co-ordinator, Rainford)

The middle ability range presented the school with its problems of control and the experiential curricula of NVEI was seen as a means of better managing it.

At Rainford then, as at Maindene (and as we see at Barton too) the desire to better control the pupil population was amongst the motivations for involvement in NVEI. However, we would stress that it would be hasty indeed were we to straightforwardly read off from this that the intention of securing greater order within these schools was one and the same thing as either the desire for or the achievement of greater control over pupils (see Hargreaves 1982). Nor would it be wise to assume that the motivations of senior teachers are the same as those teachers who ultimately realised vocational education in their classrooms. It is clearly also unwise to assume that any 'control' achieved in any one classroom is transferable to others. Indeed the levels of increased interest which were often experienced by pupils in NVEI classrooms could well have heightened lack of interest in others. In this view we need to consider that NVEI could be either dysfunctionally or functionally related to a school's concerns for order and control.

Cranfield and Barton

The response of the senior management at Cranfield and Barton were altogether different, more diffident and uncertain than those in the schools described above. Both these schools are large single sex, 12–16 comprehensives with intakes socially and academically more mixed than those of Rainford and Maindene. Neither school was particularly 'plagued' by falling rolls, though both were concerned with their public image and eager to protect the quality of their intake. In both schools the Heads received NVEI only cautiously and somewhat coldly. At Barton (the all boys school) the Head's response was to immediately devolve responsibility for NVEI to a senior 'curriculum co-ordinator' who attended management meetings in place of the Head. This was seen by some staff within the school to announce that the Head 'was only marginally interested'. In effect the NVEI co-ordinator was placed in an unenviable position (between an uninterested Head and an unenlightened staff) of having as one teacher put it 'power without credibility' (Head of Department). The NVEI co-ordinator himself however, saw NVEI as a 'tremendous chance to get the school into something worthwhile'. For him, 'money didn't matter', the new vocationalism was important because it was simply 'unrealistic to think of 100 boys going on to University. They want jobs, they need to offer the employer something'. However, while he saw this initiative as something which ideally should be available to pupils across the ability range, in practice the idea met with some considerable resistance . . .

'I would have deep discussions with the Head about whether these boys (for NVEI options) should be right across the board or whether they should be middle or lower. We reached a compromise. He wanted his high fliers doing the classical curriculum and I wanted it across the school . . .'
(NVEI co-ordinator Barton)

The ideals for the dissemination of NVEI as an idea, outlined by the Head of Rainford school (the Chairman of the Consortium) could hardly be realised in this school context. The Barton co-ordinator found the task of disseminating news about NVEI within the school very difficult indeed. Staff were 'antagonistic, resentful, they wanted it out. They perceived it as a threat. The Head didn't stop that he was quite happy to see it go down'.
(NVEI co-ordinator Barton)

This co-ordinator was then, left largely to go it alone, to identify and sell the idea to interested staff and the vocational initiative was always carefully filtered through the Head's 'traditional' classical perspective with clear effects, as we shall see, on option allocations.

At Cranfield (the girls' school) as at Barton, the Head of school had been largely indifferent to the vocational initiative and it was not until her departure in January 1984 and the appointment of a new Head and Deputy that any enthusiasm for NVEI was shown. Although the previous head had attended management meetings, NVEI had in the opinion of the new Deputy and NVEI co-ordinator, 'never been brought to a full staff meeting'. Indeed this remained the case until the Spring term of 1985. The new Head and Deputy (NVEI co-ordinator) saw NVEI as just one small component of a much broader curriculum and organisational reform needed within the school. As Ms. Richards (NVEI co-ordinator) stated 'we want to introduce curriculum change and we've been full of that really and there's so much to be done that NVEI has had to take a back seat . . . (but we've got 50 girls doing NVEI options)'.

For this teacher (as for the Head) NVEI was seen as only a small segment of a grander plan for 'improving the educational opportunities of girls within the school'. And their first priority was to ensure that the school had an organisational and management structure conducive to and supportive of curriculum change.

The ambitions of both Head and Deputy were to provide a curriculum for their girls as complete, comprehensive and 'varied as that of any co-educational school . . .' (NVEI co-ordinator Cranfield). Their efforts were directed towards the goal of improving educational opportunities and of challenging the stereotypical attitudes held by some staff and pupils.

In principle then, these teachers at Cranfield were concerned to use NVEI as part of a broad policy of introducing further vocational curricula into the school curriculum for all the children. The idea that vocational education was to be confined to a small number of pupils was firmly rejected in principle (though it was accepted that perhaps that was where the innovation had to start). The goal was to 'shift the emphasis of the whole curriculum'. (NVEI co-ordinator Cranfield)

Once again then, NVEI was very carefully filtered into the curriculum via an interpretation of the school's most immediate and pressing needs and the values of senior management. The concern was to put their 'own house in order' to equip their school with a curriculum as comprehensive as any co-educational establishment. Ironically, this ideal ran directly counter to the ambitions of other schools (like Maindene) and the principles of the consortium which, as mentioned early, suggested inter-school collaboration, a sharing of resource and so on. As the Deputy Head (NVEI co-ordinator Cranfield) remarked

'So if its going to start being the numbers game then lets have our girls here and it means that we've got to bend a little for equipment so that we can give them a good course . . . but I'm sure we can do it . . .'

TVEI, as Pring (1985) has argued provides only a 'set of criteria that spells out what the TVEI curriculum should look like'. These criteria are broad enough to 'allow for a range of interpretations and in no way can they be construed as narrowly vocational or indeed as illiberal' (p. 15). The data above would indeed tend to lend some support to this viewpoint. In each of the schools NVEI was subject to the interpretations of senior management. The scheme was adapted, adopted, resisted and exploited according to the highly localised and ideosyncratic needs of the schools, the teachers and pupils within them. Indeed, the data above has hardly touched upon the degree to which this process of mediation occurs in schools.

All these teachers were very concerned to protect the autonomy of their institution, in Bernstein's terms to re-affirm the strength of classification between the business of schooling, education and the demands of the economy. In each of these schools vocational education meant the inclusion of some (perhaps 2 or 3) new options into the upper school curriculum, along with re-orientations in old areas. The idea of a common consortium 'core' was rejected by the consortium as they asserted the independence and autonomy of individual schools and teachers to decide for themselves what was in the best interest of their teachers and pupils (though both Cranfield and Rainford adopted a core). As one NVEI co-ordinator (at Barton) reported, the idea of a common consortium core was rejected because

> 'there was some suspicions that this was a centralised curriculum, introduced by the Government indirectly through the M.S.C. and local Education Authorities'

'Relative Autonomy' in the Option System (or Fixing The Mix in NVEI?)

But Richard Pring is also substantially wrong and Bernstein (1977) and Lundgren (1983) all too right, in that while the 'systemic relations' between education and work are strongly classified, the work of social and cultural production still gets done inside schools. Although NVEI does only provide a set of criteria broad enough to allow for 'a range of interpretations', such freedom to choose is constructed and conducted within parameters which are firmly set for teachers not only by the limits of their own professional thinking about curriculum and pedagogy, but also by a range of factors, such as the principle of parental choice (bludgeon of the educational marketeers), the expectations of parents and pupils, the biographies and identities of children already established in the lower school curriculum and the awesome power of the examination system.

The power yielded by the examination system, in classifying and attributing status to particular sorts of knowledge and concomitantly to pupils is evidenced below. But we would also want to suggest that no single factor or mechanism sufficiently explains the limits imposed on the option choices of pupils in each of these schools, or by itself re-produces the 'conventional' classification and framing of knowledge.

While we again underline that the schemes we are referring to were not governed by the rigours of formal contractual relations with the MSC, we argue that the introduction of 'unsponsored NVEI' into the upper 14–16 curriculum in each of these schools did not bring with it any sudden transformation of educational categories in the thinking of teachers, or any weakening in the classification of boundaries between subjects and associated types of children, or any weakening in the frames on access to areas of the curriculum which had previously been the preserve of either high or low status pupils. In each of these schools vocational options tended to be disproportionately 'filled' by the average and less able pupils although the emphasis varied slightly from school to school. And it is difficult to see how even the much greater injection of official money alone into the system could/would alter this pattern. As the recent HMI report on first generation sponsored TVEI schemes also found (Bolton 1985) 'pupils of average and low ability were represented in all projects, but few of very high ability or very low ability appeared to have joined', though it does not go on to explain how or why this outcome or problem is so regularly achieved.

At both schools seriously concerned with their pupil intake (Maindene and Rainford) NVEI options were intentionally offered largely for the average and less able pupils. At Maindene the NVEI principle of providing access to all pupils is rationalised and interpreted as the responsibility of the consortium,

> 'now that (providing access to all pupils) is the responsibility of the consortium . . . it doesn't mean that every single school in the consortium must put in the full ability range . . .'
>
> (NVEI co-ordinator Maindene)

This is somewhat ironic, for Maindene, despite its relative lack of able children, stood nearest to having mixed-ability options thrust upon it by falling rolls. They had achieved

> 'a huge impact on our staffing, on our option system and what we can offer, irrespective of NVEI . . . we had a banded system of options up until I think last September – was the first time we departed from it. We've now got as you can see, an all through option system then in the fifth year is the banded option . . .'
>
> (NVEI co-ordinator Maindene)

In this context then, a mixed ability option system was purely an accident of falling rolls, which meant that 'in theory any child can choose any subject now which he couldn't before when it was in two bands . . .' (NVEI co-ordinator Maindene)

In practice however, a number of factors combined to ensure that this mix rarely happened

> 'you see we have a very complicated option system as you can see, that is

the top two lines of that timetable and it works out, not intentionally – but it works out that those children who want to take things like German or Integrated Science you know this 11 + double entry 'O' level cannot by the practical nature of things do a NVEI course where you need two modules of PVE [Personal and Vocational Education] because the options boxes will not allow you in the time you're allowed in a week.'

(NVEI co-ordinator Maindene)

and

'It's quite a complicated system but it does sort them out in a fairly logical way . . . self sorting if you like. It takes a lot of time but . . .'

(NVEI co-ordinator, Maindene)

These statements are of some considerable interest because they hint at not only the mechanisms by which pupils are differentiated in the upper school curriculum, but also the rationales which accompany, support and legitimise this process. Both mechanism and rhetorics are featured in the perspectives of teachers at Maindene, Barton, Rainford and Cranfield. In each of these schools, the sorting process is neither direct nor 'intentional', that is to say it is not achieved by teachers simply telling pupils which block or option he or she should choose, nor was it something which the teachers particularly desired. To the contrary, the option/selection system works by providing a framework of limited opportunity in which children are expected to recognise for themselves the limits of their own ability, and secondly to choose curricula appropriate to their 'status' and (post-school) occupational routes. Failing this, the school seems to act only in an *advisory* capacity, very often appealing to the help of parents (and the biographies of the children themselves), to ensure that any mis-recognition of talents does not take place (cf. Woods 1978).

'you see here we've got this advisory section here, we tell the kids look, you first have two choices. Your first choice . . . we advise these sets to make the first choice in this band etc . . . and PVE is open to all these sets but notice we miss out (sets) 1 and 1A which are our top two sets. So they opt for a first choice in these bands and then for the second choice they can opt across the bands . . .'

(NVEI co-ordinator, Maindene)

and

'we say to the parents and to the kids, it's no good going for German or for IS if in the years 2 and 3 you've had no experience of these. There's no point. Why deny someone else who's had experience, a place when you'll foul it up and want to leave after a few weeks? They do opt within their abilities and capabilities . . . '

(NVEI co-ordinator, Maindene)

At Maindene then, the system of selection built on pupil/curriculum hierarchies already established in the lower school curriculum (see Raffe 1985). It, of all the schools, could hardly afford to indulge in forms of curriculum re-organisation which would or could place at risk the identification of its already scarce supply of pupil talent.

At Barton and at Cranfield, the vocational options also tended to attract the middle and less able pupils. At Barton, as we mentioned earlier, NVEI was carefully filtered through the 'classical' perspectives of the Head teacher. There was something of a 'tension' between this and the more 'liberal' perspective of the NVEI co-ordinator. As a result NVEI was effectively compromised within the option system.

While in theory, all pupils had access to vocational options, in practice, pupils were 'selected from across the ability range with the exception of the top twenty per cent who are *guided* into a highly academic curriculum' (NVEI co-ordinator, Barton), while those at the lower end of the ability range had only 'a limited selection from the vocational options since some courses will be beyond their capabilities . . .' (Ibid) The NVEI options here then, as in all the other schools, were essentially for the middle range pupils, some of whom were also difficult pupils. As at Maindene and Rainford the NVEI options were intended to be more interesting to the average pupil and help lessen pupil management and control problems. As the NVEI co-ordinator at Barton stated

> 'The extreme low were . . . this is an awful thing to say perhaps, but the extreme low were too slow to create a problem because they could always be picked up easily. Problems I believe in school exist in the lower middle to middle middle . . . The upper middle were quick enough to realise that they weren't taking G.C.E.'s they were taking C.S.E.'s and that the G.C.E.'s would be in front of them in the job queue and then they became disaffected and that tended to affect some of the G.C.E. candidates . . .'

But the 'guidance' system here was both complex and subtle and involved tutors making assessments both of a pupil's social and academic credentials – an assessment which was then passed on to a senior teacher, the Curriculum Co-ordinator, for further screening. Again, the organisation of the option system firstly set limits to the choices available to pupils; the less able, for example being 'directed' into a Basic Studies course, which in taking up two option blocks effectively limited their opportunities to take up other vocational 'subjects'; while, as the NVEI co-ordinator put it, 'we steer away the top twenty five percent . . . the real high fliers in the hope that they might go on to further professional training or to University . . .'. But there was no simple intention or hope that vocational education could achieve some sort of blanket control. Here, those pupils who were of average ability and behaviourly difficult were carefully screened out of those options which demanded that they travel to neighbouring schools. The school's concern to protect its public image, to confine its behavioural problem to the boundaries of the school had thus given rise to a peculiar form of the Catch 22 of educational practice – if you can't do the practices required to learn in 'conventional' academic curriculum and you 'don't behave' then you don't get access to those alternative curriculum in which you might learn and so want to behave! Protecting school 'brand image' in the newly marketised fight for entries had set limits to the opportunities of using vocational options for the purpose of social control.

At Cranfield both Head and Deputy were, as mentioned earlier, concerned to introduce a more comprehensive curriculum to their girls. They were, at least in the first instance, concerned to weaken the frame of gender rather than ability expectations. Here the 'control' motivation did not feature in the perspectives of teachers. These teachers, (as indeed all those concerned) were very conscious of academic (ability) divisions, but they also saw the examination system along with the expectations of their 'client' parents, imposing severe constraints on any ambitions which they might have to challenge curriculum status hierarchies. As the Cranfield NVEI co-ordinator put it, 'parents won't let their children opt for anything without an examination, that hasn't an 'O level' attached to it . . .'

Moreover, the curriculum co-ordinator felt that it was their duty to help girls achieve all that was possible within the conventional subject hierarchies . . .

'we can't gamble with these girls, we wouldn't want to put a real high flier into these (vocational) options . . . if they are going on to University.'

Again, the concept of self selection is invoked to explain how the problem of differentiation and assessment works.

'They were all offered to take option X and we've got two bands. Those in NVEI came from both so it's right in the middle I'd say . . . none of them very low and none of them really high fliers . . .'

and

'It's just the way it happens . . . because the high fliers want to get their 'O' levels don't they, they can't afford to drop out . . .'

The language used by all of these teachers when describing their option systems, (including concepts such as 'self selection', 'guidance' 'advice', the denial of teacher 'intentionality') thus functioned to resolve not only a contradiction between the 'principles' of NVEI and their within school organisational practices, but also a tension in their own thinking and ideals about how educational practice ought to be. Each of these teachers would have liked to have seen more movement between the practical and academic options and a weakening of the boundaries between high and low ability pupils and subjects. But they were also, as managers, realistic enough to know that attracting a good clientele was an essential first priority. Moreover, gaining legitimation by meeting the expectations of parents meant making the most in 'conventional terms' of what available 'talent' their school had acquired. There was nothing conspiratorial or dishonest in their actions. By the age of 13–14 differences between children had already been produced within and by the lower school curriculum. Thus the task which the school saw as quite legitimate was that of ensuring that children could themselves recognise their ability, build on it and translate it into appropriate curricular routes. The interest of the school and teachers was firstly and foremostly to improve the lot of pupils within existing structures of curricular organisation and practice – to alter qualitatively not the pupils experience of post-school work, but of being *at* work in the routine conditions of their life at school. Any wider vision of either social transformation or system maintenance was not their immediate concern.

Relative Autonomy and Educational practice, ctd: Change within limits

Like others (see Wallace 1984 p. 8) we have taken the view that the education system in England and Wales enshrines a whole series of autonomies devolved from central to local government, from LEA's to governors, down to head and the teacher in his or her classroom. This indeed is 'a principle which the innovator as well as the analyst of TVEI ignores at her/his peril' (loc cit.). In practical terms, we would argue that the post-war system has developed increasing robustness in the face of possible exogenous change. LEAs and their bureaucracies have increased in size, complexity and strength. The large and deeply divided teacher base is not easily marched in any direction. And changes like comprehensive re-organisation have achieved much more than just a change in the external landscape of schooling. It has made the internal management of an educational policy or idea a much more complex operation and with it the possibilities of any direct State intervention in the internal functioning of schools (into the curriculum, organisation and content), a much more difficult thing to achieve. The direct appeal to the self-interested school consumer built into TVEI is itself good evidence of how many wires need to be snipped before there is a chance of tied response. The evolution and elaboration of pastoral and academic structures has been a concomitant of comprehensive re-organisation, and this has tended to further decentralise and complicate the development and coordination of policy, both academic and pastoral. This change has made it more difficult for senior management to influence the actions of departments and individual teachers. Schools as Bidwell (1965) has long argued, are indeed best characterised by their 'structural looseness' rooted materially in their technological and work practices rather than any tight uniformity and consensus over values and practices. In short, we should bear in mind that the professional cum-cultural autonomy of teachers has a material basis both in the organisation of schooling and in the organisation of work and it is these which generate and support the possibilities of differences, diversities of value systems and 'resistances' within schools and between them and the State. We are in a period in which an increasingly interventionist right wing education policy grows impatient with established teacher rights and practices. TVEI comes closer than anything we have seen for eighty years to direct State intervention in schools. But of course it is still only indirect, little understood and of uncertain duration. It is not all the change, vocationally directed or otherwise, taking place in secondary schools. Its importance may be less than is apparent from outward expenditures (taking the money and running is a complex educational phenomenon) and more (moral panic being what it is). We merely want to argue, after Lundgren (1983) that the pedagogic process is not 'just' determined by a number of frame factors (outside agencies or agents and the products of their decision making).

> 'But that pedagogic processes are constituted on the possible freedom for action which exists in a given situation. What the frames accomplish is to mark out the limits which pedagogic process can have. Within these limits the actual curriculum is carried out on the basis of the interpretation which it is given in a local school. Frames in combination with the character of the content of the curriculum thus provides an outer limit within which the pedagogic process can occur' (p. 159).

This lands us up in some very mundane necessities of understanding the nature and functioning of schools as places of work. Indeed we would go as far as to say that understanding much about theoretical objects like 'relative autonomy' as well as specific innovations like TVEI is conditional upon some knowledge of the latter – of teachers and pupils as workers, of teachers and pupils in work. This would not only be of some theoretical interest, it would also bring our sociological enquiry and analyses much closer to the concerns and interests of those who work inside schools (without at the same time not being confined to those interests). Yet this form and focus of analyses has hardly found a place in sociological research. As Tipton recently argued, schools as places for 'the reproduction and transmission of knowledge has never been fully explored mainly because of the habit of treating them as part and parcel of the process of social stratification' (1985 p. 35).

The image is one of schooling for work or the dole, rather than as schooling as work. This has left sociology in an ideological *cul-de-sac*, leaving people simply taking sides in debate and unable to help inform practitioners about how their material bases (of practice and ideology) might best be understood let alone altered, modified or transformed in the cause of educational change.

But to look at schools as places of work is to consider that teachers are not only concerned with (albeit at the retail and service end) the production and organisation of knowledge (cf. Apple 1985) but also with the management of time, pedagogy, resource, both human and physical and their interplay. Decisions relating to each and all of these factors might both express and set limits to the interests, thoughts and actions of teachers and pupils at various levels within the institution. In this paper we have only been concerned with the production and management of knowledge for the option systems, through the actions of senior managers/teachers, and these actions cannot be seen independently of other considerations regarding time, resource, the expectations of 'others' and so on, of utmost concern to those teachers in the management of their institutions.

We are also of the opinion that teachers work with (even if they do not often articulate it in these terms) the notion of pupils as workers and that this notion is crucial to our understanding of the limits of educational and social change and of the process of social and cultural reproduction. TVEI may be attractive to teachers because it allows them to improve the conditions of work for some of their disaffected pupils, at that moment, in school. It (TVEI) allows pupils for at least some of their time, in vocational options, to engage in curricula which come close to being work rather than labour.

'Labour which creates use value and is qualitatively determined is called work as opposed to labour; labour which creates value but is only measured quantitatively is called labour as opposed to work.'
(See Marx 1918, p. 3, footnote by Engels)

TVEI *work* then, in itself is not socially transformative – it does not challenge conventional curriculum or social hierarchies, it does not equip pupils with the knowledge to change anything outside of school, nor does it prepare them for their post school labour process (what we have seen in schools is often so unlike labour). In this sense the transformation of labour to work in schools for some pupils is ultimately conservative in its implications and outcomes. But this makes it nonetheless valid, important and meaningful for those teachers and pupils who (unlike sociologists) see themselves not preparing themselves for work but as being unavoidably there already.

Bibliography

Apple, M. (1985) *Education and Power* ARK Paperbacks.

Barnes, D. and Seed, J. (1984) Seals of Approval: An Analysis of English Examinations in Goodson, I.F. and Ball, S.J. (eds) 1984 *Defining the Curriculum.* The Falmer Press pp. 263–299.

Bates, I., et al (ed.) (1984) *Schooling for the Dole?* Macmillan.

Bernstein, B. (1971) On the Classification and Framing of Educational knowledge. In Young, M.F.D. (ed) 1971. *Knowledge and Control.* London, Collier MacMillan pp. 47–69.

Bernstein, B. (1977) Aspects of the Relations between Education and Production: in *Class, Codes and Control,* Vol. 3 (second ed) RKP. pp. 174–201.

Bidwell, C. E. (1965) 'The School as a Formal Organisation', in March, J.G. (ed) 1965, *Handbook of Organisations* Rand McNally.

Bolton, E. (1985) TVEI: very good and very bad, in *The Times Educational Supplement* 15.11.85 p. 15.

Clarke, J. and Willis, P. (1984) Introduction, in Bates et al (ed) 1984. *Schooling for the Dole?* MacMillan pp. 1–17.

Dale, R. (1985) The Background and Inception of the Technical and Vocational Education Initiative in Dale, R. (ed) 1985. *Education, Training and Employment,* Pergamon Press pp. 41–57.

Dale, R. (1986) Examining the gift horse's teeth: a tentative analysis of TVEI, in Barton, L. and Walker, S. (eds) *Youth, Unemployment and Schooling,* Open University Press pp. 29–45.

Davies, B. and Evans, J. (1984) Mixed Ability and the Comprehensive School, in Ball, S. (ed) 1984 *Comprehensive Schooling: A Reader.* The Falmer Press pp. 155–177.

Evans, J. (1985) *Teaching in Transition: The Challenge of Mixed Ability Grouping.* The Open University Press.

Glaser, B. G. (1978) Generating Formal Theory, in Burgess R.G. (ed) 1982, *Field Research: a Sourcebook and Field Manual* George Allen and Unwin pp. 225–235.

Gleeson, D. (1983) Further Education, tripartism and the labour market, in Gleeson, D. (ed) 1983, *Youth Training and the Search for Work* RKP. pp. 32–48.

Gleeson, D. (1985) Privatization of Industry and the Nationalization of Youth, in Dale, R. (ed) 1985, *Education, Training and Employment.* Pergamon Press pp. 57–73.

Grace, G. (1978) *Teachers, Ideology and Control: A Study in Urban Education.* RKP.

Hammersley, M., Scarth, J. and Webb, S, (1985) Developing and Testing Theory: The Case of Research on Pupil Learning and Examinations, in Burgess, R. G. (ed) 1985. *Issues in Educational Research.* The Falmer Press pp. 48–67.

Hargreaves, A. (1980) Synthesis and the Study of Strategies: A project for the Sociological Imagination, in Woods, P. (ed) 1980, *Pupil Strategies*. Croom Helm pp. 162–198.

Hargreaves, A. (1982) Resistance and Relative Autonomy Theories: Problems of distortion and incoherence in recent Marxist sociology of education, *British Journal of Sociology of Education* 3, 2, pp. 107–26.

Hargreaves, A. (1985) The Micro-Macro Problem in the Sociology of Education, in Burgess, R.G. (ed) 1985. *Issues in Educational Research*. The Falmer Press pp. 21–48.

H. M. I. (1983) *Curriculum 11–16 Towards a statement of entitlement.* D.E.S.

H. M. I. (1981) *Curriculum 11–16: a review of progress. A joint study by H.M.I. and five local L.E.A.'s.* London HMSO 1981.

Lundgren, U. P. (1977) *Model Analysis of Pedagogical Process.* Stockholm Almquist and Wiksell.

Lundgren, U. P. (1983) Social Production and Reproduction as a Context for Curriculum Theorizing, in *Journal of Curriculum Studies*, 1983 Vol. 15, No. 2, pp. 143–154.

Manpower Services Commission (1984) *TVEI operating manual*, Manpower Services Commission.

Marx, K. (1918) *Capital, Vol. 1*, Chicago, Charles Kew and Company.

Moore, R. (1983) Further Education, pedagogy and production, in Gleeson, D. (ed) 1983, *Youth Training and the Search for Work*. RKP, pp. 14–32.

Moore, R. (1984) Schooling and the World of Work, in Bates, I., et al (ed) 1984, pp. 65–104.

Pickard, J. (1985) The Technical and Vocational Education Initiative, in, *The Times Educational Supplement*, 3, 5, 85 pp. 23.

Pring, R. (1985) In Defence of TVEI, in *FORUM* 1985, pp. 14–17.

Raffe, D. (1985) The Content and Context of Educational Reform, in Raggatt, P. and Werner, G. (eds) 1985, *Curriculum and Assessment* Pergamon Press pp. 67–75.

Tipton, B. F. A. (1985) Educational Organisations as Workplaces, in *British Journal of Sociology of Education* Vol. 6, No. 1, 1985 pp. 35–55.

Wallace, R. G. (1984) From Concept to Reality, in *TVEI Insight* No. 1. September 1984 pp. 3–5.

Woods, P. (1978) The Myth of Subject Choice, in Hammersley, M. and Wood, P. (eds) 1984 *Life in School*. The Open University Press. pp. 45–61.

CHAPTER SEVEN

Teachers and the MSC

Patricia J. Sikes

Introduction

To a greater or lesser extent the MSC (Manpower Service Commission) has become an influence within and upon English and Welsh secondary schools and, therefore, upon the experiences of the teachers working and having careers in them. While there has been a considerable amount of discussion focussing on the political, organizational, managerial and curricular effects and implications of the MSC's incursion into education (e.g. Ball, 1984; Dale 1985a, 1985b, 1986; Davies & Evans, 1984; Exeter University, 1984; Hall, 1985; Hunter, 1981; Layton, 1985; Pring, 1985; Seckington, 1985), less time and space has been given to exploring and representing teachers' views. Yet it is important that this should be done (cf Pyart, 1985 p. 329) for teachers are the people who realise school based education and, along with the pupils, theirs is the most immediate experience of it.

Teachers are among the first to be affected by MSC involvement in schools. They go on TRIST (TVEI Related Inservice Training) courses; they are frequently involved in administrating, managing and designing TVEI (Technical, Vocational and Educational Initiative) schemes; they teach TVEI lessons; they present and discuss TVEI and YTS (Youth Training Schemes) as part of option choice and careers guidance programmes; and they use careers education materials produced by COIC (Careers and Occupational Information Centre – which is the publishing division of MSC). Even if they personally do none of these things, they work in a system where others do. Teachers are therefore mediators and gatekeepers between MSC and schools and young people (cf Kogan 1983 p. 67). What this means is that, at least to a considerable degree, the outcomes of school (and teacher) based MSC funded schemes, and perhaps to a lesser extent, YTS, depend upon teachers and their response. The same is of course true of any innovation. Even if teachers outwardly comply with and conform to official requirements be these to do with curriculum or organisation, content or process, the way in which they do this colours the nature and the appearance of the outcome (see Sikes, Measor & Woods, 1985, on 'strategic compromise'). This is the case whether or not the teacher actually believes in and is committed to what she is doing.

MSC in School

There is room for considerable speculation about the 'real', 'hidden' agenda and intentions of the MSC and its political masters. For present purposes it is sufficient to say that 'change' is both a central objective and a central motivation.

In 1976, Prime Minister Callaghan's 'Ruskin College' speech, the subsequent 'Great Debate', and the green paper (DES 1977) which summarized it placed considerable responsibility for the country's declining position as an important industrial and commercial nation upon education, schools, and teachers. The message was that schools and teachers had to change their structure, ideology and values, their (pedagogical) approaches, and the content of what they taught, in order that the country might compete more successfully on the world market. In contrast with the expansionist times of the 1960s and early 1970s the implication was that teachers 'had to be changed rather than be the agents and basis of change' (Dale, 1986). Teachers were to be acted on rather than be actors. In other words they were to lose (at least some of) their autonomy and responsibility. An associated issue is that, whether or not as a direct consequence of the 'inappropriate' education they and their predecessors received in schools, youth unemployment has also risen, and so did the star of the MSC, 'the instrument the government chose first to try to overcome it, and later to try to disguise and mitigate its worst effects' (Dale, 1986).

The MSC's relative success at coping with youth unemployment, its association with the 'world of work', the 'needs' of employers, and young people meant that it was not a totally unlikely vehicle for bringing about the changes in schools and teaching that the politicians (Labour and Conservative) saw as being desirable. By taking on this role and challenge the MSC would become an agency for centralising control of education, thus furthering a development that teachers and LEAs had long resisted.

Thus, within schools, first through COIC came the production and dissemination of materials for careers education. Then there was TVEI, which was set up as 'a pilot scheme; within the education system; for young people of both sexes; across the ability range; voluntary. Each project must provide a full-time programme; offer a progressive four year course combining general with technical and vocational education; commence at fourteen years; be broadly based; include planned work experience; lead to nationally recognised qualifications. Each project and the initiative as a whole must be carefully monitored and evaluated. The purpose of the scheme is to explore and test ways of organising and managing readily replicable programmes of technical and vocational education for young people across the ability range.' (MSC, 1984) In the summer of 1986 it was announced that TVEI was to be extended to reach more students, although with less generous funding.

Following (and contemporaneously with TVEI) was TRIST. The purpose of TRIST was to stimulate new and additional in-service training programmes for secondary school teachers. Specific areas to be dealt with included curriculum areas – particularly craft/ design/technology, information technology, micro-electronics, business studies and physical science; training to produce more practical and relevant teaching across the curriculum; training in teaching approaches designed to increase a student's responsibility for their own learning; and training to promote awareness and understanding of industry and commerce. TRIST used the pattern and the channels established by MSC for funding and administering TVEI as an interim measure, while waiting for legislation to be passed enabling the DES to change the structure for funding, and hence the nature of, inservice training. Fundamentally the change requires LEAs to bid for money for specific inservice schemes, the themes of which are nationally announced. This does away with much of the freedom they had previously enjoyed to make use of monies allocated for inservice. (It is perhaps pertinent to point out that Shirley Williams, as the Labour Party's Secretary of State for Education, had tried to earmark grants for inservice training on the grounds that some LEAs were using money intended for training for other purposes).

The extent to which LEAs and individual schools and teachers are actively involved in MSC funded schemes varies, although those most intensively involved, the TVEI schools, are in the minority. However, through TVEI, the extended TVEI, TRIST, careers education materials, and YTS which is the next stage of life for an increasing number of school leavers, the MSC has established a presence in the vast majority, if not all, schools. An important way by which this has been achieved is the take up and use by teachers of language (or jargon) and concepts which (might be described as having) originated from or have been sponsored and propagated by, MSC. Examples include; 'Occupational Families' – which is a system for categorising skills and aptitudes in terms of related occupations; 'Delivery' – the realisation of a programme/scheme agreed between various parties – e.g. MSC and LEA; and 'Ownership' – which occurs when some body, be that an LEA, a school, or teacher or a student, internalises and/or adopts and takes responsibility for some thing – such as a TVEI scheme, an experiential approach to teaching, or their own learning.

MSC coverage is, therefore, extensive (cf Dale, 1986) and, in some respects, insidious. This chapter will seek to explore what this coverage means for teachers' experiences of teaching as a career in terms of what they actually do in their job and insofar as their personal objective and subjective careers (cf Sikes, Measor & Woods, 1985) are concerned. It will look at how teachers perceive and experience the MSC; the strategies they use to accommodate aspects of the MSC's actual and philosophical presence in schools; and it will consider the implications that these perceptions, experiences and strategies have for the MSC in schools.

Data and Methodology

The chapter is based on data I have collected while working as the local evaluator, employed through the Open University, of two TVEI schemes. To a lesser extent I have also drawn on my experience as a trainer involved in a TRIST programme, and on data gathered in the course of evaluating a project which aimed to set up a national network of training teams composed of careers teachers and careers officers who would run inservice courses on the 'effective' use of careers materials. This project was developed and staffed by the Counselling and Career Development Unit based at the University of Leeds, on behalf of COIC. (It will hereafter be referred to as the CCDU/COIC project.)

The main intention is to describe how teachers themselves perceive and experience the MSC rather than to attempt to accurately measure attitudes, use of strategies and actual changes. Consequently, much use is made of quotations. These quotations were usually gathered in the course of my work and usually arise out of (tape-recorded) interview-conversations, and (noted) informal conversations with teachers, students, LEA and MSC officers, local TVEI and TRIST central staff, and CCDU trainers. At no time have I been specifically researching perceptions and experiences of the MSC and I have not asked direct questions like 'How do you see the MSC?' or 'Has the MSC in anyway affected your career prospects?' Yet the

MSC has frequently been mentioned or referred to in some way, as I have been working on, for example, the organization of a TVEI scheme, why certain students opt for TVEI, and which elements of a training course participants found valuable. I have recorded all of these references to the MSC and have taken a grounded approach to their categorisation. Thus teachers talk about Time and the MSC or Administration and the MSC, and thereby provide the categories. Where quotations are used to illustrate or support a point, unless otherwise stated, they have been chosen as representative examples of a much larger body of evidence.

Some quotations are part of the data collected while I was observing meetings, lessons, and training courses and while I have been spending time in schools. Observation and being there has enabled me to see such things as the way in which TVEI has sometimes been used to accommodate less able students, the career possibilities resulting from MSC interventions, the use that is made of TVEI financial resources throughout a school, and the different pedagogical approaches used in TVEI and student responses to them.

I have also had access to documents produced in the course of and/or relating to MSC projects.

These various sources – interview-conversation, informal conversation, observation records and documents have enabled me to check data using techniques of triangulation.

The chapter covers a wide range of issues thus reflecting the extensive coverage and the pervading influence of the MSC. It does seem important to raise these issues and, for this reason, within the space available, the aim is to provide an overview rather than a detailed, definitive argument and account.

MSC as an Outsider

Education, schools and teachers have always been criticised from some quarter, for failing to 'adequately' and 'appropriately' equip young people for the world outside of school. On the basis of their insiders' knowledge of what goes on and what they believe to be possible, many teachers would agree that the educational experience which they and/or their colleagues provide, could be improved (cf Pring, 1985 p. 14). What they are often not happy with is criticism and intervention from persons and agencies who (a) do not have practical or relevant experience and knowledge of schools and classrooms, and (b) whose philosophy, values, assumptions, actions and intentions are seen as representing particular political models and aims (cf Dale 1986, Hall 1985). The MSC can be seen to fit into both of these categories and, indeed, approximately ninety percent

(180–200) of the teachers I have talked with spontaneously referred to it in these terms.

The criticisms and interventions are perhaps made more acute because many aspects – in terms of process, content and organisation – of MSC schemes are not totally new. Given that the schemes were presented as a new (or 'pilot' or 'experimental') approach, there is an impression of a lack of recognition of what has been going on. This serves to highlight the MSC's lack of an educational background and thus reduces their educational authority and credibility. The following comments are typical:

> Are the MSC aware that what they see as innovative we have been doing for years? We started work experience for every pupil goodness knows how long ago – about fifteen years ago. Of course we're concerned to get more girls doing science, but the local culture is against us there. We keep trying though. We have always asked ourselves, 'What is appropriate to our kids' needs?' and then tried to provide it. We're involved in CPVE. We've done BEC and BTec and City and Guilds Foundation. We have intimate links with local industry. We know the needs, or some of them, and how the present situation makes things more urgent. But they come along with an attitude that suggests that we haven't done any of these things. I accept some schools might not have but many have. In some ways it's a bit insulting.
>
> (Headteacher, TVEI school)

> It isn't as if we haven't been moving in this direction for some years but it doesn't seem that MSC know this. They're here, they're new, they'll set us all to rights!
>
> (Teacher, TVEI school)
> (see also Leach and Fulton, 1984)

An associated point is that many teachers feel that MSC are ignorant of the structures and constraints within which they have to operate and that this ignorance leads to and is manifest in what are perceived and experienced as unrealistic and unrealisable requirements and recommendations. For instance;

> It's all very well them showing us this material. I'd love to use it as they're suggesting, I really would but it's totally impractical. For a start you've got to have a small group. That's not on. Then there's the cost. Just one of those sets would cost more than my year's quota. The careers department gets very little money – and that's a reflection of how important we're seen to be in the school. I don't honestly think the MSC are that in touch with the situation in schools, I don't think they can be.
>
> (Participant on a uses of careers education materials course)

For teachers and LEA officers involved in TVEI and TRIST the apparent ignorance is highlighted because they may actually have to try to meet what they see as being unfeasible conditions in order to fulfil the terms of their contract.

Different Perceptions of Time

A large proportion of complaints about the MSC's lack of awareness and consequent unreasonableness concern time. According to teachers MSC frequently expect and require them to follow unrealistic time scales, and meet unrealistic deadlines and this causes stress. They say that it seems as if MSC do not appreciate 1) that schools cannot always quickly implement organisational, managerial, curricular and pedagogical change, and 2) that teachers already have to do a great deal in a limited amount of time and consequently any additional work can put them under considerable strain. The tension is increased if the extra work is perceived to be irrelevant or unnecessary or if its value seems to be dubious.

To take these points separately:

1) In the first instance many TVEI schemes, particularly those in the first and second round of funding, were drawn up, submitted, approved and implemented in what was felt to be a relatively short period of time (MSC, 1984 p. 7, Saunders 1985 p. 5) In some instances this is partly because LEAs did not decide to respond to the MSC's invitation to submit proposals until within a few weeks, or even days, of the closing date. There are tales of LEA officers making mad dashes to London to personally hand in submissions at the eleventh hour. On the whole however it is true that LEAs and schools did have to act faster than was usual for them. This 'hurry' has meant that radical changes have sometimes had to be made in organisational and managerial structures, pedagogical approaches, and curricula, without what teachers felt would have been an adequate period of preparation. This, they say, has had implications for the development of the scheme:

> It seems to me that everything was done in indecent haste. Perhaps to get it through before too many questions were asked.
>
> (Head, TVEI school)

> We didn't have time. We could have done a much better job if we'd had time to plan properly. As it is we're left with sorting out a rush job.
>
> (Teacher, TVEI school)

> If we had had a bit more time then we'd have had all the equipment, all the resources and the facilities. As it was we had to run the first year of the scheme in totally inappropriate accommodation. We weren't able to do the course justice and that was a shame.
>
> (Co-ordinator of a specialist TVEI centre)

> The first year we had difficulty attracting students because we couldn't say 'Take this course and you'll end up with such and such qualification'. We were actually negotiating the accreditation at the same time as we were teaching the course. Now, if you put a course leading to 'O' level next to

one which at the moment doesn't lead anywhere, people are going to opt for the 'O' level aren't they?

(Head of Department, TVEI school)

As I see it the MSC want everything done yesterday.

(Teacher, TVEI school)
(see also, Leach & Fulton, 1984, Saunders, 1985, Sikes, 1985)

As Dale (1986) points out, the organisational structure of the MSC enables it to act in an immediately effective way. This is because it is,

> 'a corporate body, made up of people representing particular interests . . . This means that any decisions and actions it takes can be assumed to already have the approval of those they affect (insofar as they are represented on the commission) those actions and decisions do not have to go through further consultative, participative discussion stages.'

(Dale, 1986)

This is why the MSC was used to introduce a different approach to in-service training. The DES, on the other hand, functions in a slow, bureaucratic, rule following manner. Furthermore examination boards do not validate syllabuses overnight, and syllabuses themselves have a two year cycle. Thus schools and teachers have not been used to acting quickly or in the commercial, market response sort of way that is customary to the industrialists represented on the MSC.

Changes in the system for funding in-service training mean that unless LEAs, schools and teachers can respond quickly in identifying needs and ways of addressing them, they will lose out financially. A quick response means that needs and situations are more likely to be met by 'appropriate' and up to date solutions and provision. This is not a bad thing and many teachers welcome the change to cut through the red tape and get things done. However, initially, they would have perhaps preferred a more gentle induction that,

> 'let us see what it was all about, gave us time to gather our thoughts and then to put together the best possible package'

(Teacher, TVEI school)

2) The amount of paperwork that MSC require from TVEI and TRIST participants seems to be a constant source of dissatisfaction. Often the request is for statistical type information which takes time to compile and which does not seem to be of immediate or future use or whose use seems to some people to be potentially questionable – as with requests for data on ethnic groups. For instance

> 'Look at this! MSC want this form filling in, crediting kids with CSE, 'O' level and 16 plus grades! All three! That's them knowing all about the real world of school. When they get their meaningless statistics back then they might begin to wonder!'

(TVEI co-ordinator)

'I had great hopes for TVEI. It could have been a marvellous scheme but its been killed by all the paperwork and admin that has to be done. The time you spend on that takes away from the time you would be spending with the kids. Its sheer lunacy.'

(TVEI School co-ordinator)

'I'm up to my ears in paper. It's quite frightening really, the amount of paperwork I'm supposed to do – as well as actually do things.'

(TRIST co-ordinator)

'I get a bit fed up with all the forms I have to fill in. It takes up such a long time and some of the information they want, like ethnic group – and that to be judged on appearance, worries me rather.'

(Deputy Head TVEI school)

MSC as a Divisive Influence?

In an TVEI school the MSC administration and paperwork that has to be done directly concerns and relates to only a very small minority of students – in many cases, less than ten percent. The following comment reflects what seems to be a widely held view.

'You know, the trouble with TVEI is that it's the tail wagging the dog. We've had to re-arrange the whole school day for it, so that kids can travel to other institutions. We've had to disrupt classes, not TVEI ones, so that teachers can go on TVEI courses. The effect is tremendous and it's all for what, thirty kids.'

(Headteacher, TVEI school)
(see also Saunders, 1985)

The 'tail wagging the dog' is an aspect of one of the main anxieties about the MSC's intervention in education generally and TVEI in particular and that is of it having a divisive effect. (See for example the articles in Forum, Vol 28, No. 1, 1985 and Comprehensive Education, Issue 48, 1985).

Divisiveness is a potential effect both within and across schools and TVEI indubitably has what Saunders (1985) describes as 'enclave characteristics'. A particular fear is that there could be a 'back door' return to a tripartite education system through the separation of education and training (cf Ball 1984 pp. 125–16). Comprehensive education is threatened in that students not academically orientated might be directed towards courses with a substantial vocational and practical component. A criterion for participating in TVEI is that the scheme should cater for students across the ability range. This has been variously realised and some schools have quite openly used TVEI to accommodate less able and/or 'disruptive' students. –

'Our head said that we should have this practical course under TVEI and it would be motivating for this sort of kid. I don't mind teaching them, in fact I'd say my job satisfaction has increased. It's not been so high since before we went comprehensive. They're good lads and once you've shown them what to do they get down to it. It's better for them than book work. Too much book work and they get bored and then you get the trouble. They have a bit of trouble with them at the tech though. They don't know how to cope.

(Craft and Design Teacher, TVEI school)

Situations like that described above (which the evidence suggests are not rare) give weight to arguments that MSC are aiming, through TVEI to separate education from training and to create 'worker-pupils' (Ball, 1984 p. 15) who will then go on to become YTS trainees. The school in which the quoted craft and design teacher worked also ran TVEI courses in 'O' level electronics for high ability students (who also had to take and be capable of 'O' level physics) and so were fulfilling the MSC criteria. While MSC are responsible for the conditions which allowed this situation to arise it was the school, the headteacher and some of the staff who exploited the 'divisive' potential, and this is true whether or not MSC expected or intended that this would happen.

A perhaps inevitable source of divisiveness, particularly at a time when the majority of schools are experiencing financial cuts and contraction, are the resources enjoyed by TVEI schools and specific departments within them. This can lead to resentment and jealousy and a categorisation into 'haves' and 'have-nots'. TRIST has similar potential although perhaps to a lesser extent because the sums of money involved are smaller and more teachers are involved. (TRIST and the system following it is however potentially divisive in the higher and further education sector insofar as institutions compete to provide training courses). In general, use of TVEI resources and specialist staff skills is extended across the school. Computers and CNC lathes for instance are usually used by others when not time-tabled for TVEI groups.

Experimentation and Evaluation

Extension or rather 'replication' is a declared aim of TVEI. The emphasis has been on TVEI as an experiment and a pilot study – and this is one reason for the intensity of the various evaluations which many have found onerous, disruptive and threatening.

It may be that, with regard to the concept of TVEI as experiment and pilot, the differences in structure and background of the MSC and schools (and the DES) lead to differences in interpretation.

On-going research and development and the need and the ability to quickly respond to market demands – experiences and understandings shared by many of the commission's representatives – are not as common to or hitherto possible for educationalists. It is therefore suggested that the latter tend to take a reflective, long term, rather than an immediate, basis for action view of and approach to experimentation. That in at least one TVEI scheme headteachers did not share or subscribe to the same official concept or view of experiment is demonstrated in the following exchange concerning the wording of a combined working paper/policy statement/publicity document about TVEI.

Headteacher 1: Leave out 'TVEI is an experiment'
LEA Adviser: Those are MSC's words
Headteacher 2: That's all the more reason to leave them out.
Headteacher 3: We can't really do that but I'm not happy with it all the same. People don't like the idea, parents especially, that we are experimenting on children.
Headteacher 1: And I don't either. After all they only really get one chance.

The fears expressed here are essentially that the 'experiment' may go 'wrong' and the students suffer as a consequence. This is a reasonable fear – but 'failure' is a constant possibility in all experimentation. MSC accept this possibility – although perhaps in more economically oriented than child centred terms. For instance, as one MSC officer explained to a TVEI project steering committee:

'We've put this vast amount of money in because you're experimenting. In an experiment you may take wrong directions; and these can be expensive, so we've budgeted to account for that, so that you can cover them. That's the whole point. When it comes to reproducing the best parts of the scheme it shouldn't need so much money because you'll know where you're going'.

It is self-evident that perception of TVEI and TRIST schemes as successful depends upon the criteria by which they are evaluated. The various evaluations (by MSC, DES, the NFER, Leeds University, Institutes of Higher Education and local and individual studies) may all have certain different orientations, compasses and foci and they may be used (or not) in different ways, yet it is unlikely that any would not make at least passing reference to MSC's original aims and intentions (which were quoted earlier). After all, MSC are paying for the schemes and for the (majority of) evaluations (and this can cause tensions for both those doing the evaluation and those being evaluated).

Since they are paying and consequently might therefore be seen to have some say over what they are buying, there has been much concern and speculation over the extent to which they might direct and determine the curriculum, the pedagogy and the organisation and management of schools. In the first place MSC defined the criteria and topics, then accepted local schemes with or without modification, then, through a system of reviews and 'planning dialogues' which draw on evaluation reports, they chart out and set goals for further development.

Participation in a TVEI scheme or TRIST 'requires some sacrifice of institutional autonomy' (Pring, 1985 p. 16) – in terms of organization, management, pedagogy and curriculum (cf Ball, 1984). This 'sacrifice' has implications for the autonomy, the job content and job satisfaction of individual teachers at all levels (see Sikes, 1985, Stoney, Pole and Sims, 1986). What remains to be seen is the extent to which the MSC, through TVEI and TRIST – and YTS to a lesser direct degree – serves as a Trojan horse (maybe in the guise of a mouse) – for introducing a directed centralised and politically influenced secondary school curriculum and system.

Incoherence?

While centralisation is frequently viewed with some apprehension there is scepticism about whether the different departments within the MSC are sufficiently co-ordinated and in touch with each other and with other agencies to be able to develop and realize a coherent centralised plan,

> Does the right hand know what the left hand is doing? The evidence suggests not.
>
> (Teacher, TVEI school)

> What happens in MSC is that one day they say one thing and the next it's something totally different.
>
> (Teacher, TVEI school)

> It's my belief that MSC shift the criteria about to suit themselves. There doesn't seem to be any real plan.
>
> (Teacher, TVEI school)

Changes in emphasis immediately following review and evaluation may be partly responsible for the view that many teachers share of MSC incoherence. That this may not necessarily be a fair view because a fast response reflects and is in line with the MSC structure, composition and preferred methods of working has already been suggested. Having said that, the lack of continuity and congruence between TVEI and YTS is not so easily explained in teachers' eyes. In short, TVEI is, essentially, a four year scheme for 14 to 18 year olds yet staying on rates post 16 are likely to be adversely affected by students leaving to take up 'waged' YTS places. Another point is that youngsters who do go into a YTS placement may well have covered much of what they will be doing in their 14–16 TVEI course. MSC officials do accept the discrepancy but, at the time of writing, have not resolved it.

So far the emphasis of this chapter has been on negative aspects of MSC involvement in schools. This is, perhaps, a distorted picture, at least in terms of the immediate experience of many teachers. In the next section certain positive aspects will be briefly discussed.

Resources

Participation in TVEI and TRIST has brought resources, facilities and money to spend. At a time when most schools and LEAs are experiencing cuts and contraction the apparent wealth of the MSC is particularly obvious. The fact that some schools within an authority and some departments within a school do have considerably more and often superior equipment, work with smaller groups of students and frequently have money available to them can be and is divisive, but for the teachers teaching in those schools and departments it is a marvellous opportunity.

> 'TVEI has meant that it's possible to do all sorts of things that I'd always wanted to do but never could because the money wasn't there. It's great. You don't have to scratch around to find materials for the kids to work with – I've kept up my links with the firms that give me their throw-outs because when the money stops we'll need them. But it really has changed things.'
>
> (Craft & Design Technology Teacher, TVEI school)

> With each youngster being able to work on a computer or a typewriter at the same time you can get so much more done. The only problem is that these typewriters are far superior to what they have to use out on work experience.
>
> (Business Studies Teacher, TVEI school)

> I don't actually teach any TVEI courses but the equipment is there and we can use it so there is spin-off value for everyone.
>
> (Teacher, TVEI school)

New Approaches

One way in which TVEI money has been used is to 'buy' smaller classes by improving the teacher:pupil ratio. Indeed the largest proportion of TVEI expenditure has been on staffing (MSC 1985 p. 25). Smaller classes and different subject content and forms of accreditation e.g. profiling have required that, and enabled teachers to, experiment with teaching styles. In general, the move has been towards encouraging students to take greater responsibility for their own learning and development, and giving them more opportunities for practical experience (see MSC, 1985 p. 14). TRIST aims to promote the move among a wider teacher audience. Some teachers, even if theoretically willing, have found it very difficult to change their approach (see Sikes, Measor & Woods, 1985 on teacher insecurity). Others have been more successful – and have found their job satisfaction has increased.

'When you've only got 10 or 15 kids it's a whole different ball game. You can treat them better, you've more time, you're not so pushed. You can allow them to experiment and there's time to talk and question. The relationship between you and them can be so much better – especially if sometimes you're only a page ahead of them anyway. Much of what we're doing is new to me too. With TVEI, sometimes, it's like what I hoped teaching would be like in college. Not always of course – but quite often.'
(Technology Teacher, TVEI school)

'I went on this course for teaching TVEI life skills and it bloody changed my life. I used to hit kids. I don't mean I was a sadist but it was in the good old tradition of a clip round the earhole if you deserve it then we're friends after. You know what I mean. I now realise how I wasn't, what, respecting the student's dignity. That sounds pat, sorry!, and contrite but it's hard to say I get on so much better with kids now, not that I didn't before but the relationship's more equal. I do sometimes feel like belting certain little sods now and again, but so far I haven't and I hope I never do.'
(Life Skills Teacher, TVEI school)

Students' experiences of being taught and treated in a different way do have implications for their relationships with staff throughout the school. TVEI students are frequently said to be more mature, more self-confident and more curious.

'You can tell the TVEI kids without knowing. They look you in the eye, they can express themselves, they have an idea of where they want to go, they're more confident. It's quite uncanny.'
(Careers Officer in a 'TVEI town')

'The TVEI students who come to us are identifiable because they can organise themselves much better than most of the others can.'
(Vice principal, TVEI sixth form college)

'You can tell the TVEI kids. They do seem more mature. But they must realise that in a school situation, with younger people then the regulations have to be much more, well, strict. It's quite odd having a class of half TVEI and half non-TVEI – there is a difference, the TVEI talk to you more as an equal while the others are kids!'
(Teacher, TVEI school)
(see also Sanders 1985 p. 8)

Curriculum Content

A condition for receiving TVEI funding was that it should only be used 'to deliver those identifiable elements in the curriculum that are different from what was on offer previously' (MSC, 1985, p. 6). In practice, and with MSC's knowledge this definition has sometimes been rather stretched. However, different courses perhaps leading to different qualifications (e.g. pre BTEC) have meant that many teachers teaching TVEI students are dealing with different and/or new subject content. Inevitably some teachers will prefer to stay with the 'old' content. For example, among craft teachers there is a fundamental division (described simplistically here) between those who believe in the initial development and practice of specific skills and techniques such as making joints and forge welding and those who favour a problematic, design approach. Others welcome the opportunity to become involved in curriculum development, either at the initial stage of syllabus design and construction or later, in actually teaching content which is new to them or to their experience of teaching. For instance:

'I'm teaching concepts and theories that I didn't do until I was at university. I enjoy the challenge of putting it over in a way that the students will be able to understand.'

(Electronics Teacher, TVEI school)

'I tell you, it's true, sometimes I'm only a page ahead of what we do in class. It keeps you on your toes. It's very enjoyable.'

(IT teacher, TVEI school)

'I found it particularly stimulating being in the curriculum working parties, hammering out new syllabuses.'

(TVEI Teacher)

One reason why teachers sometimes prefer the 'new' curriculum is because students often respond to it more positively and a positive pupil response is a crucial requirement for the majority of teachers' job satisfaction (Sikes, 1986).

Inservice Training and Staff Development

If the argument that the MSCs are concerned to change teachers is accepted, inservice teacher training might be expected to be prominent. This is indeed the case, with the MSC heavily financing INSET largely by paying for additional staff to cover for those released. INSET programmes have dealt with a wide range of areas, including the subject-based, the management of change, teaching/learning processes, profiling and assessment, lifeskills and education industry links. As well as taking the form of courses (of varying length) and secondments, MSC 'sponsored' INSET has also involved teachers observing and working alongside others with specialist knowledge.

The chance to further their own professional and personal development is very attractive to many teachers (cf Nixon, 1981 and Sikes, Measor & Woods, 1985, Woods 1985, Woods & Sikes, impending). Although it can be exciting it can at the same time be quite threatening (see Stenhouse, 1975). While there will always be some who are reluctant, others are eager to take advantage of what is available.

> 'I'm very glad to be able to come on a course like this. It's a day out! No, seriously, you get the chance to reflect on what you do, to see what others are doing, to pick up some ideas. There's some things you think well, we do that or, we do that better but it's important that we should get this opportunity.'
>
> (Participant on Careers Education Course)

> 'I think the most valuable thing of TVEI for me personally has been the chance to work alongside Colin (a peripatetic TVEI teacher) and see how he does things. I've learnt a lot, I'm about to retire and I'm sad I've never had the chance to do it before. But it's changed a lot of what I do. Changed it for the better, I think.'
>
> (Craft & Design Teacher, TVEI school)

Career Opportunities

It is not exaggerating to say that TVEI and to a lesser extent other MSC interventions have created a new career path for teachers (see Sikes, 1985). Again, in this area as with resources, the comparative wealth of the MSC is highlighted by the contraction being generally experienced. There are new posts, temporary and permanent as, for example (TVEI and TRIST) scheme co-ordinators or directors, as peripatetic staff, and within school as co-ordinators (Bell, 1985 McCabe, 1985) and specialist staff. Having had TVEI experience is said (in staff-rooms) to be a valuable qualification for those seeking senior posts in other, and particularly new TVEI schools. (Lacking objective evidence this must at the present time remain a 'myth'.)

Entrepreneurial teachers (cf Taylor, 1986) have recognised and grasped the opportunities:

> 'I've totally changed my career plans as a result of my involvement in TVEI. I was previously thinking in terms of staying with physics for as long as I could but now I've got interested in curriculum development, assessment, profiling and a more general area. The opportunities are there and I'm going to take them.'
>
> (TVEI Teacher, involved in a Consortium Development Working Party)

I thought I'd put in for the School Co-ordinator's job. I was doing much of it anyway and it's an extra point, extra interest and it'll look good on my C.V.

(TVEI School Co-ordinator)

Taking advantage of the career opportunities created by the MSC is a strategic move. Teachers make use of various strategies in order to accommodate the MSC in school or, in other words to implement policy arising from MSC schemes. Some of these will now be described.

Strategies for Accommodation

Saunders defines policy implementation as

'a process of modification and adaption of policy messages by participants . . . at each point in the implementation staircase from the MSC to the classroom teacher. These adaptations occur as the practical implications of the policy become apparent and adjustments are made in the light of the different sets of priorities, preoccupations and interests participants may have' (1985 pp. 1–2)

This definition accurately reflects many teachers' experiences. For example:

'Initially we had very funny ideas about the MSC. Initially they weren't there, they just provided the money. Then because we kept having it drummed in that we had to 'deliver' and satisfy their criteria they became an ogre. But now we've stopped worrying. The MSC is in the background and we, or I, have become much more concerned with getting on with what we wanted to do. As I say we don't worry because if the MSC want something they'll come and ask and if they see or get to hear about something they don't like they'll let us know. So where in the beginning we were always looking over our shoulders and saying "Oh, will that be alright for the MSC?" now we just get on with it; I forget all about them.' (TVEI teacher – member of various TVEI Curriculum Development Groups)

The teacher quoted had characterised the MSC as an ogre, others have referred to the 'Task Master', 'Whip Cracker', 'That lot', 'Them' and a range of other appelations and epithets. What is interesting is that the MSC has (usually) been reified, it is an It which has become the independent sum of the elements (e.g. individuals and schemes) which come together in the commission. Thus although individuals from the MSC frequently visit the scheme and/or are known of by their name because documents bear these (perhaps a deliberate strategy to 'personalise' the MSC), the trend among teachers is to depersonalise and homogenise. This may well be a distancing strategy, which casts the teacher in the role of individual facing the organisation. On the other hand it may just reflect a view of the commission as a coherent entity and force, although this view is inconsistent with criticisms of the MSC's lack of internal co-ordination.

On occasion advantage has been taken of the way in which the MSC can be characterised and anthropomorphised.

> 'I use the MSC as a bogeyman. I tell the heads "Oh you've got to get this or that done because the MDC want it quickly. They might make things difficult for you if you don't do it". – and all along it's me who wants it done. Wicked I am!'
>
> (TVEI Scheme Co-ordinator)

> 'You can use us as a big stick. If it gets the schools or the elected members going that's fine. Feel free to take our name in vain.'
>
> (MSC Regional Adviser)

Perhaps one of the most common strategies that teachers at all levels use is to treat the MSC and the demands and possibilities of its schemes as just another part of their job, and as Saunders suggests, prioritise and participate according to their interests, orientations and commitments. Thus, on the whole, strategies to accommodate the MSC and it's interventions are not markedly different in nature from those used to accommodate any other aspect of the job.

Discussion

While it is relatively easy to see the immediate effects that the MSC has had upon teachers' experience of teaching, the implications for the future are more elusive. Over the years initiatives and innovations have tended to have a limited effect in schools (cf Rudduck 1986), although they have been significant for the subjective and objective career experiences of some teachers. Comprehensivisation and ROSLA inevitably had more impact, although the experiences of individual teachers and schools varied, with some being minimally affected while others were completely changed (cf Sikes, 1984).

The MSC interventions are however different because they 'challenge basic assumptions about the purpose of educational institutions' (Pyart, 1985 p. 324). They have also put the spotlight on subjects and subject areas which have tended to have low status in the traditional academic hierarchy. Furthermore they have introduced a different, industrial/commercial model of administration and management which emphasise doing (experiential learning) delivery, and evaluation of processes (teaching), personnel (teachers and pupil) and products (what students learn). All this has involved a change – a loss – in the amount of autonomy available to individuals and individual institutions.

It has meant a diminution of freedom over what is done, when and how and by whom; it has meant more surveillance and control of teachers and pupils (through evaluation, through profiling and records of achievement) (see Hargreaves, 1986) and through measurement and testing of specific skills (see Ball, 1984 p. 169). It has meant more centralised control, in that the MSC has achieved an extensive if not intensive coverage of schools. Indeed, the fact of the existence of TVEI and TRIST affects all schools and all teachers whether or not they are personally involved.

Many teachers and pupils have had, and have created for themselves positive experiences as a result of MSC intervention, many more have just incorporated the new requirements into their basic job, and carry on as before. For this reason it may be that, in terms of educational innovation, few changes will be achieved – so far there is little evidence that TVEI has had much impact on gender, inequality and sex-stereotyping. While it may be possible to legislate for change it is a much harder task to change individuals.

The effects that the MSC will have on teacher careers are likely to tend to be structural. Career prospects for teachers of different subjects and with different experience may and perhaps already have altered with the balance coming down much more in the favour of scientists, technologists, mathematicians and craftsworkers. This bias will be reflected in school with favoured subjects being allocated more resources and money. There will be more pressure to be accountable and there will be more evaluation. These things will undoubtedly have an effect upon how teachers perceive and experience their careers. And yet, after all, teachers will continue to make the situation in which they find themselves their own. The MSC may well promote 'ownership' but whether or not it will serve their own ends is a question for the future.

Bibliography

Ball, S. J. (1984) 'Becoming a Comprehensive? Facing Up to Falling Rolls' in Ball, S.J. (ed) *Comprehensive Schooling: A Reader* Lewes, Falmer.
Bell, L. A. (1985) 'An investigation of A New Role in Schools; The Case of the TVEI School Co-ordinator' (Paper or British Educational Management and Administration Society Conference, Sheffield Polytechnic, 22/11/85).
Comprehensive Education (1985) Issue 48.
Dale, I. R. (1985a) 'The Background and Inception of the Technical and

Vocational Education Initiative' in Dale, I.R. (ed) *Education, Training and Employment: Towards a New Vocationalism?* Oxford, Pergamon.

Dale, I. R. (1985b) Examining the Gift-Horse's Teeth; a tentative analysis of TVEI (unpublished).

Dale, I. R. (1986) Buying Change? The Technical and Vocational Initiative in England and Wales (unpublished).

Davies, B. and Evans, J. (1984) 'Mixed Ability and the Comprehensive School' in Ball, S.J. (ed) *Comprehensive Schooling; A Reader* Lewes, Falmer.

D. E. S. (1977) *Education in Schools, A Consultative Document* London, HMSO.

Exeter University (1984) *T.V.E.I.* Exeter School of Education.

Forum (1985) Vol. 28, No. 1.

Hall, J. (1985) 'The Centralist Tendency' *Forum*, Vol. 28, No. 1, Autumn 1985 pp. 4–6.

Hargreaves, A. (1986) 'Record Breakers?' in Broadfoot, P. (ed) *Profiles and Records of Achievement* London, Holt, Reinehart & Winston.

Hunter, C. (1981) 'Politicians Rule OK? Implications for Teacher Careers and School Management' in Barton, L. & Walker, S. *Schools, Teachers & Teaching*, Lewes, Falmer.

Kogan, M. (1983) 'The Case of Education' in Young, K. (ed) *National Interests and Local Government* London, Heinemann.

Layton, D. (1985) 'From Nuffield to TVEI: science or technology for citizens?' *Education Today* Vol. 35, No. 2 pp. 37–45.

Leach, M. & Fulton, O. (1984) *The Evaluation of Three TVEI Schemes, 1983 – 84: Final Report* Lancaster, University of Lancaster.

Manpower Services Commission (1984) *TVEI Review 84* London, MSC.

Manpower Services Commission (1985) *TVEI Review 85* London, MSC.

McCabe, C. (1985) 'The TVEI Co-Ordinator' (paper given at Conference on the *Organisation and Management of TVEI*, University of Newcastle-Upon-Tyne, 22/11/85.

Nixon, J. (1981) *A Teachers' Guide to Action Research* London, Grant McIntyre.

Pring, R. (1985) 'In Defence of TVEI' *Forum* Vol. 28, No. 1 pp. 14–17.

Pyart, B. (1985) 'An Overview of TVEI' *School Organization* Vol. 5, No. 4 pp. 323–330.

Rudduck, J. (1986) *Understanding Curriculum Change* (University of Sheffield Inaugural Lecture, 19/2/86).

Saunders, M. (1985) *Emerging Issues in TVEI Implementation* University of Lancaster, TVEI Evaluation Unit.

Seckington, R. (1985) 'TVEI Defending the Indefendable' *Forum* Vol. 28, No. 1 pp.26–28.

Sikes, P. J. (1984) 'Teacher careers in the Comprehensive School' in Ball, S.J. (Ed) *Comprehensive Schooling: A Reader* Lewes, Falmer.

Sikes, P. J. (1986) *The Mid-Career Teacher: Adaptation and Motivation in a Contracting Secondary School System* (Unpublished Thesis, University of Leeds).

Sikes, P. (1985) 'Headteachers and the Organization and Management of TVEI' (paper given at Conference on the *Organization and*

Management of TVEI University of Newcastle-Upon-Tyne 22/11/85.

Sikes, P. J., Measor, L. & Woods, P. (1985) *Teacher Careers: Crises and Continuities* Lewes, Falmer.

Stenhouse, L. A. (1975) *An Introduction to Curriculum Development and Research* London, Heinemann.

Stoney, S. M., Pole, C. J., Sims, D. (1985) *The Management of TVEI* London NFER for MSC.

Taylor, M. (1986) 'Educating Entrepreneurs' (unpublished paper).

Woods, P. (1985) 'Conversations with Teachers: Some aspects of Life-history method' *British Educational Research Journal* 11, 1, pp. 13–26.

Woods, P. & Sikes, P. (Forthcoming) 'The Use of Professional Biographies in Planning Self Development' in Todd, F. (ed) *Planning Continuing Teacher Education* London, Croom Helm.

CHAPTER EIGHT

Studying Education Policy through the Lives of the Policy-makers: An attempt to Close the Macro-micro gap

Jenny Ozga

Education policy as a field of study

To a considerable extent the shape of the study of education policy is determined by where it is studied. Before the 1970s and '80s, when sociologists of education began to show an interest in policy, it found a space within social policy and social administration, government and politics (notably at Brunel), and as an important strand in the history of education. Education policy was also the concern of those who worked in educational administration as a field of study, though the label 'educational administration' often indicated on emphasis on the structures within which policy making took place and on the workings of educational government. Policy content and the politics of education occupied a secondary place. Recently, two developments have changed that rather fragmented picture: educational administration has been largely subsumed by educational management, a change which has considerable consequences for the type and form of activity which used to find some shelter under the broad umbrella of educational administration. The strong applied orientation of educational management, with its emphasis on improved performance, and the 'development of capability' (Glatter 1979) is flourishing in a sympathetic political climate, and the tradition of detailed historical work, or work concerned primarily with politics or policy content is in danger of being squeezed out.

The second development has been the growth of interest among sociologists in education policy. Beryl Tipton (1974, 1980, 1985) has drawn attention to the way in which educational administration has ignored certain areas of work, especially work on teacher unions, and provided an early diagnosis of the tense relationship between educational administration and sociology. That general failure of communication between the two areas has become more significant for the study of education policy, as, in recent years, much work on education policy has come not from the scattered and disparate sources outlined above, but from within the sociology of education, especially from those working within, or influenced by, the 'new' sociology of education, and, especially, those of a Marxist or neo-Marxist persuasion or at least concerned with the relationship of the state to education as a central problem. Thus the 1980s have seen the publication of Ahier and Flude's *Contemporary Education Policy*, the Open University Course E353 *Society, Education and the State,* Salter and Tapper's *Education, Policy and the State* and many other more theoretical works on the state and education, notably those of Offe (1984), and Flora and Heidenheimer (1981). The economic crisis and resultant growth of conflict in most western education systems have encouraged sociologists of education to examine a range of education policy issues from 'welfare' policies to race, gender and vocationalism, very often as part of their concern to explore the relations between education, the state and capitalism. This growth of interest in education policy has had little impact on what I will term, for the sake of convenience, the 'traditionalist' study of educational administration, where the very use of the term 'state' is uncommon, 'government' being the acceptable term, despite the rather obvious failure of the area to move away from reliance on a now superceded model of distribution of control and 'partnership' in education.

The lack of communication between the two groups results from a number of reasons, principally ideological, or to do with methodological differences, which are themselves often reflections of ideological difference. Although the 'traditionalists' come from varied disciplinary backgrounds, there are distinguishing features of much of the work in educational administration/policy which may be identified. A major characteristic is a cavalier, uncritical and eclectic attitude to theory, which often seems to be no more than a source of working tools, or is 'bolted on' rather insecurely to the case in question. Case study methodology dominates, in a huge variety of forms, but lacking in self-consciousness or open discussion about selection of material, representativeness, etc.

In Heclo's words:

'There remains great untapped potential in the use of case study for policy analysis, but without the use of theoretical perspectives such studies provide at best an interesting contribution to historical scholarship, at worst an uninteresting episodic narrative'

(Ribbins and Brown 1979)

Education Administration/Policy and Educational Sociology: Methodological and other differences

There have been two recent major discussions of the state of education policy from outside the 'traditional' field – those by Andy
Hargreaves (1983, to some extent continued in 1985) and Roger Dale
(1986), which approach the subject from slightly different angles but
which both highlight the differences between what I have called the
'traditionalists' and those working with the sociology of education,
and provide some explanation for the lack of communication
between the two camps. Hargreaves in his article in Ahier and
Flude's 'Contemporary Education Policy' sees the division in the
area as one between pluralism and Marxism, and argues that such a
division hampers the development of the subject and should be overcome. The different traditions, he said:

> 'differ greatly in the theoretical and methodological approaches they
> adopt to the extent that they are professionally embedded in distinctive
> kinds of discourse and in separate, relatively insulated communities of
> academic exchange. As is usual in such circumstances, each tradition
> tends to neglect the work of the other, or to construe it in terms of a
> limited number of unflattering stereotypical features which do little
> justice to the complex positions and nuances of argument that would be
> involved though a more thorough examination. This is a pity for such
> neglect, hostility and mistrust serves only to inhibit the traditions from
> appreciating and building upon their very real complementary strengths
> in the service of improved understanding of the educational policy
> making process, its determinants and effects'

(Hargreaves 1983)

In his recent discussion of *The Macro – micro problem in the
Sociology of Education* (1985) Hargreaves seems less optimistic
about the 'complementarity' of approaches, admitting that attempts
at bridge building were rather unspecific about how connections and
syntheses could be made. Although this article deals with the sociology of education, not education policy, it is to some extent a continuation of his earlier argument and reveals interesting parallel
problems. Hargreaves sees sociology of education as increasingly
divided between micro-level interactionists and macro-level theore-
tians of the state, but sees the potential for the closing of the gap
through linked micro-studies:

> 'For instance, many of the so called macro-constraints which teachers
> face that are usually attributed to the operation of vast social structures
> could actually be analysed by studying interactions outside the classroom
> – in the headteacher's Office, County Hall, the Department of Education
> and Science, and so on . . . It is a mistake, then, to regard education
> policy as belonging exclusively to the worl of macro-theory (as in Ahier &

Flude 1983, Dale, 1981) not just because classroom teachers have policies too, (Pollard 1984), but also because even outside the school, policy still has to be negotiated and implemented through interaction. . . . The growth of linked micro studies could be one of the most significant future developments in the sociology of education, not only for micro-macro integration as an interesting if esoteric theoretical project but also for the much needed attempt to understand the schooling process in the context of policy changes, economic pressure and so on, and not in isolation from them. . . . Of course, these linked micro-studies would still not remove the need and relevance for concepts like state, class and economy which transcend space and time, but they would prevent us relegating much of our analysis to that level by default simply because we chose not to study them empirically'

(Hargreaves 1985).

Hargreaves, then, still sees the possibility of closing the micro-macro gap, despite increasing division with the sociology of education. Development of 'middle level' analyses, especially in LEA structures, work on teacher unions and study of historical and public documents, plus interactionist studies of LEA administrators and heads and school staffs outside the classroom all look like promising ways of bridging the micro-macro gap. But do they offer a solution to the distance between 'pluralists' and 'Marxists' in the study of education policy? Can the pluralist/Marxist divide be reduced to the micro-macro problem?

The Pluralist/Marxist divide

To assume this might be to underestimate the extent of the division in the study of education policy. Although the hostility of the 'traditional' educational administrator/policy analyst to sociological work on education policy making is often conveyed in criticisms of its macro-level and abstract analyses, and its lack of detailed empirical evidence, these form only part of the barrier to communication. In the new Open University course E333 *Policy-making in Education*, Roger Dale presents a view of the study of education policy which suggests that the divisions cannot be easily overcome. He argues that it is not so much that education policy/administration has been dominated by work uninformed by theory, but more that the theoretical framework of this work is underdeveloped and implicit. He calls the pre-theoretical, informing and framing concepts 'projects' and identifies 3 major projects in the study of education policy. These are briefly: –

1) the *social administration project*: which is reformist in character, concerned to improve not just efficiency but social con-

ditions, and directed toward potential policy problems,

2) the *policy analysis project*: which is essentially concerned with finding ways of ensuring effective and efficient delivery of policy, and

3) the *social science* 'project' which is concerned with finding out how things are and how they came to be that way and is not concerned with a specific policy problem or its implementation. This is a vital and serious distinction, which lies at the heart of the difference between sociologists and practitioners of educational administration.

Maurice Kogan illuminates this difference in making a distinction between social scientists and administrators. He says:

> 'I assume that it is the task of social scientists to take things apart. I assume that it is the task of politicians and administrators to make sure that things are brought back together again . . . Whilst the social scientist has license to engage in the study of phenomena for its own sake, the creed of the administrator has to be 'I must act, therefore I must think! It is not the other way round'.
>
> (Kogan, 1979)

Many of those who work within the first two projects do so within traditional educational administration/policy, and have that preoccupation with action, with practice rather than analysis. That tendency is even more marked in educational management, as is shown in, for example, its treatment of teacher unions or ancillary staff as potential management problems. Though many working in education policy/administration would consider themselves adherents of the 'social science' project, their interest in problems and, as Dale points out, their definition of what constitutes a problem increasingly stems from a search for solutions, and for improvement in the system. This orientation is not necessarily explicit, but it is powerful. Pressure for work which can be seen to increase efficiency and secure improvement is growing in the current climate and increases the strength of education management at the expense of educational administration and history. The dominance of the applied, practical orientation precludes others which concern practitioners of the 'social science' project. The differences between project 1 and 2 and project 3 are sharpened if we follow Dale's analysis through to the theoretical underpinnings of the projects. While summary does less than justice to the original, in broad terms Dale suggests that neo-liberalism, systems theory and pluralism have dominated projects 1 and 2, while Marxism and neo-Marxism have provided a major, but not the sole inspiration for many working within the social science project. Practitioners of the social science project share, among other things, a concern to place the role of the state as a central focus of enquiry, and a tendency to produce what Cox (1980) terms 'critical theory'. The divisions, therefore, are not merely methodological. The 'traditionalists' are nearly all pluralists, often, of course, they object to any label, and some subscribe to modified and complex forms of pluralism which draw on resource dependency theory or 'Open' or modified systems theory. Whatever the variation, it is essentially a variation on a broad and deeply felt pluralist theme, which is all the more difficult to counter because of its vagueness – even its revision (Lindblom 1983) leaves it, as Dale points out, less of an account of distribution of power and influence than a statement of how things ought to be in Western, democratic societies. Dale's analysis, then, lends weight to the conclusion that there are irreconcileable differences between 'traditional' education policy and work on education policy which comes from within the sociology of education. These differences are likely to deepen as the reduction of certain areas of current educational sociology seems to be an item of education policy, and as education management grows, and the policy/administration strand follows the trend in the U.S. and elsewhere and becomes dominated by policy analysis (Harman, 1984). The reaction of education management to qualitative research methods, to ethnography and to feminist – inspired styles of research is further cause for assuming that little result will follow from that area in carrying out the 'linked micro studies' which Hargreaves calls for.

Ethnographic work has made little impact on school management because it is not obviously linked to system improvement and indeed reveals the contradiction and untidiness in any 'system'. Literature on heads' tasks and heads' roles grows, but whatever happened to Wolcott's 'Man in the Principal's Office'? Nor is there much evidence of consciousness of these problems. For example Janet Finch (1985) provides a sensitive and illuminating discussion of the problems of using qualitative research in attempts to influence social and education policy, but supports Payne *et al's* (1981) concept of 'policy sociology' and 'the recognition that sociology is involved in the policy field of necessity', rather than any attempt to shift the direction and ethos of education policy studies.

There are exceptions to the general division of interests, of course. Stewart Ranson (1980, 1984, 1985) has consistently attempted to inject broader theoretical considerations into his studies of central-local relations and DES policy making, and has demonstrated a willingness to draw on a variety of research methods to produce work on education policy which is historically grounded, theoretically informed and uses experienced practitioners as source material. (See Ranson 1985 and the article with Gray and Hanson in this volume for examples of the richness of interview material). A major figure in the study of education policy, Maurice Kogan, has consistently extended his analysis of policy beyond the conventional pluralist mode, and concerns himself especially with the connection between values and policy (Kogan 1979, 1985, 1986). His work and that of his colleagues at Brunel is often historically based, and draws on practitioner experience.

Do these relatively isolated, though highly significant examples, give us sufficient grounds for belief that the micro-macro gap can be bridged, especially if we accept that the division is not merely methodological, but represents different preconceptions? The grounds for pessimism are clear: the depth of the division, the dominance of applied educational management studies, the neglect of historical work and the tendency of educational sociology to restrict itself to macro-level and relatively abstract theorizing. However, there are more hopeful signs; most significant among them being the failure of pluralist-inspired theorizing about education policy to cope with the degree of conflict and change in the area in the 1980s. Pluralist-dominated education policy studies appear increasingly as the product of their time. For this reason the time is ripe for the development of policy sociology, rooted in the social science tradition, historically informed and drawing on qualitative and illuminative techniques. The second part of the paper sketches out what such an approach might involve if applied to the re-examination of one of the central explanatory themes of pluralist educational policy studies.

The 'partnership': a Pluralist article of faith re-examined

The 'partnership' thesis stresses the sharing or distribution of power over education policy-making between DES, LEAs and teachers. There is more or less emphasis on consensus in the partnership, depending on the commentator or the policy under scrutiny. Some accounts emphasise tension and stress in the relationship (Briault 1976) but the idea of shared control is common to all, and central to pluralism. Pluralists, quick to condemn Marxists for their selection or misrepresentation of evidence, have been remarkably slow to recognise the extent to which the dominance of the relatively unquestioned paradigm of DES decentralisation, LEA independence and teacher autonomy has shaped and guided their work.

One of the most significant and least questioned examples of the dominance of the partnership model is the status given to the 1944 Act as the cornerstone of educational devolution. Yet the evidence exists, in primary sources, contemporary accounts and historical research, which allows for a different interpretation. Certainly Sir

Keith Joseph was able to interpret the Act as supporting his increased 'control and direction' of education policy. Those responsible for framing the Act and for its successful passage came from a small group of educational administrators who wanted a strong, efficient central administration capable of co-ercing recalcitrant LEAs into providing a new education system. The tone of the Act, as Britton (1985) points out, if it is read as a piece of literature rather than a piece of legislation, is centralist and directive. There were, of course, political considerations which made it necessary for Butler and his supporters to compromise (Fenwick, 1985, Lawn & Ozga 1986), and to emphasise local autonomy. But the administrators at the Board of Education and Butler himself were greatly concerned that without strong leadership from the centre, the new system of secondary education provided for in the Act would not be successfully established, particularly in some of the more dilatory or conservative authorities.

Had education not subsequently suffered financial cuts, and had the task of secondary provision not been complicated by post-war reconstruction, the 'baby boom' and teacher shortage, the Ministry of Education might have emerged as the most powerful policy-making government department in Whitehall. But control of the system on the scale necessary in the post-war crisis was impossible. The fledgling Ministry failed to impose strong central direction, and the LEAs, staffed by a new breed of trained educational administrator, and the teachers were able to exploit its weakness and retrieve some policy-making territory. The ministry reverted to the tradition of 'Indirect Rule' (Lawn 1986) and the encouragement of 'professionalism' among teachers as a method for the management of the system. (Ozga 1981, Ozga and Lawn 1981).

If this interpretation is sustained, it has consequences for the period following the post-war crisis, especially the 1960s, often viewed as the apotheosis of 'partnership'. Examples often cited are the introduction of comprehensive education through long and incomplete persuasion, and the achievement of teacher control over the curriculum through the transformation of the Curriculum Study Group into the Schools Council. However if the Ministry, (subsequently the Department), is viewed as essentially frustrated in its ambition to achieve greater central control, and forced to rely on indirect methods, then continuity may be appreciated in its activities from the 1940s to the 1980s, which is only partially obscured by the 'partnership' of the 1960s. The Department allowed the convention of partnership to flourish, and indeed encouraged it and the related idea of teacher professionalism. But the underlying trend was towards central control – of finance and curriculum. This is not to suggest that LEA and teacher autonomy did not exist; both the concepts of autonomy and the related idea of professionalism are far from amenable to straightforward manipulation, but they were restricted and formed an essential part of a management strategy with a long history (Lawn 1986). This critical approach to the concept of partnership could be further developed using some of the micro-level techniques described by Hargreaves, and which could reveal the extent of teacher and LEA autonomy, its working out in practice, the differences between rhetoric and reality, the extent to which the Department consciously pursued a coherent strategy, and the extent of internal Departmental differences. The use of in-depth, unstructured or semi-structured interviews with policy-makers (not just politicians, but administrators) who have worked in LEAs and government departments in the period since 1944 is, from a brief experience of it (Open University 1986) extraordinarily revealing. The richness of reflections on experience, especially from those no longer actively involved, but with a continuity of service to education, is hard to convey without intensive quotation, which is impossible here.

The combination of such material with careful historical work and the development of an education policy archive would do much towards bridging the micro-macro gap. This is not a mere extension of the traditional education administration/policy methodology, as pluralists – as well as neo-Marxists – tend to ignore the part played by people in policy making. People do not feature in pluralist accounts except as members of groups-interest or pressure groups, mainly, or as occupants of roles, that is as CEOs, Party Leaders, Ministers etc. They do not appear as themselves, but as occupants of roles which largely determine their behaviour. Pluralists, because of their belief in negotiation and bargaining among groups as the basis of social organisation, are not interested in individuals. This contributes to the lifelessness of much case study material, even on exciting topics. It is difficult to avoid: most of us who have, for example, carried out case studies of LEA policy-making are aware of the gap between the finished account and the reality where individual personality and personal relations were vital in affecting policy outcomes. The framework simply does not allow for this to be adequately expressed. And if this is true of studies of education administration, it is even worse in education management.

Using Interview Material

Stewart Ranson's (1985) work on the DES gives an indication of the richness of interview material, even where there are problems of confidentiality and access. The brief quotations convey the internal divisions in the Department following Sir Keith Joseph's assumption of control of policy. Here is one official, holding out for tertiary reorganisation against the Minister. He says, after the defeat of the tertiary model:

> 'We will challenge, react. They cannot deny us that: If not, they must staff with yes men. They cannot expect intelligent people to behave like automata. In public we will try to defend, in private we will express conviction. We will wait for *'le moment venue'* to change the situation to match the facts'.

> (Ranson 1985)

This quotation, and indeed, the whole article, conveys an image of the DES far removed from the accounts of dispassionate officials (Weaver, 1979, Pile 1979) and the inexorable bureaucratic machine of Salter and Tapper (1981). Obviously, there would be problems about pursing the extent of contradictions in the DES as officials come under increased political pressure, (see Tomlinson 1985) but material can be gathered, and the problems are much less acute if the enquiry is historically based. Recollections present different sorts of problems, but historians have worked with incomplete and partial accounts, and the techniques of oral historians and ethnographers can help to overcome some of the difficulties.

Work directed at a reassessment of the 'partnership', informed by critical theory and carried out through linked micro-level studies would be enriched by the gathering of interview material. The project is not impossibly ambitious. Accounts of the post-war education system and of the experience of working in it, at least at a fairly senior level, can be developed from research on a relatively small group. A further point of interest is the extent to which we are dealing with a homogenous self conscious group. Certainly connections between those working in the education service were very strong indeed, and 'networks' are easily identified. Toby Weaver, ex-Deputy Permanent Secretary at the DES, gives an account of his years as an educational administrator (Weaver 1979b) in which he refers to the 'Young Contemporaries', a group of university trained educationalists who included Clegg, Fisher, Houghton, Braithwaite, and Alexander and whose godfathers were Henry Morris and Salter Davies. He describes them as a 'beneficent mafia'. This interconnectedness and shared culture and social connection is important and must have made a major contribution to the idea of 'partnership' and to the ways in which things were done in education. These networks may have had more to do with the idea of devolution of control then the supposedly devolved structure of the 1944 Act. Sensitive exploration of the connections between these people, and knowledge of their backgrounds, and of the experiences which led them into education could provide a dimension on education policy which is currently absent.

Nor should such work be rejected as too individualistic and too far removed from the macro-level of theorising and Hargreaves' 'timeless' concepts of state, class and economy, although the argument outlined above does stress the richness of the human document, and it is easy to become engrossed in the account for itself. Furthermore the material reveals complexities and contradictions in the internal structures of education policy-making which macro-theoretians have found easier to deal with as relatively autonomous (and homogenous) agencies. But it is this over-determined structure that pluralists have been most successful in attacking, and which presents an impasse to those who wish to explore the potential for resistance, confusion and contradiction in the education state apparatus. Moreover, there are available what might be called 'middle level' theories, which could be tested against data gathered from policy makers. Much elite theory (e.g. Pareto, Mosca), has fallen into disfavour and indeed it seems dependent on massive generalisation and a kind of circular conspiracy theory. But the relationships between elites and the state is one that might fruitfully be explored in the light of material on senior educational administrators, and here there are a number of relevant sources (for example Mills, Giddens, Gramsci). Some of the ideas which might repay development concern the opposition of elites to the proliferation of state power, the idea of service being the obligation of elites, and the basis of elite power in non-economic sources, i.e. through ideological and moral leadership.

The separation of economic and political power helps us to examine the problem of the relative autonomy of the state, and points to the potential for the further development of the idea of fractions within the state, following Poulantzas. The elite and the state are not separate intrinsic entities, but evolve within each other, and further, more sophisticated conceptualisation would attempt to identify the contradictions and complementarities. The kind of work that I have outlined, combined with 'linked micro studies' would continue the growth of education policy sociology, and retrieve some of the territory of enquiry from the traditionalists, and, even more importantly, assist the survival and growth of education policy as a field of study, as distinct from education management.

Note

This is a much revised version of a paper given at the International Sociology of Education conference on Teachers, Policy and Education in January 1986. The original paper concentrated more on giving extracts from interviews with former policy makers. I hope to continue and extend this work in 1986. My thanks to conference participants who commented on the paper, and to members of the E333 *Policy Making in Education* course team who have contributed, in various ways, to the ideas in this paper.

References

Ahier, J. and Flude, M. (1983) *Contemporary Education Policy* Croom Helm.
Briault, E. (1976) 'A distributed system of educational administration' *International Review of Education* Vol. 22 No. 4.
Britton, E. (1985) Interview for Open University TV Programme 'After the Act': Programme 1 of E333.
Cox, R. W. (1980) 'Social Forces, States and World Orders'. Millenium: Journal of International Studies 10/2.
Dale, R. (1986) *Perspectives on Policy-Making*. Module 1 Part 2 of E333 Policy-making in Education. Open University Press.
Fenwick, K. (1985) 'Changing Roles in the Government of Education' *B.J.S.E.* Vol. XXXIII (2).
Finch, J. (1985) 'Social Policy and Education': problems and possibilities of using qualitative research' in Burgess R. (Ed). *Issues in Educational Research*. Falmer.
Flora, P. and Heidenheimer (1981) *The Development of Welfare States in Europe and America*. Transaction Books.
Giddens, A and Stanworth, P. (Eds.) *Elites and Power in British Society* C.U.P.
Glatter, R. (1979) 'Education 'Policy' or 'Management': one field or two?' in Fowler G. (Ed) *Educational Analysis* Vol. 1.2 Falmer.
Hargreaves, A. (1983) 'The Politics of Administrative Convenience' in Ahier, J. and Flude, M. (Eds.) *Contemporary Education Policy*. Croom Helm.
Hargreaves, A. (1985) 'The Micro-macro problem in the Sociology of Education' in Burgess, R. (Ed) *Issue in Educational Research*. Falmer.
Harman, G. (1984) 'Conceptual and Theoretical Issues' in Hough, J.R. (Ed.) *Education Policy; an international survey*, Croom Helm.
Kogan, M. (1979) 'Different frameworks for education policy-making and analysis' *Educational Analysis* 1 (2).
Kogan, M. (1985) 'Education Policy and Values' in McNay I and Ozga J. *Policy-making in Education; the Breakdown of Consensus* Pergamon Press/The Open University Press.
Kogan, M. (1986) *Education Accountability: an analytical overview* Hutchinson.
Lawn, M. (1986) 'The Spur and the Bridle': Indirect Rule and the rise of professionalism. *Westhill Conference Paper 1986*.

Lawn, M. and Ozga, J. T. (1986) 'Unequal Partners: Teachers under Indirect Rule' in *B.J.S.E.*, special issue *'Whatever Happened to Equality'*.

Lindblom, C. E. (1983) 'Comments on Manley' *American Political Science Review* 77 (2).

Mills, C. W. (1956) *The Power Elite* New York.

Offe, C. (1984) *Contradictions of the Welfare State*. Hutchinson.

Ozga, J. T. (1981) 'The Politics of the Teaching profession' Unit 14 of E333 *Society, Education and the State*. The Open University.

Ozga, J. T. and Lawn, M. A. (1981) *Teachers, Professionalism and Class* Falmer.

Open University (1981) *Society, Education and the State* (E333).

Open University (1986) Policy-making in Education (E333).

Payne, G. Dingwall, R., Payne, J., and Carter, M. (1981) *Sociology and Social Research* R.K.P.

Ranson, S. (1980) 'Changing Relations between Centre and Locality in Education' *Local Government Studies* Vol. 6 No. 6.

Pile, W. D. (1979) *The Department of Education and Science*. George Allen and Unwin.

Ranson, S. (1984) 'Towards a tertiary tripartitism' in Broadfoot P. (Ed) *Selection, Certification and Control*. Falmer.

Ranson, S. (1985) 'Contradictions in the government of educational change' *Political Studies* 33.1.

Ribbens, P. M. & Brown, R. J. (1979) Policy-making in English local government: the case of Secondary School reorganisation. *Public Administration* 57 (2).

Salter, B and Tapper, E. (1981) *Education, Policy and the State* Grant McIntyre.

Tipton, B. F. (1974) 'The Hidden Side of Teaching: the teachers' unions in Taylor W. (ed) *Teaching as a Profession*. London Educational Review Vol. 3 No. 2.

Tipton, B. F. (1980) 'The tense relationship between educational Administration and Sociology' *B.J.S.E.*

Tipton, B. F. (1985) 'Educational Organizations as Workplaces' *B.J.S.E.* Vol. 6 No. 1.

Tomlinson, J. (1985) 'From Projects to Programmes; The view from the top in Plaistow (Ed) *Life and Death of the Schools Council*. Falmer.

Weaver, T. R. (1979) 'The DES: Central control of education' Unit 2 of E222 *The Control of Education in Britain*, Open University.

Weaver, T. R. (1979b) 'Education: retrospect and prospect: an administrator's testimony' *Cambridge Journal of Education* Vol. 9 No. 1.

Wolcott, H. (1973) *The Man in the Principal's Office: An Ethnography*, Holt, Rhinehart, Winston.

Wolcott, H. (1981) 'Mirrors, models and monitors; educator adaptations of the ethnographic innovation'.

PART 3

New Policies and New Practices?

Introduction

The papers in this section of the book examine the question of the reproduction of sexual divisions within society and the particular part schools do, and can play, in both legitimating and challenging such divisions.

An overview of the ways in which the question of gender differentiation has been viewed in past work is provided. It has been used as a means of raising awareness, as a vehicle for changing the organisational practices of schools and as a basis for support and resources (Deem). Whilst not denying the importance of such endeavours, for the authors in this section, they are viewed as insufficient without a recognition of the question of power and power-relations within society and schools.

These papers emphasize the demand for change and argue, that a basic prerequisite for this is to understand the nature and impact of dominant ideologies. These include 'make physical aggression' (Scraton), 'motherhood' (David) and 'sexual equality' (Deem). Nor is the concern to be equated with mere questions of equality of access. The commitment is to sexual equality and thus to question the ways in which identities, expectations and relationships are gendered.

Teachers are viewed as crucial agents in the pursuit of anti-sexist policies and practices within schools. However, we are reminded that they are not a homogeneous group in so far as ideological commitment is concerned and that schools are also varied in terms of their ethos and organisation. Therefore, the ways the promotion of sexual equality in schools is being received by some teachers can be characterised as either one of apathy or resistance. Whilst the authors are sensitive to the contradictory work context of teaching and wish to disassociate themselves from the general criticism of teachers inspired by supporters of the New Right position in education, they offer both a critique and a call for educators to be more involved in the task of achieving sexual equality in schools.

Given the pressures arising from the new ideology and policies of education outlined in the previous sections of this book, the task facing teachers and schools in attempts to effect change relating to sexual equality can be seen as a very complex and difficult one.

Teachers need the support of other interested parties and one item on the agenda for immediate action is to find ways in which teachers and sociologists of education can work together in a form of common struggle in order that laudable rhetoric may be realised in practice.

CHAPTER NINE

Bringing Gender Equality into Schools

Rosemary Deem

Introduction

The issues concerning gender and gender inequalities in schools have
been the subject of intensive sociological discussion and research for
over a decade in the U.K. Many books and articles have analysed
what is wrong and put forward various explanations for why sexism
is so endemic to our schooling system. Research projects have been
launched to try to bring about changes which reduce gender inequality (e.g. Kelly 1984, Millman and Weiner 1985, Whyte 1985) and
assess the impact of changes already made (Pratt, Bloomfield and
Searle 1984). Individual teachers and groups, mainly but not entirely
feminists, have developed their own strategies for dealing with
sexism (see G. Weiner 1984 and Stantonbury Campus Sexism in
Education Group 1984) in particular schools. Local education
authorities have begun to develop policies and guidelines on equal
opportunities for both sexes.[1] National initiatives like the MSC financed TVEI schemes for 14–18 year olds in full time education have
adopted gender equality as part of their criteria. HMI and the DES
have 'noticed' gender equality, and refer to it in reports.

The whole process of educational reform however is a chancy
business (Deem 1984a) as the move from selective to comprehensive
secondary education has shown.[2] Things do not always turn out as
expected: moves that look like real changes may be circumvented or
stifled; the outcomes may be different to those required or may
throw up new problems (e.g. if there are single sex girls groups in
mixed schools for subjects girls find difficult, the problem often lies
in persuading anyone to teach the inevitable single sex groups of
boys left over). There are large, sometimes seemingly insurmount-
able gaps between theory and practice, or between policies/

guidelines and their implementation. Although some things have changed in schooling, girls are still underachieving in the labour market, and distinctive patterns of subject choice between the sexes in secondary and post-school education in England and Wales remain discernible; sexual harassment in schools (see Jones in Weiner 1985) continues to be a problem in schools; women teachers are still failing to achieve promotion (WNC 1983) in the same proportions as male teachers.

What I am particularly concerned to look at in this paper is the kind of roles sociologists might play in the process of bringing gender equality into schools, whilst at the same time taking into account some of the major gender issues too. With the rise of the comprehensive school, sociologists like Banks, Floud and Halsey were influential in shaping national policy and sometimes acted as government advisers. In relation to gender equality, a rather different political climate has made it much more difficult for sociologists (other than those on the extreme right) to play similar policy advisory roles in relation to education. Hence, Hargreaves' (1984) condemnation of sociologists for failing to be sufficiently involved in practical policy-making within education is an unfair attack. It fails to recognise that most sociologists are neither going to be a Chief Inspector of ILEA nor are likely to be in a power position to greatly influence national educational policies at a time when the social sciences, together with humanities, are increasingly seen as non-relevant, non-vocational, and indeed as positively dangerous, by a government concerned to shift school and further/higher education curricula towards science, technology and vocationally relevant subjects. Nevertheless, despite the severe constraints it is possible for sociologists to continue to play a role in shaping educational policy. There are indeed a number of different roles 'available' from the detached objective academic consultant through to the fully-fledged politician. But the process of influencing educational change has many potential pitfalls. It is also important to recognise the need to exploit the possibilities offered by the current prevalence of local and central educational policy discussions, documents and papers which recognise gender equality as an important goal, and to accept that whilst equality in education covers a wide field besides gender, gender is an important social division in our society, and tackling that when a policy lever already exists may then prepare the ground for tackling other dimensions of inequality such as class and race.

Roles, modes and levels of influence

(1) The researcher
The time-honoured conventional approach has been to do the research, write a book about it, or an article, often several years later, and then retire from the field to wait for the impact (sometimes silence or a dull thud). There is clearly a role for this approach, but it is a rather indirect one, and there is a longstanding antipathy between teachers and 'academic' experts, who are regarded, often quite rightly, as having no relevant practical experience of the educational grassroots. One way out of this dilemma has been the so-called 'action research' which actually involves the researchers in establishing or contributing to change (for example the Girls into Science and Technology project in Manchester, see Kelly 1984, Whyte 1986). Another strategy has been to try to disseminate research findings in a form more accessible to teachers and policy makers and making use of publications teachers already read, or writing books specially addressed to teacher audiences and often including contributions by teachers (e.g. Deem 1984b; Weiner 1985a; Whyld 1983; Mahony 1985; Spender 1982).

(2) The consultant
The range of possible interventions ranges from one-off lectures to INSET courses and may also include advising on the drawing-up and implementation of policies designed to reduce educational sexism. This mode is much more direct than many forms of 'pure' research intervention because there is often face to face contact between consultants and schools, but it has the disadvantages that teachers may still see such interventions as being made by remote experts, or associate what is happening with a 'management' rather than an 'classroom' viewpoint. The latter of course depends on the context within which consultancy takes place and who initiates it. Whilst there is an important role for consultancy through the medium of LEAs or advisers, it may also be as or more satisfactory if it is arranged through groups of interested individuals or through a third-party like a teachers centre or teacher training institution.

(3) Political involvement
This is a much more fraught route than that of either the researcher or consultant not only because it has no pretence at being 'objective' but also because it may involve many things seemingly having no connection with the pursuit of gender equality, like canvassing for votes on doorsteps and sitting all night in 'smoke filled rooms'. Nevertheless it is and can be important because it provides firstly a

way of introducing issues like gender equality onto the political agenda and secondly it can provide access to spheres of influence otherwise difficult for social scientists to reach (for example interviewing panels, and 'closed' meetings, or elected members of local authorities). There are a number of possible channels available

a) through involvement with a political party at national or local level
b) through a pressure group
c) by actually becoming a local politician
d) by becoming a school governor (there are of course non-political routes to this too e.g. parent governors – but it would be a mistake to think that being a governor is non-political, even if it is not always party-political). This route offers the possibility of greater involvement at the level of an individual school and can include being part of appointments panels, reviewing the curriculum and looking at school organization.

Many local authorities already have some kind of policy or guidelines on equal opportunities, not necessarily just about gender, and not always just confined to education. But equal opportunities is a vaguely defined term – does it convey equal facilities, equal access or equal outcome for example? However the existence of a policy already means that the task isn't so much convincing someone that equal opportunities are a good idea (as was previously the case in many areas, Headlam Wells 1985, Cant 1985, Taylor 1985a, b) but rather of trying to make those policies effective. This in itself implies coming to terms with what it may be possible to achieve. Paper policies are a good start, but don't necessarily achieve anything other than a 'pat on the back' for the LEA concerned; there may be an initial flurry of activity which then fizzles out or is ineffective (Cant 1985). Some authorities (by no means all) have very little conception of what being an 'equal opportunities employer' (often emblazoned in all their job adverts) or having a policy on equal opportunities means in practical terms. So, for example, discriminatory practices may continue amongst an authority's existing staff, or the policy, rather than its implementation, may be seen as an end in itself. Even where there is commitment to change, what outcomes are required may vary enormously and any change needs to permeate all levels of the educational system. An input of resources (including people) is required and there is also need to establish a network of support for those who are expected to bring about changes, particularly classroom teachers.

What kind of changes?

One of the biggest problems with the shift to comprehensive school-ing was the plurality of models of what a comprehensive school was (was it a form of social engineering, an open access grammar school or a community school?). Deciding what is wanted has also been a major stumbling block in the field of gender equality; there is no consensus about what it would look like. It may involve any of the following

(1) achieving equal access to educational opportunities for both sexes, including pupils and teachers.
(2) ensuring conditions of 'neutral' treatment for girls and boys in schools. As Pratt (1985) has noted, many teachers think this already happens, especially with regard to option choices. The notion of individualism is very prevalent in the comprehensive system, implying that social divisions have no real effect on what happens in schooling (Shaw 1984).
(3) eradicating sexism from the organisation and content of schooling.
(4) promoting equality of outcome for girls and boys, although there is a problem about at what levels and age. Is outcome to be measured in terms of labour market entry or who does what in the home; in exam results, HE and FE entry or what?
(5) providing positive discrimination in favour of girls and women [Smith 1984, Weiner 1985a] and indeed in favour of boys where appropriate (e.g. in languages and music where boys currently underperform)
(6) changing the views and behaviour of girls and boys, so that both are prepared for all aspects of adult life, including housework and parenting as well as employment.

Much of the work done so far has concentrated on

(1) raising awareness of the issues surrounding the need for gender equality through courses and other INSET (Arnot 1984). But as Adams (1985) and others have noted, such courses may have less impact on men than on women. Men may see any raised aware-ness of sexism in school and the need to try to be anti-sexist as separable from what happens in their outside school lives, whilst women are more likely to make connections between sexism in their public and private lives.
(2) changing the organisational practices in schools – e.g. on option choice (Pratt, Bloomfield and Searle 1984) or single sex setting (Smith 1984) or opportunities for promotion.
(3) offering support and resources e.g. The Schools Council

'Reducing Sex Differentiation' project (Millman and Weiner 1985, Weiner 1985b).

Where and on whom/what is change to be located?

Much of the focus in Britain during the 1980s has been on trying to change schools, and the ways teachers see the world. This is clearly important, but is also extremely difficult. As Whyte (1985) notes, in her GIST project teachers were reluctant to admit they had changed, as this implies they were previously sexist in their practices and outlook. Some of them also didn't want to accept that a research project could influence them. Teachers will of course vary in their reactions to attempted changes. Feminist teachers, already committed to improving the lot of female pupils and women teachers, will value the support offered, but others may be indifferent, hostile (Pratt 1985; Witcher 1985) or apply anti-sexism only in school, and hence never really change their attitudes (e.g. the headteacher of a comprehensive who proudly tells everyone about the efforts in his school to attract girls to physics, but who never bothers with housework or childcare at home because that's 'his wife's job'). Teachers at the present time are under tremendous pressure; they feel demoralised and undervalued by a whole variety of factors; falling rolls, cuts in capitation, low teacher pay and massive curriculum intervention by outside agencies like the MSC. Teachers are continually being asked to implement changes of all kinds – from vocationally relevant curricula to more primary science – and within the field of 'equality' there may be what are perceived as competing demands – race versus gender or special needs. Personal beliefs and values are bound to influence what is seen as a priority. Furthermore in the period 1984–6 teacher action over pay meant that in many areas curriculum development, meetings and INSET almost ceased, so that normal channels of influence weren't really available.

Recently emphasis has begun to shift to other groups, focussing on strategies to change pupils (Arnot 1984) or getting school governors to raise the issues (Labour Party 1986; Headlam Wells 1985). Parents and employers are harder to reach than teachers and may be the cause of major headaches especially when encouraging pupils and school leavers to make untraditional (for their sex) choices of subjects or jobs, because employers and parents may think this is 'unnatural' or upsetting the 'balance between the sexes'. It is important also that we are reflexive and critical about what we are trying to achieve. So, we need to ask about 'more girls into science and technology' for example, what jobs are available to those girls and what are the implications of them being employed in areas like weapons technology – is this necessarily better than trying to raise the ambitions of girls who enter traditionally female jobs like hairdressing? In areas of high unemployment, gender divisions may tend to be reinforced despite efforts to overcome this in schools, because pupils want to get any job they can, and because employers may fear 'spoiling the chances of good male applicants' if they take on females too. There is obviously less possibility of sociologists or educationalists influencing employers. But it is important to think about the relationship between education, certification and the labour market and about the connections between schools and their communities. The naive belief that if schools change, so will the rest of society, without recourse to other strategies outside the field of education, is likely to lead to failure.

Equal Opportunities versus Feminism

Weiner (1985) raises an important issue about the underlying philosophies and intentions of 'gender in education' intervention strategies. She distinguishes between equal opportunities approaches (i.e. those moderate policies which are concerned principally with equal access of both sexes) concerned not to 'rock the boat', make radical changes or bring in 'positive discrimination', and feminist approaches (which takes the subordination of women to men as its political starting point) concerned to improve the social position of women *vis-a-vis* men in a radical way using any means seen as appropriate. The latter approach sees positive discrimination for girls and women as crucial, and is unconcerned about 'rocking the boat'³. Although the difference between these approaches is according to Weiner analytically distinct, the situation is actually more complicated than Weiner allows:

(1) in practice the 'equal opportunities' approach has brought in committed feminists to posts and responsibilities in LEAs, schools and elsewhere who are then more able to achieve their objectives, even if the covering 'rationale' is more limited than they would like. This ought not to be seen as 'selling out' because as I have pointed out elsewhere (Deem 1984a) it is necessary for women to infiltrate the formal political and policy making process as well as the informal, if real changes are to occur. It is also important for the same reason to form alliances with male groups as well as having autonomous women – only groups (see also Rowbotham 1985).

(2) there are some overlapping aims and intentions between the two

strategies, including a desire to achieve eradication of at least some of the elements of sexism from education.

(3) the legitimation of the approach used to make change seem acceptable is crucial to the success of any policy. All social change of more than the most piecemeal and trivial kind needs the consent of those likely to be affected. In a political climate where some forms of social change are seen as unacceptable (particularly, for example, women taking power from men) then it may be legitimate to couch proposed changes in more moderate ways. Otherwise the outcome may be the political wilderness rather than the radical changes required (for example as Barnett (1985) points out, the real political alternative to Thatcher and Owen is not Kinnock but Wedgewood Benn, – but who mentions Benn in serious politics now?) Also, teachers, schools, LEAs and communities differ. What is acceptable in one place may not be elsewhere. If 'equal opportunities' can be used as a lever to achieve changes in the educational experiences of girls and women (and boys and men too) then surely it is better than no change at all? Of course equal opportunities may be seen as a catchphrase, involving little beyond a paper policy – but this is also true of more 'radical' policies such as the declaration of Nuclear Free Zones. What counts is what happens afterwards and where and to whom, rather than the ideological purity of those involved, and the rationale within which it is all cloaked.

Two projects: limitations and possibilities

What follows is a brief discussion of two projects concerned with promoting awareness of the importance of gender equality in the classroom. There are several reasons for examining these two projects. One is that they involve different kinds of roles for sociologists; the Bucks project is based on conventional academic research, and was carried out in an authority which has no specific policy on eradicating sexism in education, but was partly made possible by contacts developed as a local politician. The Manchester project uses a consultancy role in an LEA which already had a policy on gender equality in education and is based round a brief INSET course drawing heavily on teaching methods developed in order to raise issues about sexism with adult students in the Open University (principally within the Social Sciences Foundation Course Summer School Module developed by Helen Lentell and Angela Coyle). The second is that both projects illustrate some of the pitfalls which are likely to confront sociologists trying to bring about controversial changes in education (including in both instances the effect of the

1984–6 teachers dispute on research and consultancy of all kinds). The third reason is that the problems encountered in the experience of carrying out these projects throw new light on the difficulties of implementing Hargreaves (1984) plea for sociologists to be more involved in policy-making. Finally the Bucks project in particular illustrates the conflicts and difficulties which trying to wear both an academic and a political hat at the same time may present. It is also not without relevance to note that, in this period of reduced funding for social scientific research, that both projects have been carried out with minimal funding.

The Milton Keynes (Bucks) project

Buckinghamshire is a Conservative LEA (albeit with a woman Chair of Education) with no definite policy on equal opportunities in education, although it has adopted the 'we are an equal opportunity employer' slogan. Three quarters of the county retains selective secondary education and the 12 + (reflecting the wealth of the south Bucks commuter belt whilst 'hiding' socially disadvantaged and substantial ethnic minority groups in Wycombe and Aylesbury). However, Milton Keynes, the base for the research has comprehensive secondary schools and is therefore seen as 'different' to the rest of the county (indeed in 1985 a controversy about the allegedly poor exam results of the Milton Keynes comprehensives compared to the grammar and secondary modern schools of South Bucks, developed, and in 1986 was still continuing). Milton Keynes itself is a new town which has changed quite rapidly from being mainly rental housing to having a large amount of owner-occupied housing, some of it expensive 'executive' homes. Its employment structure includes high technology, retailing, banking, insurance and building societies, warehousing and a fairly small manufacturing sector. The two largest employers in the city are British Rail Engineering Ltd (currently in 1986 facing the possibility of large-scale redundancies) and the Open University! Unemployment rates are slightly above those for the region as a whole. Many of the hi-tech firms recruit little or no local labour, and there is some concern about this. Milton Keynes schools are currently in their second year of the MSC-financed TVEI scheme, and this plus concern about the possible underachievements of girls in the labour market are principally what gave rise to the idea of the present project.

I was approached by the City's Education-Industry Liaison Committee to undertake some research on what was happening to girls in Milton Keynes schools, including identifying examples of 'good practice'. Some if not all of this group were certainly aware that I was both a local councillor (and on the Education Committee) and an academic sociologist. It was decided initially to focus on secondary schools because TVEI (which has equal opportunities between the sexes as one of its criteria) has raised some awareness there. The first stage, after discussion with various teachers, officers and other interested parties, was to send a questionnaire to all the Milton Keynes secondary schools focussing on staffing, curriculum (including subject choice) exam performances and entry, books and materials, pupil groupings, classroom behaviour and practices, school organisation and the extent of awareness about the need for gender equality.

The intention was then to disseminate the results of this survey at a seminar for all Milton Keynes teachers [in March 1985 an OU/BERA seminar we ran entitled Gender and Classroom Life attracted a number of local teachers] and then to follow this up by interviewing 4th year pupils and appropriate teachers in each secondary school. Some kind of work in first and middle schools was seen as a possible second stage. The questionnaire was sent out in May 1985, with a supporting letter from the Area Education Officer. By September 1985 five out of eight had been returned, a sixth was lost in the post and the other two schools said they were too busy. Actually it seems likely the heads concerned were hostile and used the excuse of the teachers dispute to avoid completing something they regarded as irrelevant and trivial. The schools which did respond have in all cases displayed at least a basic understanding of the issues surrounding sexism in education. There are some very positive things going on, including monitoring TVEI for gender bias, the arrival of a TVEI curriculum leader who is particularly interested in gender, the appointment of a deputy head with special responsibility for equal opportunities, curriculum changes and the establishment of a working group in one school. The three schools which did not respond may be doing equally positive things, but the teachers' dispute has made it difficult to chase two of them where the heads claim that they are already over-stressed by guerilla strikes and dinner supervision problems. Furthermore a series of meetings held between heads and governors over the teachers dispute in early 1986 actually made any efforts to follow up the research in non-co-operative schools very difficult, since I, as a governor, have been at those meetings in a political rather than academic role and the Heads concerned are certainly aware of this. But we have now completed 4th year pupil interviews in four schools, all of which were extremely helpful and supportive. Teacher interviews, possible in only one school before the summer term of 1986 because of the dispute, have gone ahead subsequently. One of the projects researchers has also been able to go into two schools in connection with a TVEI project about the social and pastoral aspects of the curriculum. There are a number of problems with the project as a whole

(1) I am walking a delicate tightrope between the role of academic researcher and local politician and some heads and certainly some teachers are suspicious. LEA officer help was initially good but became significantly worse after the 1985 May county council elections and the continuation of the teachers dispute into 1986.

(2) It is difficult to reach hostile heads and schools where it is felt there is no problem; successful access to schools has largely been based on existing personal contacts including being a governor, or knowing that someone on the staff is interested in the issue.

(3) The research is so far having no impact on Middle or First schools – there is no entry point, or lever comparable to TVEI or employment prospects.

(4) The teachers dispute has made it so far impossible to disseminate the results of the questionnaire through a seminar.

(5) The LEA has no real commitment to doing anything about gender equality, and locally the TVEI gender equality criterion receives only grudging acceptance in some quarters. Pursuing equality issues has proved no easier in relation to race; continued pressure by a few elected members has produced so far a brief discussion of the Swann Report, a tiny 'share' in an advisor and the change in role of an existing area multi-cultural co-ordinator to a county-wide brief.

(6) The teachers dispute has made it impossible to work with groups of teachers on a school basis, which would probably be more effective.

(7) The Milton Keynes Area Education Office has been in a panic about 'O' and 'A' level results in the city. This controversy has been stirred up by Tory Councillors who want a city grammar school, and everything else except that has taken a back seat for the time being.

(8) The LEA is likely to impose severe cuts in 1986/87 (already 1985 saw a twelve percent capitation cut) so that there are few possibilities of new appointments or additional resources being devoted to equal opportunities.

The Manchester Project

I want to compare the Bucks project with a different kind of intervention made in Manchester during 1984 which was INSET rather than research-based, and which drew heavily on OU experience of small group work and used OU video and research materials.

Manchester was one of a large number of LEAs approached by Gaby Weiner and myself in 1983/84 when we were seeking finance to launch a pack on gender equality in classroom (non award-bearing Open University courses have to be externally financed). Manchester gave us a sum of money towards the pack, but as no other funding was forthcoming it was decided to run a seminar weekend for some of their teachers. In 1980 an initiative on sexism in education in the authority had led to Working Parties being set up to review what could be done. In 1982 the LEA produced guidelines on good practice in secondary schools and each secondary school nominated one member of staff to meet regularly to plan projects and bring about implementation of the guidelines. Despite this, there was a feeling (Waldron 1984, Cant 1985) that not much was happening. I met one officer, an Inspector and a group of teachers twice in the Spring and Summer of 1984 to plan the seminar. In October 1984 a workshop weekend took place in Buxton with a mixed group of 16, mainly teachers (from scale 1 to Heads), one Inspector and an LEA officer and five academics, researchers and students from the Open University. The objects of the weekend were

(1) to mix their and our expertise – so there was a mixture of sessions with the whole group and some smaller group work. There was emphasis on both our research and on things they had done (e.g. drama, role play and videos and various resources already in use) as well as on problems they had encountered.

(2) to give each individual teacher some INSET ideas they could take back and use to raise awareness in their own school. The introductory exercise was adopted from the OU Foundation Social Science course and is about our own beliefs in relation to masculinity and femininity, but is less threatening than some exercises about gender because it initially revolves around photographs of other people. We also used the work of a Ph.D student Jenny Griffin, on 'trigger starts' to writing a story about women teachers and promotion.

(3) to offer some support for Manchester's own projects, and provide a sense of breaking down their isolation.

(4) to develop materials for wider use – otherwise there is the problem of re-inventing the wheel each time a new person or school develops materials (Taylor 1985a).

Issues covered during the weekend were: stereotypes of women and men, the use of OU videos showing schools and classrooms and the identification of sexist practices and occurrences in them; the situation of women teachers; language and classroom interaction; girls and writing; role-play and drama; mixed P.E. and what is happening in other LEAs. We experimented with mixed and single sex small groups. Like Adams (1985) we have found the latter work much better with women than men. We found the men on the course were on the whole more critical and less willing to relate it to their own situation than the women. The whole thing was a very limited exercise, but it did increase contact between the teachers and those with a specialist knowledge of gender equality. It also allowed the production of materials and the spreading of ideas developed in OU teaching about how to approach gender issues without arousing undue hostility.

It is of course impossible to fully evaluate the effects of this kind of INSET exercise, but this is also a problem with more elaborate projects, including action research (Whyte 1985). It would also be difficult to undertake a Manchester type project in an LEA without at least some interest in gender equality. But there is perhaps more likelihood of changes arising from the Manchester project than the Bucks project; the latter is likely to reveal simply what is wrong. At the same time, the Manchester project where we had few personal contacts and little local knowledge was much more difficult than working in Bucks. In the former case there was a lack of awareness of issues which could be influential – other local political and educational developments, personalities, and so on. Also the Manchester weekend was remote from actual schools. Nevertheless, the Manchester exercise drew on joint teacher/sociological expertise and tried to focus on developing techniques and materials which could be used in schools elsewhere too – although the funding situation of the OU means it is unlikely that a 'pack' will emerge from the project. Both the more detached stance of the consultancy role and the more involved academic/politician mode have their advantages. But my experiences in Bucks show up some of the pitfalls of the 'sociologists should be more involved' role which Hargreaves (1984) and others have urged. Both projects, however limited, do suggest however, that it is possible for sociologists to intervene in educational change in a variety of ways and without necessarily having the advantage of large research funds. The contrasting situation of the two LEAs also illustrates how different the climate is now from that prevailing in the late 1970s, when almost no LEA had developed any policy around gender equality – at the present time even LEAs not overtly interested in the issue have nevertheless been pushed to do something, and there is a lever for commencing change. The legitimation for that change is, as I have said earlier, less important than the possibility of exploiting any base for trying to bring about gender equality. Nevertheless the path to such equality is strewn with many rocks.

Conclusion

I have attempted in this paper both to sketch out some of the issues surrounding endeavours to bring gender equality to the classroom, and to examine some of the roles and intervention strategies which sociologists can use in order to bring the elimination of gender differentiation in schools closer. I have also looked at two projects I am currently involved with, which were arrived at by very different routes and are based in two very different LEAs. These projects suggest ways forward both for LEAs who already have policies on gender equality and the levers which may be possible in those without. Whichever strategies are used, there is still a very long way to go. The question of the role played by sociologists in policy making and implementation is a much more complex one than Hargreaves (1984) suggested two years ago at Westhill and has to be carried out in a climate unsympathetic both to the social sciences (except economics) and to feminism. But at the same time, perhaps because of the very benign nature of the maligned 'equal opportunities' policies which some LEAs, TVEI, HMI and others have adopted, interventions and changes are still possible. However, what is most important I believe, is that sociologists of education continue to be involved in trying to shape educational policy, and exploring the different routes through which this may be possible.

Notes

1. I am well aware that 'equal opportunities' policies covers other aspects of inequality than gender; but increasing awareness of the pervasiveness of gender divisions has been an important springboard for the development of such policies.
2. Changes may of course be of different kinds; reform is not everyone's idea of a desirable change because it is felt to be too limited. But within the educational system and social structure as they presently exist, it is difficult to see how any kind of more radical or revolutionary change could be feasible.
3. Some commentators have drawn parallels between the equal opportunities versus feminist approaches in the field of gender, and the controversy between multi-cultural and anti-racist approaches in the field of race. But quite apart from the obvious differences between race and gender as social divisions, this doesn't seem to me a very apt parallel because whereas in the field of race the two approaches have both different methods and different objectives, this isn't necessarily the case in relation to gender equality.

References

Adams, C. (1985) 'Teacher attitudes towards issues of sex equality' in J. Whyte, R. Deem, L. Kant and M. Cruickshank (eds) *Girl Friendly Schooling*, Methuen.

Arnot, M. (1985) *Race and Gender*, Pergammon.

Arnot, M. (1984) 'How shall we educate our sons' in Deem, R. (ed) *Co-education Reconsidered*, Open University Press.

Arnot, M. (1986) 'Political lipservice or radical reform? The response of education policy-makers to race and gender inequality' paper given to International Sociology of Education Conference, Westhill, Birmingham.

Barnett, A. (1985) 'The void Kinnock can't fill' in the *Guardian*, December 30th, p. 6.

Cant, A. (1985) 'Development of LEA policy – Manchester' in J. Whyte, et al *Girl Friendly Schooling*, Methuen.

Deem, R. (1984a) 'Women, educational reform and the process of change' Occasional paper series, Faculty of Educational Studies, SUNY Buffalo and OISE.

Deem, R. (1984b) *Coeducation Reconsidered*, Open University Press.

Hargreaves, D. (1984) 'Sociology, Education and Policy: Some reflections' paper given to Westhill Sociology of Education Conference.

Headlam Wells, J. (1985) 'Humberside goes neuter: an example of LEA intervention for equal opportunities' in J. Whyte (ed) op cit.

Kelly, A. (1984) 'Promoting societal change through schools: the Girls into Science and Technology project' paper given to Westhill Sociology of Education Conference.

The Labour Party (1986) Pack on 'Gender and Equal Opportunities' for school governors.

Mahony, P. (1985) *Schools for the Boys*, Hutchinson.

Millman, V. and Weiner, G. (1985) *Sex Differentiation in Schooling: is there really a problem?* Longmans/Schools Curriculum Development Council.

Pratt, J., Bloomfield, J. and Searle, J. (1984) *Option Choice*, NFER.

Rowbotham, S. (1985) 'What do women want? Women centred values and the world as it is' *Feminist Review*, No. 20, pp. 49–69.

Shaw, J. (1984) 'The politics of single sex schools' in Deem, R. (ed) (1984b) op cit.

Smith, S. (1984) 'Single sex setting' Ibid.

Taylor, H. (1985a) 'A Local Authority initiative on Equal Opportunities' in M. Arnot (ed) *Race and Gender: Equal Opportunities Policies in Education*, Pergammon.

Taylor, H. (1985b) 'INSET for equal opportunities in the London Borough of Brent' in J. Whyte et al *Girl Friendly Schooling*, Methuen.

Spender, D. (1982) *Invisible Women: the Schooling Scandal*, Writers and Readers Co-operative.

Weiner, G. (1985a) (ed) *Just a Bunch of Girls*, Open University Press.

Weiner, G. (1985b) 'The Schools Council and Gender: a case study in the legitimation of curriculum policy' in Arnot, M. op cit.

Whyld, J. (1983) *Sexism in the School Curriculum*, Harper and Row.

Whyte, J. (1985a) 'Girl Friendly Science and the girl friendly school' in Whyte, J. et al (eds) *Girl Friendly Schooling*, Methuen.

Whyte, J. (1985b) et al *Girl Friendly Schooling*, Methuen.

Whyte, J. (1986) *Girls in Science and Technology*, Routledge and Kegan Paul.

Witcher, H. (1985) 'Personal and professional: a feminist approach' in Whyte 1985b op cit.

Women's National Commission (1983) *Report on Secondary Education*, Cabinet Office.

CHAPTER TEN

Gender and Physical Education: Ideologies of the Physical and the Politics of Sexuality

Sheila Scraton

Introduction

> The ideology in the legal treatment of rape corresponds closely with general ideologies about masculine and feminine behaviour. It is acknowledged that women have a sexuality, but it is a sexuality which pervades their bodies almost in spite of themselves. It is up to women to *protect* themselves by only allowing this sexual message to be transmitted in contexts where it will be received *responsibly*, that is, in heterosexual, potentially permanent situations.
>
> Coward 1984:42. (My emphases).

Coward (1984) identifies a situation whereby ideas around acceptable female sexuality have become institutionalised into the criminal justice process to the extent that they have serious implications for the treatment and protection afforded to women who have suffered male physical violence. (Toner 1977; Smart and Smart 1978; Hutter and Williams 1981; Wilson 1983). Consequently the victims of rape, sexual assaults and sexual harrassment have to 'prove' that they are morally responsible women and any hint of overt sexuality evident in their appearance, style or past sexual experience usually is construed as inviting or at least contributing to a physical sexual attack (Jeffreys and Radford 1984). It is in this way that women are seen to be responsible for acceptable female sexuality which by definition implies an asexual presentation of themselves.

The politics of sexuality has become a central concern in the understanding of sexual divisions and, more specifically, of patriarchal power relations.[1] Feminist work which places sexuality as central to its analysis emphasises the construction and use of male sexuality as a multi-dimensional form of social control over women:

by confining us in terms of the space we may move in, by dictating the way we look, by restricting the work we do and how and when we do it, ..., and by constraining the social life we engage in. The effect is to undermine our confidence and reinforce our inferior status, to alienate us from our bodies, and to induce a timid and careful response to men.

Coveney et al 1985:19.

Jackson (1982) argues further that sexuality is inextricably tied up with power and dominance. This exists at both psychological and physical levels and, as Coveney et al explain, results in severe restrictions for women in terms of time, work, space, social life and confidence. This paper is concerned specifically with the physical aspect of male power and domination. Female and male sexuality both incorporate an ideology of the physical which has become so internalised and a part of everyday life that it appears as natural and inevitable. Ideas and images of what the 'physical' means for men and women incorporate expectations about appearance and behaviour. The stereotype for men is one which emphasises strength, power, activity and a muscular physique. Women, however, should be bodily firm but not muscular, relatively inactive, weak and project a central concern for their personal appearance – as defined by men. For women the primary objective in relation to the 'physical' is to look good for others. As Coward (1984:81/82) states:

> Every minute region of the body is now exposed to this scrutiny by the ideal. Mouth, hair, eyes, eyelashes, nails, fingers, hands, skin, teeth, lips, cheeks, shoulders, arms, legs, feet, – all these and many more have become areas requiring work. Each area requires potions, moisturisers, conditioners, night creams, creams to cover up blemishes. Moisturise, display, clean off, rejuvenate – we could well be at it all day, preparing the face to meet the faces that we meet.

Ideas about the 'physical', however, are not restricted to the level of commonsense assumptions to be 'achieved' by some individuals and challenged by others. Taken together they form ideologies of the physical which are formulated and articulated in cultures of masculinity and femininity. In relation to women it is the institutionalisation of an ideology of the physical – incorporating ideas about their biology, physiology and psychology which define 'womanhood' – which in the criminal justice system, media, health service and schooling helps to construct and maintain sexual divisions in society. It is central to the restriction and subordination of women in their participation and potential in social practice. Similarly the ideology of the physical, implicit and often explicit in the culture of masculinity helps create the powerful, active and dominant position of men which has repercussions for the daily experiences of men and women (Weeks 1981). It is reflected and reinforced by the politics of sexuality. Male-female power relations are portrayed and popularised exclusively within the framework of heterosexuality and it is this politics of sexuality which radical feminist theorists (e.g. Coveney *et al* 1984; Mahony 1985) place centrally within their analysis of sexual divisions.

Schooling as an institution concerned with the maintenance and reproduction of a sexually differentiated power system has received considerable analytical attention. Research has focused on the relationship of schooling to the reproduction of the sexual division of labour (Deem 1978, 1980; Wolpe 1977, 1978; MacDonald 1981) and the reinforcement of ideologies of femininity and motherhood through both overt and covert curricula (Sharpe 1976; Stanworth 1983). Recent classroom interaction studies have contributed to an understanding of how schooling influences the process whereby girls (and boys) emerge from the classroom with gendered identities, prepared to take their place in a sexually differentiated society, (Spender and Sarah 1980; Spender 1982; Mahony 1983, 1985; Weiner 1985). While acknowledging the complexity of this process, with contestation from both teachers and pupils, the overall 'success' of the system in maintaining male-female power relations has remained depressingly secure. The explanations for this reiterate the need to consider schooling within the broader construct of advanced capitalist society (Wolpe 1972, 1978; Deem 1980; MacDonald 1980), male-female power relations (Spender and Sarah 1980; Spender 1982; Mahony 1985), or the complex integration of the two (Arnot 1981).

The following discussion sets out to extend the work on gender ideologies and schooling by considering the relationship of schooling to the maintenance and reproduction of an ideology of the physical and the attendant implications this has for the politics of sexuality. The area of schooling most overtly concerned with the physical is physical education[2] and it is this area of curriculum which will be analysed. The discussion focuses on girls' secondary schooling, although similar work on male physical education is central to any future analysis of the relationship between ideologies of the physical and the culture of masculinity.

Secondary schooling is considered not least because this covers the period of adolescence crucial to the development of female sexuality. However, it must be recognised that by the age of 11 years, images and ideas held about girls' physicality in relation to 'femininity' are well established and strengthened through children's literature, television and the schooling process (Belotti 1975; Whyte 1983; Clarricoates 1980). This paper considers whether commonsense assumptions around the physical can be identified universally in the teaching of secondary PE during this adolescent period and whether such assumptions have formed an ideology of the physical which defines and contributes to the formation of 'acceptable' female sexuality. Contemporary material is drawn from a research project carried out in the secondary schools of a large city LEA during 1984. This research involved in-depth structured interviews with advisory staff, peripatetic PE teachers and heads of PE departments throughout the city, followed by observation and informal discussion in four case study schools. These case study schools were selected as representative of the different catchment areas and school organization (i.e. mixed or single sex) covered within the authority. Half a term was spent with the girls' PE department in each of these schools.

The first section of the paper considers the relevance of physical power relations to an understanding of gender divisions in society. This is followed by a brief introduction to the historical development of PE where an ideology of the physical can be identified throughout the development of the subject from its formal beginnings in the girls' secondary schools of the late nineteenth century. Necessarily this is a brief overview of the historical work, but it provides the historical context through which the ideologies of the physical have developed and, consequently, have informed the policies and practice of PE teaching in today's schools. Finally the paper considers the importance of physical power relations both within schooling and in wider society and the inevitable implications for future policy orientations concerned with encouraging anti-sexist strategies within the schooling system.

Physical power relations

> Socialist feminist theory has abandoned a concept of the superior physical effectivity of men on account of a very reasonable fear of that biologism and essentialism which may nullify our struggle. I suggest however that we have thrown out something we need with the radical feminist bathwater. We cannot do without a politics of physical power.
>
> Cockburn 1981:4.

Explanations of physical sex differences based on biological determinants have been the subject of much academic, as well as popular, debate (Ferris 1978; Dyer 1982). Whether differences in physical ability are primarily biologically determined or socially conditioned remains controversial albeit, to some extent, irrelevant (Cockburn 1981). What has become increasingly clear, is that the social construction of physical differences has given the appearance that differences between men and women are 'natural' and 'inevitable', while differences between women or between men are not considered as being important. Radical feminist work (Jeffreys 1981; Dworkin 1981; Coveney *et al* 1985) locates sexuality centrally within its explanation of women's oppression. The importance of such work is, as Cockburn suggests, the identification of physical power relations at both ideological and political levels. The ideological construction of male physical dominance is an integral part of male sexuality used directly and indirectly in order to control and discipline women (Coveney et al 1985). Female sexuality also incorporates an ideology of the physical relating to strength and appearance. In terms of the generally accepted stereotype of 'ideal female sexuality' women are expected to be passive, dependent and, therefore, vulnerable. In their appearance women are defined by men in relation to sexual attractiveness. Dominant images of women create a polarity between the 'Page 3 girl' and the 'caring wife and mother'. Female sexuality stresses the need to be attractive but not active (Jackson 1982). Women who project their sexuality through dress/style and promote active sexuality are unacceptable and considered to be 'dangerous' for they are 'asking for trouble'. Women ultimately are responsible for morality.

Ideologies of the physical do not exist only in the minds of individuals whereby physical power is considered the prerogative of the male. More importantly these ideologies have consequences in social practice which are experienced by women at different levels. First, through a monopoly on physical strength and technical capability, men maintain control over technology and manual occupation. Cockburn (1981)[4] suggests:

> The appropriation of muscle, capability, tools and machinery by men is an important source of women's subordination, indeed it is part of the process by which females are constituted as women.

In a more thorough and developed account of her research into the male domain of the printing industry she argues:

> Small biological differences are turned into bigger physical differences which themselves are turned into the gambits of social, political and ideological power play . . . . . . women are first tendered weak; the weakness is transformed to vulnerability; and vulnerability opens up the way to intimidation and exploitation. It is difficult to exaggerate the scale and longevity of the oppression that has resulted.
>
> Cockburn 1983:204.

Furthermore ideologies of the physical reinforce women's dependancy in domestic situations. The image of the male 'handyman' i.e. changing the tyre, mending the fuse and performing the physically 'skilful' tasks, remains powerful. In reality women perform many arduous domestic tasks but these are defined as everyday mundane chores. The sexual division of labour in the home and the ideology supporting it leaves women dependent on men to perform the more 'skilful' jobs such as maintaining the car, putting up shelves, mending the windows etc.

However ideologies of the physical have consequences at a far more serious level in relation to men's direct physical control and domination of women. Evidence from recent feminist research into male violence against women highlights the extent of direct physical dominance by men. (Hanmer and Saunders 1984; Hall 1985; Radford and Laffy 1985). Radford and Laffy emphasise the discrepancy between official statistics on male physical violence and the results of surveys and studies by women themselves. They found that three quarters of the women in their study who had suffered male violence did not report it. The extent to which women experience both the threat and the reality of male violence is considerable. Hanmer and Saunders (1984) found that of the 129 women interviewed fifty nine percent had experienced 'threatening, violent or sexually harassing behaviour'. This is supported by Hall (1985) who reports that out of the 1,236 women asked, more than one sixth had been raped and thirty one per-cent sexually assaulted. Furthermore in addition to the actual experience of male violence Hall also found that the majority of women felt restricted and fearful of rape and assault. Indeed Radford and Laffy report that ninety two per-cent of the women in their study did not experience the streets as safe territory for women either during the day or at night. These studies highlight the significance of both the reality and the threat of physical violence by men on women. The consequence of which is the pronounced restriction on the social freedom of women.[3] This physical advantage and oppression of women is maintained at an ideological level. The strength of ideologies of the physical and sexuality make many situations of male sexual harassment and violence seem inevitable. Men's physical power is an acceptable feature of male sexuality and the line drawn between acceptable and unacceptable violence is often arbitrary. The consequences of which are demonstrated in the popularity of films using male physical violence as entertainment (e.g. 'Dressed to Kill'), the treatment of rape victims and rapists by the police and courts, and the reluctance of the police to 'interfere' in situations of domestic violence. As Stanko (1985:70) comments:

> Women's experience of sexual and or physical intimidation and violence – much of it the result of what is assumed to be typical male behaviour – is an integral part of women's lives.

> The physical and or sexual abuse of women is a manifestation of male domination itself, it has been seen to be a natural right of man.

Physical education and the reproduction of physical power relations

The Beginnings

Physical education developed in the pioneering girls' day schools of the late nineteenth century which were primarily middle class institutions for the daughters of the 'new' bourgeoisie. (Kamm 1958; 1966; Atkinson 1978). Indeed it emerged out of a radical movement as the pioneers of girls schooling (e.g. Frances Mary Buss, Dorothea Beale, Emily Davies) were intent on demonstrating that women were fit to undertake sustained academic work and were not the frail, helpless creatures defined by the male Victorian medical and educational professions. (Hargreaves 1979; Fletcher 1984). Maudsley, a professor of Medical Jurisprudence at University College, London, writing in 1874 expressed his concern about women's entry into secondary and higher education in arguing that the 'intellectual' race would produce in girls:

> . . . lifelong suffering which might incapacitate them for the adequate performance of the natural functions of their sex – motherhood.
>
> cited in Burstyn 1980.

Although the entry of physical education into the curriculum challenged the physical stereotype of the weak Victorian 'lady', it was not a radical change to the definition, rather an adaptation to allow for and to accommodate new educational initiatives for girls. While opportunities for physical activity improved, the activities were clearly under-pinned by commonsense assumptions about women's 'natural' physical abilities and capacities. For example, Swedish gymnastics, which formed the central core of PE from its inception through until the 1950's, retained a commitment to an ideology of women's biologically determined abilities. Although more energetic than the former callisthenics, Ling, the founder of Swedish gymnastics, based its development on an assumption that:

> . . . women's physiological disposition demands less vigorous treatment. The law of beauty is based purely on the conception of life and must not be abused. The rounded forms of women must not be transformed into angularity or nodosity such as in man.
>
> cited in Webb 1967:49.

The view that women's 'natural' physical abilities and capacities involved a delicacy which required protection also can be found in the teaching texts of rhythmical gymnastics, the only other form of gymnastics which had a limited impact on PE in secondary schools during the 1920's and 1930's. Eli Bjorksten the originator of rhythmical gymnastics stated:

In a comprehensive review of the most noticeable differences in physique between men and women we find that women are in every respect *inferior*. Disregarding the fact – which may be *taken for granted* – that this difference is in accordance with the *purposes of nature*, we who have developed women's gymnastics must start from existing conditions. A woman's more delicate physique requires appropriate exercises . . .

Bjorksten 1918:172 (my emphases).

The belief that women were physically different and inferior to men and, therefore, required different physical exercise was reinforced by the development of team games. This second strand of PE developed alongside gymnastics and together with it created the formal comprehensive system of PE which has continued throughout this century in secondary schooling (MacIntosh 1952). Again the emphasis was that girls required different games and sports due to their 'natural' disposition. Sports were either adapted to accommodate womens assumed natural abilities or new activities were introduced which did not carry the 'stigma of overt masculinity' (McCrone 1982:78) e.g. netball, hockey, lacrosse.

Historical research into physical education identifies the deeply embedded traditions relating to an ideology of the physical at the core of the subject. The dominant ethos which was established stressed 'different' physical exercise and sport for girls and women with complementary features encouraging specifically 'feminine' attributes. However, implicit within an ideology of the physical was its relationship to female sexuality. Throughout the development of PE morality held a central place. For example, Woodhouse, the head of Sheffield High School in discussing PE in 1898 stated that

. . . moral effects are of greater importance than any increase of measurement or muscular vigour.

Special Educational Reports 1898:133.

Morality encompassed all forms of exemplary behaviour and standards and its foci were appearance, discipline, conduct, clothing and social graces. Girls were expected to demonstrate respectability through their behaviour and general demeanour. Throughout the Victorian development of PE sexuality was seen to require 'responsibility' and 'protection' (Bland 1982; Jackson 1982). Women's sexuality required regulation if women were to be successful in the fulfilment of their future female adult role. Fletcher (1984) describes the training of PE teachers in the early colleges as a sexless 'Peter Pan world'. This 'sexless' world involved no contact with the opposite sex, no male visitors and a general emphasis on morality and modesty. Any hint of young women's sexuality was denied. In both teacher training and secondary schooling 'standards' were encouraged to develop discipline, neatness, self control, respect for authority, dedication and service to others (Crunden 1974; Fletcher 1984). Swedish gymnastics, with its emphasis on 'precision and smartness' (Lawrence 1898, p. 134), provided the perfect activity to encourage these standards. Furthermore it encouraged increased moral consciousness and health through its emphasis on remedial and therapeutic work.

Games playing, also, was seen to develop these 'qualities'. Young men were encouraged into games to develop 'masculinity' through the promotion of leadership, dominance and decision making on the rugby pitch or cricket field (Springhall 1985). The development of masculinity was associated intrinsically with mature male sexuality. This sexuality involved activity, initiative and control. For girls, however, sexually-appropriate behaviour involved modesty, passivity and responsibility. While team games allowed for energetic activity they were controlled by restricted direct contact with other players or with the hockey ball. Netball, while allowing contact with the ball was adapted to restrict space, reduce speed and avoid physical contact. As Okeley (1978:132) argues, in all activities:

> girls' bodies are extended and constrained in this choreography of their future which they learn unconsciously in legs, arms, hands, feet and torso.

Women needed 'protection' not only for their future reproductive function but from any hint of sexual contact or sexual awareness. They were responsible for maintaining modesty and the connections between childhood, femininity and asexuality were supported by their experiences of physical education. The image of woman faced in two directions – the virgin or the whore (Jackson 1982:169). By undertaking 'masculine' pursuits young women were seen to be in danger of developing in the latter category. Thus the pioneers of PE trod a new path of physical activity with restraint. At no time was the new ideology of women's sexuality challenged and new physical pursuits were adapted and encouraged which incorporated this ideology and thus contributed to its continuation.

Physical education, however, did contribute to the release of women's clothing from the restrictive bustles, corsets and stays of the Victorian era. The development of the gymslip and tunic allowed for greater freedom of movement than previously had been considered socially acceptable or sexually appropriate. Yet these changes retained an emphasis on modesty and masked any hint of developing sexuality. As Okeley (1978:131) suggests:

> . . . our bodies were invisible, anaesthetised and protected for one man's intrusion later. As female flesh and curves, we were concealed by the uniform. Take the traditional gymslip – a barrel shape with deep pleats

designed to hide breasts, waist, hips and buttocks, giving freedom of movement without contour.

It is ironic that today's image of the gymslip is used in pornography as a tantalising symbol of the young woman as virgin!

From this brief and schematic excursion into the origins of physical education, ideologies of the physical and sexuality can be seen to underlay the development of PE and, consequently, to be part of its traditions and ethos. Although PE contributed to the liberation of girls and young women in relation to dress, opportunities for physical activity and access to a future women's profession, PE also reaffirmed clear physical sex differences in ability and capacity within generalised boundaries and limitations of women's sexuality.

More recently Weiss (1969:215–216), whose work formed a core element in many PE teacher training courses wrote:

> One way of dealing with these disparities between the athletic promise and achievements of men and women is to view women as truncated males. As such they could be permitted to engage in the same sports that men do . . . but in foreshortened versions . . . So far as excellence of performance depends mainly on the kind of muscles, bones, size, strength that one has, women can be dealt with as fractional men.

The following section will look more closely to see whether similar attitudes prevail within contemporary PE and whether an ideology of the physical can be identified in the practices and policies of PE teaching.

Contemporary PE

> PE is the part of the curriculum that can contribute most to the physical experience of the pupils. It's aims are concerned with the development of psycho-motor competence in order to facilitate participation in worthwhile activities during the critical years of puberty and maturation to adulthood. Its unique contribution is that it focuses on the body and on experience in activities in which bodily movement plays a significant part.
> HMI Report 1979

In this statement about PE there is no distinction made between boys' PE and girls' PE. In considering ideologies of the physical and sexuality it is imperative to unpack what the 'physical experience' of the pupils actually means in practice. The unique contribution of PE is that it 'focuses on the body' but it is important to understand what that actually means for girls' PE. This following section therefore, draws on the research material which identifies the commonsense assumptions determining girls' physical abilities and capacities as they exist currently in the teaching of PE and the inevitable implications for the politics of sexuality. The historical material demonstrated the presence of powerful ideologies of the physical and sexuality in the origins of girls' PE. Do such ideologies exist in contemporary PE teaching?

'Natural' physical sex differences?

Out of the 56 interviews with those in a position of responsibility for decisions relating to the teaching of PE in the authority, i.e. advisory staff, heads of department, peripatetic teaching staff, 53 referred to the existence of 'natural' physical sex differences which had implications for their teaching content, organisation and style. For example:

> 'boys can give girls much more daring, adventure, excitement and of course girls can give grace and "finish", those things they are better at.'

> '. . . boys and girls are taught separately for physical reasons – basic natural power. . . . boys have no finesse but all little girls are poised. Little boys just throw themselves about.'

> '. . . boys have far more strength, speed, daring. Women are much more the devious species.'

> '. . . I support the fact that there are clear natural differences between boys and girls most definitely.'

> (Heads of Departments – taped interviews.)

These powerful stereotypes held by teachers are not supported so definitively by research evidence. Dyer (1982) suggests that in relation to sporting ability and physical capacity physical sex differences are relevant only at the highest competitive level and even here it remains difficult to identify 'biological fact' from the social effects of socialisation, training opportunities etc. Certainly observation of PE classes of 13 year old girls suggests that there are as many physical differences in relation to physique, strength and co-ordination within the group as there are in comparison to a similar age group of boys.

Common sense assumptions and stereotypes concerning girls 'natural' physical abilities and capacities, however, do have consequences for the teaching of PE. Girls' activities within the LEA researched remain traditional sporting activities developed specifically for girls. In the first three years of secondary schooling over half the total PE teaching time is spent on the team games rounders, netball and/or hockey. The remaining time prioritises the 'feminine' pursuits of gymnastics and dance with some athletics (including restrictions in some of the events for girls[4]) and swimming. As the girls reach the 4th or 5th year most of the schools offer 'options' which include the choice of traditional team games plus badminton, trampolining etc. Some schools have broadened the options offered but only to provide gender 'appropriate' activities such as 'keep fit' or 'health and beauty'.[5] It is interesting to note that self defence, a physical activity clearly relevant to girls living in Britain today, does not appear in any of the schools' curricula or extra-curricula programmes. All the schools within the LEA teach PE as a single sex activity up to the age of 16 years. While not suggesting that mixed teaching necessarily provides a more 'progressive' situation for girls[6], the justification for separate girls' and boys' PE is identified as the need to 'play the games to suit our abilities' (PE adviser – taped interview). As in the historical legacy outlined earlier girls are seen to have different 'physical' abilities and capabilities determined by the limitations of their biology and consequently separate departments offering restricted, gender appropriate activities are justified.

Physical contact is taboo?

The issue of physical contact remains a central worry for those involved with the teaching of PE. The PE adviser stated her position quite clearly:

> 'I have yet to see an elegant footballer. Maybe I'm just prejudiced but they just look horrible. I just don't like seeing women play football. But if they did I would definitely modify it. The pitch is too big and the ball to hard . . . in fact I am very concerned about any sport involving physical contact. I believe in 'feminine charms' and hard contact sports just wouldn't be right.'

This was supported by other PE teachers. For example:

> 'Physical contact – all that rolling in the mud – no way for girls. Now cricket's not bad, I think it's more ladylike.'

> 'There's nothing more sorer to my feminine eyes than a big bust and a big behind – girls are not put together to play football, even the sporty girls. I won't let my girls play because to me it is very, very unfeminine.'

The argument does not hinge on a belief that violent contact sport might be considered unsuitable for *anyone* but that 'contact' is not suitable for girls.

> 'I don't mind boys playing rugby but I don't think it's a girls sport. It's like boxing really. They might enjoy it but I wouldn't enjoy seeing them battering each other.'

Girls are considered physically capable of contact sport but it is deemed undesirable physical behaviour. There appear to be two major objections to physical contact between women both of which relate to female sexuality. The PE adviser puts forward the first argument with clarity:

> '. . . there is a physiological point. If we put adolescent girls into that situation I am very concerned about the damage they might do to their breasts with hard knocks. After all hockey, although a tough game, there is an implement between yourself and the ball. You can protect yourself, it isn't bust to bust.'

This is the same argument put forward in the late nineteenth century to justify the development of separate and 'suitable' games for girls. The need for protection for the female body relates specifically to the damage that might be caused to young women's reproductive capacity. Yet work by Ferris (1978), Dyer (1982) debunks many of the myths surrounding women's supposed physiological vulnerability. The vulnerability of women's bodies is a curious assertion given the location of male reproductive organs!

The second objection to physical contact for women is explained by Hall (1979:25/26):

> For a woman to subdue another woman through physical force and bodily contact is categorically unacceptable, the inuendo sexual and the act considered unnatural. There exists an age-old prohibition against aggressive physical contact between women.

Thus the demonstration of power and assertion between women is not acceptable in relation to female sexuality. Desirable female sexuality is a passive, responsive heterosexuality and women engaged in contact sports immediately raise doubts about the status of their sexuality.

Young (1980:153) argues that girls learn to protect their bodies and to inhabit a limited personal body space. As a girl reaches adolescence she:

> . . . learns actively to hamper her movements. She is told that she must be careful not to get hurt, not to get dirty, not to tear her clothes, that the things she desires to do are dangerous for her. Thus she develops a bodily timidity which increases with age. In assuming herself as a girl she takes herself up as fragile.

The restrictions on contact and the use of physical space in girls' sports encourage the position whereby young women learn that their bodies need protecting and they must remain enclosed within personal space. Young (1980:153) emphasises physical development whereby girls, 'acquire many subtle habits of feminine bodily comportment – walking like a girl, tilting her head like a girl, standing and sitting like a girl, gesturing like a girl, etc'. Whereas physical exercise and sport encourage a wider and explorative use of space the activities offered and the attitudes held by many people responsible for their teaching reinforce a limited extension of bodily use. As Young argues (1980:154):

> To open her body in free activity and open extension and bold outward directedness is for a women to invite objectification. . . . She also lives the threat of invasion of her body space. The most extreme form of such spacial and bodily invasion is the threat of rape . . . I would suggest that the enclosed space which has been described as a modality of feminine spatiality is in part a defence against such invasion.

PE teaching accepts these limitations and the responsibilities women have for their own protection. An ideology of the physical incorporated within PE relates directly to a politics of sexuality which defines women as responsible yet vulnerable and, therefore, in need of protection.

Acceptable 'standards' for girls?

Every head of girls' PE throughout the city LEA studied, identified the maintenance of 'standards' relating to dress, appearance, discipline and good behaviour, as first or second in their priorities for PE teaching.

> 'I think the standards in all the school need to be high but we expect a higher standard of behaviour, attitude and appearance in PE – loyalty almost.'

This priority, however, is not extended by the heads of girls' PE to the teaching priorities for boys. As one teacher commented:

> 'I think we do stipulate more trying to make them into "young ladies".'

Certain standards of appearance are expected of 'young ladies' and although dealing with physical activity, PE teachers are careful to encourage the 'correct' conforming standards.

> 'We don't just teach the girls PE, we always include a lot of other bits and pieces e.g. hygiene, cleanliness, dressing well in PE kit, uniform.'

> 'I teach them to have correct uniform, kit, hair tied back, attention to detail.'

The notion of 'Playing like gentlemen while behaving like ladies' (Hargreaves 1979) remains as clear an objective for girls' PE in 1987 as it did in the late nineteenth century!

As discussed earlier, 'appearance' is central to female sexuality. The female body is defined and portrayed in a specific form geared to an 'ideal' image of femininity. As Coward argues (1984:77):

Because the female body is the main object of attention, it is on women's bodies, or women's looks that prevailing sexual definitions are placed . . . The emphasis on women's looks becomes a crucial way in which society exercises control over women's sexuality.

PE reinforces in girls the need to be concerned with appearance, dress and presentation of self. The message in relation to female sexuality remains clearly articulated through PE. Women's bodies are physically developed in order to look good and presentable (particularly to men), yet they must be protected from overdevelopment and physical contact in order to avoid 'unnatural' or 'unhealthy' touch and danger to 'delicate' parts. This ideological construction of the 'ideal woman' is clear in practice. In the case study observations, up to one third of the total teaching time for PE was spent on discipline over appearance and correct dress or uniform.

The implications for girls' PE

Coward (1984:41) suggests that the ideal sexual image of woman today:

is not of a demure, classically 'feminine' girl, but a vigorous and immature adolescent. Nevertheless it is not a shape which suggests power or force. The sexually immature body of the current ideal . . . presents a body which is sexual – it 'exudes' sexuality in its vigorous and vibrant and firm good health – but it is not the body of a woman who had an adult and powerful control over that sexuality. The image is of a highly sexualized female whose sexuality is still one of response to the active sexuality of a man.

Very few women 'achieve' this ideal image although it remains powerfully reinforced by media presentation. This paper argues that this image is upheld also through the institution of schooling and, more specifically, physical education. PE encourages girls to be 'vigorous', 'vibrant' and to develop 'good health' but within the constraints of an ideology of the physical which sets limitations on female activity and physical contact and concentrates attention on personal appearance. Together this contributes to the development of acceptable female heterosexuality. This is by no means a straightforward process and considerable conflict is experienced by both teacher and pupil within a subject that is centred on 'the physical', yet limited by social expectation and ideologies of the physical relating to cultures of femininity and masculinity. Adolescent girls often experience conflict within this process. The broader social emphasis, via the media, advertising and popular culture, is on a desired body shape, culturally determined and strongly informed by an ideology of sexuality which views women as sexual objects to be admired, viewed and used by men. PE provides a platform where physical differences in appearance during adolescence are unmasked and, for many young women, the enforcement of showers or the wearing of 'childish' PE kit – a memory of so many adult women – creates a difficult situation negotiated through various strategies of resistance.[7] Furthermore teachers face a situation of encouraging physical activity (albeit limited) during a period of time in young women's lives when the culture of femininity encourages young women to adopt a passive, inactive role centred on attracting the opposite sex (McRobbie 1978; Nava and McRobbie 1984; Griffin 1985). Consequently the strategies for coping within PE teaching often respond to the development of possibilities which will 'appeal' to young women (i.e. keep fit, health and beauty) but which inevitably reinforce the culture of femininity.

If, as this paper suggests, male-female physical power relations are reinforced and reproduced (albeit in a complex manner) by the teaching of PE what are the implications for policy which emerge from this analysis? First, if policy is to confront the issue of sexual divisions, then it must be concerned with the physical education of both boys and girls. If girls' PE reproduces an ideology of the physical which constructs young women as physically subordinate to men, equally male PE reproduces an ideology of the physical which underpins a culture of masculinity emphasising strength, toughness, competitiveness and physical domination. It is for male PE to respond to the ideology of the physical reflected in the culture of masculinity. Without challenging the dynamics of gender in the schooling of boys, male-female power relations cannot change. Wresting power from the powerful, however, involves men accepting that physical domination and the control of women, both inherent in the politics of sexuality, is a problem for women. The powerless can attempt to appropriate their rightful situation but for the powerful to relinquish their position demands considerable material change. Yet change in PE must be placed within a broader context of patriarchal power relations that goes beyond the equal opportunities reform of liberal feminism. As was discussed earlier in this paper male-female physical power relations have direct and serious consequences for women. PE is part of this process which constructs and reinforces ideologies of the physical experienced in everyday situations faced by women, outdoors or in the home. Pessimism, however, provides no route towards change and although physical power relations remain an integral part of an overarching patriarchal power system, reforms in schooling at a local level can provide a challenge to these relations. As Yates (1985:225) comments:

> Schooling is a limited venue for producing social change, but it does help to form the consciousness of the next generation.

Weiner (1985:5) makes a useful distinction between equal opportunity approaches to policy initiatives which concentrate on gaining 'equality of access for both girls and boys to existing educational benefits', and anti-sexist approaches which 'concentrate on the development of a girl-centred education'. This latter approach identifies a male-female power structure within schooling and thus places 'patriarchy, power and women's subordination . . . at the centre of their thinking' (ibid: 9). It is this approach which needs to be developed within PE if physical power relations are to be eroded. Superficial changes creating equality of access (e.g. mixed PE) have limited impact on the reinforcement of ideologies and it provides a weak move towards equality of outcome (Scraton 1984). A more radical questioning of the content, organisation and teaching of the subject should be of central importance. While being unable to provide an immediate panacea to the 'problem', the following are suggestions for some initial considerations.

In line with Weiner's (1985) arguments, girl-centred organisation of PE should be retained. This raises the problem of retaining boy-centred organisation in male PE and the attendant implications. However, in the short term girls require both the time and the space to develop their physical potential. Whether this can be achieved through selective single sex grouping within a predominantly mixed sex organisation is debateable. The real problems of sexual harrassment in mixed physical activity cannot be ignored. Jones (1985) has found that male violence in the form of visual, verbal and physical sexual harrassment is a part of everyday school life. Mixed PE places girls and young women in a particularly compromised position and, therefore, such 'progressive' moves need to be approached with considerable caution.

In relation to sporting activities, which occupied over fifty percent of the total teaching time in the research schools, there is a need to move away from the dominant, competitive ethos. Willis (1982:134) suggests:

> Sport could be presented as a form of activity which emphasises human similarity and not dissimilarity, a form of activity which expresses values which are indeed immeasurable, a form of activity which is concerned with individual well-being and satisfaction rather than comparison.

The emphasis should be on the collective experience of shared physical activity with the associated experience of developing personal physical skill, rather than on the result of the sporting contest. The fundamental enjoyment of working and playing together should be encouraged. That this can be achieved within the present structure of team sports, however, is debateable and it could be that a redefinition of sport for women should be a priority for attention.

The most important consideration for PE is in the development of individual potential in physical strength and power for girls. The priority must be to challenge the ideology of the physical discussed in this paper, so that girls can develop more confidence and assertiveness and, ultimately, greater control over their bodies. Consequently, the reality of male physical violence in society should make the inclusion of self-defence essential as a core element of PE teaching.

In order to achieve these objectives, teachers, advisers, pupils and parents need to develop an awareness of the significance of these issues. By implication this suggests the need for more research into this area and the instigation of in-service courses, staff meetings and pupil-teacher discussion. In practical terms, a more positive 'female' atmosphere could be developed in PE through the presentation of positive physical images of women on wall displays etc. However Deem (1986) emphasises that, in relation to policy implementation, teachers must first admit that there is a problem before they will question their practice. If, as Pratt (1985) suggests, PE teachers are generally unsympathetic to the notion of equal opportunities between boys and girls in school, then teacher commitment to change will be difficult to achieve. Initially the setting up of teacher support groups for those with a personal commitment to anti-sexist strategies within PE, would be a positive move of support for those isolated in sceptical and even hostile environments.

Over a decade ago Simone de Beauvoir (1974:178) defined the objectification of the female body and its resultant inactivity:

> The ideal of feminine beauty is variable, but certain demands remain constant; for one thing, since woman is destined to be possessed, her body must present the inert and passive qualities of an object. Virile beauty lies in the fitness of the body for action in strength, agility, flexibility; it is the manifestation of transcendence animating a flesh that must never sink back on itself . . . Her body is not perceived as the radiation of a subjective personality, but as a thing, sunk deeply in its own immanence; it is not for such a body to have reference to the rest of the world, it must not be the promise of things other than itself: it must end the desire it arouses.

Today 'fitness of the body for action in strength, agility, flexibility' remains the ideology of male physicality. Men's control over women is generated by a perceived heterosexuality reinforced and justified by this ideology. For women, the ideology of the physical is, as De Beauvoir suggests, constrained in action and experienced as subordinate to and defined (in appearance especially) by men. Physical education needs to question whether, or indeed how, it contributes to this definition of woman-as-object. For women to gain equality, they need to control their sexuality which implicitly requires a redefinition of the 'physical' for both men and women.

Acknowledgements

Many thanks to Pat Craddock, Rosemary Deem and Phil Scraton for their help, support and critical comments. Also personal thanks to Sally Channon.

Notes

1 The term 'patriarchy' is used here in its most general sense to denote the male domination of women. See Delphy, C. (1984) *Close to Home* Hutchinson; Beechey, V. (1979) 'On Patriarchy' *Feminist Review* No. 2; Rowbotham, S (1979) 'The trouble with patriarchy' *New Statesman* 21–28 December, for a fuller discussion of the complexities of its usage.
2 For the purposes of this paper PE will be used to denote girls' physical education.
3 The restrictions on the social freedom of women include their experiences on the street, in the home, at work and in their social life. See Coveney, L. *et al* (1984, p. 17–19) for a fuller discussion.
4 Girls and women are restricted from the triple jump, pole vault and in some areas from long distance running events.
5 It should be noted that one of the case study schools did offer soccer as an option to the 4th and 5th year pupils. However, there remained considerable constraints on girls who might opt for this activity both in terms of their previous experience and having to handle comments such as the following:

'football in this weather, you must be mad. You really should have been born a lad.'

(Head of Department – recorded observation.)

6 For further discussion of the debates around mixed v. single sex PE refer to Scraton, S. (1984) *Losing Ground: The Implications for Girls of Mixed Physical Education*. Paper presented to Girl-Friendly Schooling Conference, Manchester and Graydon, J. et al (1985) *Mixed Physical Education in the Secondary School – An Evaluation*. Paper presented to the International Council for Health, PE and Recreation World Congress. West London Institute of Higher Education.
7 See Scraton, S. 'Boys muscle in where angels fear to tread' – the relationship between physical education and young women's subcultures' in Horne, J. et al (1987) *Sport, Leisure and Social Relations*, R. K. P.

Bibliography

Arnot, M. (1981) 'Culture and Political Economy: Dual Perspectives in the Sociology of Women's Education. *Educational Analysis* Vol. 3, No. 1.
Atkinson, P. (1978) 'Fitness, Feminism and Schooling' in *The Nineteenth*

Century Woman: The Cultural and Physical World. Delamont, S. and Duffin, L. (Eds) Croom Helm.

Belotti, G. (1975) *Little Girls*. Writers and Readers Publishing Co op.

Bjorksten, E. (1918) *Principles of Gymnastics for Girls and Women*. London: J. and A. Churchill.

Bland, L. (1982) *'Guardians of the Race' or 'Vampires upon the Nations Health?: female sexuality and its regulation in early twentieth century Britain*. Paper presented to B.S.A. Conference Manchester.

Burstyn, J. (1980) *Victorian Education and the Ideal of Womanhood*. Croom Helm.

Clarricoates, K. (1980) 'The importance of being Ernest . . . Emma . . . Tom . . . Jane' in *Deem* (Ed).

Cockburn, C. (1981) 'The material of male power' *Feminist Review 9*.

Cockburn, C. (1983) *Brothers* Pluto.

Coveney, L. et al (1984) *The Sexuality Papers* Hutchinson.

Coward, R. (1984) *Female Desire – Women's Sexuality Today*. Paladin.

Crunden, C. (1974) *A History of Anstey College of Physical Education 1897–1972*. Anstey C.P.E.

De Beauvoir, S. (1974) *The Second Sex* Vintage Books.

Deem, R. (1978) *Women and Schooling* RKP.

Deem, R. (1980) Ed. *Schooling for Women's Work*. RKP.

Deem, R. (1986) *'Implementing gender – equality policies in schools: an analysis'*. Paper presented to International Sociology of Education Conference Westhill College, Birmingham.

Dworkin, A. (1981) *Pornography: Men Possessing Women*. The Women's Press.

Dyer, K. (1982) *Catching up the Men: Women in Sport*. Junction Books.

Ferris, E. (1978) 'The myths surrounding women's participation in sport and exercise' in *Report of the Langham Life 1st International Conference on Women in Sport*. CCPR.

Fletcher, S. (1984) *Women First*. Athlone.

Griffin, C. (1985) *Typical Girls* RKP.

Hall, A. (1979) 'Women and the Lawrentian Wrestle' *Canadian Women's Studies* 1. 39–41.

Hall, R. E. (1985) *Ask Any Woman* Falling Wall Press.

Hanmer, J. & Saunders, S. (1984) *Well Founded Fear: A Community Study of Violence to Women*. Hutchinson.

Hargreaves, J. (1979) *'Playing like gentlemen while behaving like ladies.'* MA Thesis University of London Institute of Education.

Hutter, B. & Williams, G. (1981) *Controlling Women*. Croom Helm.

Jackson, S. (1982) *Childhood and Sexuality*. Blackwell.

Jeffreys, S. (1981) 'The Spinster and her Enemies: sexuality and the last wave of feminism'. *Scarlet Women* No. 13 part 2.

Jeffreys, S. & Radford, J. (1984) 'Contributory Negligence or Being a Woman? The Car Rapist Case' in Scraton, P. and Gordon, P. *Causes for Concern* Penguin.

Kamm, J. (1958) *How Different From Us: A Biography of Miss Buss and Miss Beale* London Bodley Head.

Kamm, J. (1966) *Rapiers and Battleaxes*. Allen and Unwin.

MacDonald, M. (1980) 'Socio-cultural Reproduction and Women's Education' in *Deem (Ed)*.

MacDonald, M. (1981) 'Schooling and the Reproduction of Class and Gender Relations' in Barton et al *Schooling, Ideology and the Curriculum*. Falmer.

Mahony, P. (1983) 'How Alice's chin really came to be pressed against her foot: Sexist processes of interaction in mixed sex classes!' *Women's Studies International Forum* Volume 6 No. 1.

Mahony, P. (1985) *Schools for the Boys*. Hutchinson.

McCrone, K. (1982) 'Victorian women and sport: Playing the game in Colleges and Public Schools'. *Canadian Historical Association*.

McIntosh, P. (1952) *Physical Education in England Since 1800*. London, Bell.

McRobbie, A. (1978) *Jackie: An Ideology of Adolescent Femininity* CCCS.

Nava, M. & McRobbie, A. (Ed) (1984) *Gender and Generation* MacMillan.

Okeley, J. (1979) 'Privileged, schooled and finished: boarding school for girls' in Ardener, S. (Ed) *Defining Females*. London: Croom Helm.

Radford & Laffy (1985) *Violence against women: women speak out*.

Scraton, S. (1984) 'Losing Ground: The Implications for Girls of Mixed Physical Education', unpublished paper.

Sharpe, S. (1976) *Just like a Girl* Harmondsworth, Penguin.

Smart, C. & Smart, B. (1978) *Women, Sexuality and Social Control*. RKP.

Special Reports on Educational Subjects. (1898) Volume 2.

Spender, D. & Sarah, E., (Eds) (1980) *Learning to Lose*. Women's Press.

Spender, D. (1982) *Invisible Women: the Schooling Scandal*. Writers and Readers Publishing Co op.

Springhall, J. (1985) 'Rotten to the very core: leisure and youth 1830–1914.' *Youth & Policy No. 14.*

Stanko, E. (1985) *Intimate Intrusions*. RKP.

Stanworth, M. (1983) *Gender and Schooling*. Hutchinson.

Toner, B. (1977) *The Facts of Rape*. Arrow.

Webb, I. (1967) *Women's Place in PE in GB 1800–1966*. Unpublished thesis, University of Lancaster.

Weeks, J. (1981) *Sex, Politics and Society* Longman.

Weiner, G. (1985) *Just a Bunch of Girls*. OU Press.

Weiss, P. (1969) *Sport – a philosophic inquiry*.

Whyte, J. (1983) *Beyond the Wendy House: Sex Role Stereotyping in Primary Schools*. Schools Council/EOC Longman.

Willis, P. (1982) 'Women in Sport in Ideology' in Hargreaves, J. (Ed) *Sport, Culture and Ideology*. RKP.

Wolpe, A-M. (1978) 'Education and the sexual division of labour' in Kuhn, A. & Wolpe, A-M. (Ed) *Feminism and Materialism* RKP.

Wilson, E. (1983) *What is to be done about violence against women?* Penguin.

Yates, L. (1985) 'Is "girl-friendly schooling" really what girls need?' in Whyte, J. et al (Ed) *Girl Friendly Schooling* Methuen.

Young, I (1980) *Throwing like a girl – a phenomenology of feminine body comportment, mobility and spatiality*. Human Studies. 3, 137–156.

CHAPTER ELEVEN

The Dilemmas of Parent Education and Parental Skills for Sexual Equality

Miriam David

Current proposals and policies for parent education, also known as
parental skills, education for family life or preparation for parenthood and child care, sex education, moral, social and personal development merit careful scrutiny by teachers and teacher educators,
especially those interested in promoting equal educational opportunities between the sexes. The aims of parent education are usually to
reinforce traditional relationships between the sexes – particularly
within the privacy of the family but also within adult working life.
This is the very antithesis of policies to promote sexual equality in
education, where the aim is to modify and revise traditional relationships between the sexes. This is to be achieved by providing girls with
wider educational opportunities, with the ultimate intention of
giving girls better careers and opportunities in paid employment.
However, this 'educational solution' to the 'problem' of sexual
equality may itself be too limited to achieve a major social transformation of the relationship between the sexes in both public and
private life.

In this paper, I want to suggest some new policies, which would go
beyond the conventional 'educational' solution to sexual equality in
employment and the parent education approach. Such policies
would aim to achieve sexual equality in both the public world and the
privacy of the family. They would entail teaching about adulthood
in both the family and in the labour market. Parental responsibilities
would be taught as indeed parental rather than as specifically
paternal or maternal duties, bearing with them social commitments
to caring relatonships. Such curricula also require, for their success,
transformations in the actual existing relationships between the
sexes in the private family and world of work.

The aims of proposals for parent education are to teach about the conventional relationships between the sexes, particularly within the family, but extending to the implications of these familial roles for participation in paid employment and public life more generally. Put simply, motherhood is to be taught as a 'vocation'; a full-time, but unpaid occupation, or pre-occupation; covering such activities as the care and nurturance of other family members from dependent children to husband to elderly or handicapped relatives. As regards dependent children, the social expectations of motherhood are not only care but also education. Indeed, it is almost a truism nowadays to speak of mothers as the first educators of their children. By contrast, fatherhood is hardly a term in common parlance but is used mainly to refer merely to the act of procreation. The expectations about fatherhood are, indeed, a contrast with motherhood. Fathers' responsibilities are usually seen as 'economic' – to participate in the labour force to provide for their offspring.

Moreover, the aims of these education for family-life courses are also class-specific. They are to ensure that working-class or poor girls become parents and bring up their children with appropriate attitudes and behaviour for their working lives. Implicit within the proposals is the notion of middle class standards of parental behaviour, as the norm. Berger and Berger in *The War over the Family*, a book published initially in the USA and more recently in Britain argue explicitly for what they call 'the Bourgeois family' – a particular style and method of commitment to children and family life. (1983, 1984). There is also an element of religious or spiritual commitment in many of the proposals. Whitfield who, as a professor of education, wrote the first text in Britain entitled *Education for Family Life* (1980) ended it with a poem of devotion to Christ. Pugh and De'Ath, however, are the main adovocates, in Britain, of 'parent education' and are themselves somewhat more eclectic in their approach. But they argue that their aims are drawn from those of the late director of the National Children's Bureau. They say:

'Mia Kellmer Pringle argued that parenthood, and particularly motherhood, has been undervalued for far too long; children are our future and their upbringing and care is a skilled, responsible and demanding job in which the community as a whole should invest considerable resources (Pringle, 1975, 1980a, 1980b, 1982). She campaigned tirelessly for parenthood to be a deliberately chosen role, undertaken with the full understanding of what it involved – "warts and all" – . . . and she was one of the first to argue for a compulsory "core" element in the school curriculum of all young people which would include human psychology, child development and preparation for parenthood.'

(1984, p. 2).

They go on to define parent education as:

'a range of educational and supportive measures which help parents and prospective parents to understand themselves and their children and enhance the relationship between them'.

(*ibid*, p. 7)

They try to argue that the term 'parent' should be gender-neutral and that, according to Schaffer (1977), men can mother too – 'it is basically a matter of personality'. However, they acknowledge that the term parent at the moment usually refers either to biological mothers – 'most schemes attract mainly mothers' (*op. cit.*, p. 7) – or women as carers – 'step parents, foster parents, members of the child's extended family, childminders or other professional child care staff'. (*ibid*.) They do go on to acknowledge dilemmas in advocating parent education. They say 'for many women parent education is likely to intensify the conflict between their dual roles as mother and worker' (*ibid*, p. 206). They then add:

'The emphasis on equal opportunities, which we would heartily endorse, has left many women feeling that in an attempt to maintain an equal status with men at work, their roles and abilities as mothers are being under-valued'.

(*ibid*, p. 207)

However, their solution to this dilemma of parent education versus equal educational opportunities is limited and underdeveloped, since their chief focus is on trying to enhance the status and value of motherhood for poor and working class women. They advocate 'shared parenting', or bringing fathers back into the home, where it is possible. They assume that current trends in male unemployment will usher in such developments. Campbell (1984) amongst others, has provided anecdotal evidence to suggest that high rates of male unemployment do not domesticate men but tend rather to make them feel emasculated. Pugh and De'Ath also hint at necessary changes in other social policies, such as housing and social services. They do not comment on the organisation of education, child care or paid employment as necessitating change to provide the context for the new parent education.

This particular focus on valuing motherhood and the various other parent education proposals are a response to what is now seen as 'the problem of the family': namely the apparent growth since the post-war period of both lone parent families created by divorce, separation, out-of-wedlock, under-age or teenage sexual activities and also 'working mothers' whether in one or two-parent households. These changes in family structure have indeed taken place over the last two or three decades, although the new 'family worlds' are very complex. The Centre for Educational Research and Innovation (CERI) in an international report has summarised these changes:

> 'In modern advanced societies, the entourage in which children grow up has undergone profound changes over the course of the last few decades . . . The magnitude of certain transformations . . . (for example, the large-scale entry of women into active life) have given rise to the idea that major upheavals are affecting the organisation of family structure . . . between the generations within the family or the household.'
>
> (CERI, 1982, p. 12).

It goes on to specify the variety of changes:

> 'There is an enormous number of different family worlds in which [children] may grow up . . . It must also be remembered that households undergo changes of environment for the child whose parents have divorced and remarried. Such families are often "corporations" including a mixture of adults and children from two families. These observations are important because very often the variety of "realities" is under-estimated. Through stressing the role of the parents, one ends up forgetting about all the others, as if the majority of families consisted just of one couple and their families. Certainly this is the majority situation, in the sense that it applies to a great number of children, but a good number of other situations exist alongside it'.

What is regarded as the conventional family and the ideal to which to aspire is no longer the norm in Britain. As the Study Commission on the Family puts it:

> 'the proportion of all families which might be regarded as typical, that is a married couple with dependent children, has declined from thirty eight percent in 1961 to thirty two percent in 1980 . . .'
>
> (1983, p. 10)

Even in these families, many of the women will be in paid employment since fifty six percent of mothers with dependent children work for money. (Martin and Roberts, 1984, p. 13). People seem to be taking the fact of marriage less seriously, since more men and women live together without it. Most people still get married, but one in every three marriages ends in divorce. Almost sixty percent of divorces involve dependent children, a quarter of whom are under five. One and a half million children in Britain lived in one parent families in 1980; many others had a period in such a family during their childhood. Many then moved into reconstituted families, since eighty percent of those who divorce under the age of 30 remarry within five years, and often divorce again. (Study Commission, *op. cit.*, pp. 11–14).

> 'In 1982 about a third (29,000) of all illegitimate births in England and Wales were to mothers aged under twenty. For the first time (at least in the

recent past) illegitimate births actually outnumbered legitimate births (27,000) to mothers in this age group. Many of these illegitimate births are jointly registered by both parents . . .'

(*Social Trends 14*, 1984, p. 38).

In fact, almost half of these young unmarried mothers, registered the child in the father's name, too. The trends for illegitimate births are even greater for women aged 20 to 24 since it is double the increase for teenage mothers, which itself was fifty percent between 1977 and 1983. The total number of illegitimate births of 100,000 in 1983 is the highest ever, and nearly double the figure for 1977. (*New Society*, 1984, p. 443).

The important question is how to respond to such changes. Some, such as Whitfield (*op. cit.,*) advocate 'education for family life' in schools as a means of stemming the growth, in the belief that education can indeed change social behaviour. Whitfield recognises the need, however, for concomitant social policy changes. Mrs. Whitehouse argues for a sex education based on traditional notions of chastity before marriage. (1977, pp. 227–8). Others suggest a harsher approach. Digby Anderson, in an article entitled 'Ripe for a British Moral Majority' argues for 'the cause of the normal family . . . husband and wife living with their own children, the husband the major earner, the spouses intending and trying to stay together' as against what he chooses to call the 'anti-family lobby' who are 'disposed to help casualties of the traditional family such as abandoned wives or children brought up by one parent'. (The *Times*, October 15, 1985, p. 12) His views echo those of the American Moral Majority and New Right. George Gilder, in *Wealth and Poverty* (1981), has voiced the view that men need marriage and the family to give a purpose to their economic activities. Liberal policies, which allow women to rear children alone, destroy men's purpose in life.

"It has destroyed the role of the father: his key role and authority . . . he can no longer feel manly in his own home . . . the man has the . . . gradual sinking feeling that his role as provider, the definitive male activity from the primal days of the hunt through the industrial revolution and on into modern life has been largely seized from him; he has been cuckolded by the compassionate state" (1984, p. 251).

Gilder, amongst others, has advocated making it harder for women to leave their marriages and seek state support. In the Family Protection Act, a bill presented twice to the US Congress, by the American New Right, an attempt was also made to limit the teaching of 'liberal' courses at school. Indeed, it was proposed that school textbooks should be reviewed to ensure that they only contained traditional sex roles. (Petchesky, 1984, p. 265)

In Britain, similar views have been expressed by Ferdinand Mount in *The Subversive Family* (1983). He, too, argues against state interference in family life, especially defending the privacy of the family for the working class.

He aims to reinstate the privacy of the family, removing all external controls by government, church and other organisations. He argues that there is sufficient evidence amongst the working class already to show its resentment of state interference in family life. He writes

> "The family's most dangerous enemies may not turn out to be those who have openly declared war. It is so easy to muster resistance against the blatant cruelty of collectivist dictators. . . . It is less easy to fight against the armies of those who are 'only here to help' – those who claim to come with the best intentions but come armed, all the same, with statutory powers and administrative instruments: education officers, children's officers . . . welfare workers and all other council . . . which claim to know best how to manage our private concerns . . ." (1983, p. 173).

In this attack on the welfare state, he argues that it is an invasion of the privacy of the family.

> '. . . what is always affronting, offensive and distressing is the simple fact of their intrusion into our private space. Our feelings are mixed even in the case of the most helpful of all public visitors. The District Health Visitor who visits mothers with babies is often sweet and sensitive and genuinely useful . . . But [mothers] cannot help being continuously aware that she is there as an inspector as well as an advisor . . . The Visitor – grim, symbolic title – remains an Intruder.
> . . . In all the revolts against big government and high taxes . . . resentment has played its part . . . the feeling that the State is intruding into private space more and more and ought to be stopped – is growing. The Visitor is being made to feel unwelcome. His or her claim to moral superiority is being disputed.
> What few have yet grasped is that the working class is the true defender of liberty and privacy . . . The material triumph of the masses is not to be used for making society more public and collective . . . it is to be used for dispersing the delights of privacy to all'.
>
> (1983, pp. 174–5).

Yet others argue to accommodate the education system and social services to the current reality of family life. On the one hand, there are proposals, on the lines of Pugh and De'Ath, for more liberal parent and social education, including sex education. On the other hand, there are proposals for what Bland (1985, p. 21) has called a 'radically different sex education' which would aim to teach about both sexual morality as well as family life and child care. Such proposals depend for their success on concomitant social policy changes, such as the extension of pre-school education, and the relationship between family responsibility and paid employment. (New and David, 1985, pp. 330–354).

To respond to such apparently fundamental changes in family life by means of education is certainly not new. Indeed, education as the antidote to poverty and inadequate parenting amongst the working class has a very long pedigree. Dyhouse has written that

> 'There was a strong current of opinion in mid-Victorian society which would hold the poor – through their attitudes, behaviour and domestic disorganisation – personally responsible for their own poverty. It followed that most reformers bent on tackling a whole variety of social ills channelled their energies into attempts to change behaviour rather than conditions. They sought to reform working class lifestyles as a first means towards altering the environment in which working people lived; frequently looking towards education for solutions to poverty.
>
> The educational policies devised by church and state in the second half of the nineteenth century aimed to "civilise" the working class and to bring the structure and organisation of working-class family life into line with middle class values and canons of "respectability" '.
>
> (Dyhouse, 1981, p. 79)

The education provided in late Victorian times was not to all the working class, just to the women. It had, then, the double aim of preparing girls for wifehood and motherhood as unpaid occupations and, in the interim, of maintaining the supply of adequate domestic servants for middle class housewives. Dyhouse continues:

> 'If so much depended on women's domestic skills, and if working class women were generally perceived to be so ill-equipped as wives, mothers and housekeepers, it followed in the minds of contemporaries that schooling might supply the remedy. And there was, of course, a further very important dimension to middle-class discussion over the desirability of domestic training for girls – a dimension supplied by the middle-class demand for domestic servants throughout the period'.
>
> (Dyhouse, 1981, pp. 81–2)

The kinds of education provided then were very often called 'schools for mothers' and courses taught not to young girls at school but through the health and welfare services. Dyhouse has written that:

> '. . . "educative" institutions – "schools for mothers", infant "welcomes" and health visiting networks . . . aimed to teach women to become better mothers . . . Infant Welfare centres performed valuable information services, disseminating advice on care and feeding, and must be seen in the widest sense as "educational" institutions. It seems unlikely that lessons in "mothercraft" supplied to girls of twelve and thirteen in the elementary schools were on anything like the same scale of importance . . . lessons in home management provided in school seemed "artificial" and of little value'.
>
> (*ibid*, pp. 100–101)

These parallel kinds of education are both being proposed afresh now – changes in the curriculum of compulsory schools and post-school education to include social and parent education and specific courses for parents at family centres, day nurseries run by social service departments and ante-natal classes provided by maternity hospitals. Again, their chief, but not only, target is working class or poor, disadvantaged girls. The aim is not to provide universal family-life education for all girls, although some components of the proposals are for all schoolchildren or all pregnant women. For example, the Parliamentary Select Committee on Social Services Report, *Children in Care* recommended to the Government that both kinds of education be provided.

> 'Children sometimes have to be received into care because their parents simply lack parenting skills. It cannot unfortunately be assumed that all young parents will have had an opportunity to learn parenting skills either from their own parents or their friends. The education system does not seem to recognise that children who have not had such an opportunity could benefit from acquiring basic home-making and parenting skills *before* rather than after they become parents . . . It is no good teaching children how to be good citizens if they become incompetent parents. *We recommend that the Department of Education and Science take account of the need to impart parenting skills in curriculum development'*
> (1984, para 48, p. xxv) (their emphasis).

It also went on to recommend more informal parent 'education' to be provided to girls or women who had already become parents and were not coping very well:

> 'At present much practical help and advice is given by social workers, health visitors and so on – albeit on a *remedial* rather than prospective basis. Several witnesses emphasised the value of giving families under strain practical help in their own homes . . . *Family aides* or *'home-makers'* can pass on some of the *simple and practical domestic skills such as buying, cooking, washing and budgeting.* Evidence was received on Home Start schemes which provide *practical support and friendship from volunteers to families* with young children facing particular difficulties. The value of such help cannot be over-emphasised: its prompt provision could help avert a number of receptions into care.'
> (1984, para 49, p. xxv), (my emphasis).

These new recommendations for parent education are only dissimilar from those that Dyhouse discussed in their language. In Victorian and Edwardian times, policy-makers had a clear view of the sexual division of labour in both family life and the economy. Ehrenreich and English have called that approach the 'sexual romantic' solution to the 'Woman Question' (1979, pp. 20–21).
They describe it as:

'Sexual romanticism cherishes the mystery that is woman and proposes to keep her mysterious, by keeping her outside . . . If she became a female version of "economic man", an individual pursuing her own trajectory, then indeed it would be a world without love, without human warmth . . . Sexual romanticism asserts that the home will be . . . (the) refuge, woman will be . . . (the) consolation . . . The world of private life and biological existence has become suffused with a holy radiance'

(1979, pp. 20–21).

Indeed, there is plenty of evidence to show that early social reformers held such views. Herbert Samuel, a Liberal MP, put the official view very clearly in arguing for changes in maternity provision and for 'mothercraft':

'The conclusion is clear that it is the duty of the community, so far as it can, to relieve motherhood of its burdens, to spread the knowledge of mothercraft that is so often lacking, to make medical aid available when it is needed, to watch over the health of the infant. And since this is the duty of the community, it is also the duty of the State. The infant cannot, indeed, be saved, by the State. It can only be saved by the mother. But the mother can be helped and can be taught by the State.'

(Davies, 1978, p. xvii)

Nowadays, social reformers are not so explicit about their intentions and use gender-neutral language to describe their proposals – parent or social life, family centres, "parenting skills". Indeed, their aims may well be laudable – to improve the status of parenthood in contemporary society – but, given the contemporary 'family worlds', are unlikely to reach men as well as women, boys as well as girls, without concomitant social policy changes.

Indeed, the current evidence would suggest that most recipients of such education, where it exists, are girls or women. Pugh and De'Ath (*op. cit.*) provide the most comprehensive review of the evidence, looking at curricula in primary and secondary schools; post-school education through the youth service, the youth training schemes, special schemes for deviant pupils and teenage parents. They also investigate antenatal education; provision for parents with preschool children such as mother and toddler groups, preschool playgroups, family centres and home-visiting schemes, and finally parents with school age children:

'In brief the extent of family life education in schools shows that whilst this is still not a part of every school's curriculum, some schools are beginning to adopt a more coherent approach to the social and emotional development of their pupils. Courses whose primary aim is family life education tend to fall within the ambit of child care and development, and as optional subjects offered at CSE or O-level *are taken almost entirely by girls and often less-able girls*. Where relevant courses are a compulsory part of a core curriculum taken by all pupils, they are often a secondary aim of broad-based non-examined courses in personal social or health education . . . There are as yet few courses which offer to boys and girls alike an opportunity to develop self-confidence and self-knowledge, to build up satisfactory relationships, to consider whether or not they wish to become parents, to discuss values and attitudes towards parenting, to develop some insight into child development, and to gain some first hand experience of life with young children.'

> (*ibid*, p. 199). (my emphasis)

In their review of post-school schemes, they conclude:

'Outside the school classroom, such opportunities are even more limited. Despite the fact that thirty three percent of all women and twenty percent of all men marry before they are 21, and that teenage marriages have a particularly high breakdown rate, neither the youth service nor further education seem to see family life education as part of their brief. Social education is a primary goal of the youth service and social and life skills are an important feature of the new Youth Training Scheme yet the current emphasis in both these services is on skills related to work rather than personal relationships and family life . . . Although antenatal clinics and classes are now widely available they are attended by only half of all pregnant women. They have been consistently criticised for failing to reach the most vulnerable women – the young, the single, ethnic minorities.'

> (*ibid*, pp. 199–200)

In commenting on facilities for parents, they add;

'. . . An appreciation of the value of the support that parents can give each other is reflected in the growing number of informal post-natal and mother and toddler groups, and of parent education groups . . . Adult and community education, family groups and family centres are developing strategies for working with more vulnerable families, and along with playgroups are often offering mothers both increased insight into their own children's development and opportunities for widening their own horizons and developing their own confidence as parents. Home visiting schemes and crisis telephone services are also growing . . . given adequate preparation and support, parents are well able to lead groups, visit other families and run 24 hour crisis telephone services.'

> (p. 201)

But as Finch has made so crystal clear, all this kind of community care and support depends on women. She writes:

'. . . is "caring" in these schemes necessarily women's work? All such schemes seem to envisage developing a pattern of front-line daily care for highly dependent individuals in which services are provided by a mixture of volunteers, paid workers, and "informal" carers, usually relatives but possibly neighbours. It comes as no surprise to discover that, on evidence of such schemes to date, almost all carers in all three categories are women . . .'

> (1984, p. 10).

Since Pugh and De'Ath surveyed school curricula there have been
some significant developments that appear to alter the courses provided. In 1983, the government, through the Manpower Services
Commission, launched a pilot scheme of education and training for
14 to 18 year olds, entitled the Technical and Vocational Education
Initiative (TVEI). It provided funds to a select number of local education authorities to develop schemes in certain schools and monitor
their progress. A year later, before the scheme had been evaluated, it
was extended to most LEAs although some, such as the Inner
London Education Authority (ILEA) refused to participate. One of
its first aims, according to the initial statement of principle, was to
provide equal opportunities for boys and girls.

> 'Equal opportunities should be available to young people of both sexes
> and they should normally be educated together on courses within each
> project. Care should be taken to avoid sex stereotyping.'

The Women's National Commission, reviewing the initial impact of
TVEI and the above aim, commented:

> 'Because of the short time available it was not easy for LEAs to make pre-
> paration to meet the very considerable challenge of equal opportunity
> before the projects began. It was therefore probably inevitable that, if the
> design of projects involved immediate choice between courses on sex
> stereotyped lines, boys and girls reacted predictably. Sex stereotyping has
> therefore emerged to a very marked degree in some projects, though not
> in others . . .'
>
> (WNC, 1984, p. 52, para 32).

In their recommendations to the Manpower Services Commission,
they suggest:

> 'using sex-neutral terminology to describe courses e.g. it is better to
> describe the course as "Food, Nutrition, Catering" rather than "Home
> Economics" or "Cookery" '.
>
> (*ibid*, p. 55)

They also reviewed the evidence about the workings of the Youth
Training Scheme revised in 1983, for school-leavers aged 16 or 17
and unemployed. They found that there was 'a smaller number of
girls' than boys on any of the schemes, ranging from forty four percent of girls on Mode A schemes to a mere twenty one percent on one
of the Mode B1 schemes. They comment somewhat sanguinely:

> 'The smaller number of girls on YTS overall is probably accounted for by
> the fact that in a very difficult market for young people there are rather
> more "girl's type" jobs (e.g. in service industries) available than "boy's
> jobs" '.
>
> (*ibid*, p. 57, para. 36).

They also comment on how 'girls predominated . . . in care place-ments' (p. 58). Moreover, they identified as a problem for girls gain-ing access to YTS the limited age range:

> 'Some girls have difficulty in relation to the restricted YTS age group. It is common for girl school leavers to be expected to help at home for a period before finally going into the employment market. We were told of three categories of girls –
> — Asian girls whose families seek to keep them at home
> — West Indian girls with working mothers
> — Girls in rural areas where jobs for women were often scarce.
> who might at the more mature age of 18–20 decide they want a YTS placement, but will be then have lost their opportunity. The Group would like a study to be made of the prevalence of these cases and, if a significant number of girls experience such difficulties, a policy of deferral to be considered.'
>
> *(ibid*, pp. 60–61 para. 43)

The WNC make clear that there is a sexual division in home-based activities, such as care of family members, as well as in training for care work, but do not acknowledge the contradiction in seeking a deferral policy. They argue that this might help girls to become interested in 'non-traditional work', having presumably had an experience of unpaid, traditional work. In summarising their recom-mendations they put the point forcefully:

> 'A deferral system under which urgent family responsibilities might be one acceptable ground should be considered. If it became generally possi-ble for girls to begin YTS at 18/19 this would prove a more appropriate age to interest girls, by then beyond the uncertainties of adolescence, in non-traditional work'.
>
> *(ibid*, p. 16, para. 14)

MSC see 'care placements' or child care courses as training for important paid or unpaid work. They certainly have not begun to value parenthood on a par with work such as 'craft, design and tech-nology'. The aim of the WNC, in reviewing education and training courses for women, is to ensure that girls have opportunities to con-form to the traditional forms of male employment, rather than seeking to get boys and men into female patterns of family-based 'work'.

Indeed, changes in contemporary patterns of work, especially voluntary and low-paid jobs, are exacerbating rather than eroding the differences between male and female patterns of employment. The expansion of schemes for preschool children such as home-start, befriending schemes and family centres rely on the availability of women, usually themselves mothers. The aim is usually to teach 'parenting skills', to mothers of pre-school children who have expressed an inability to cope alone. Obviously women who have already reared their own families are seen as most appropriate recruits for this kind of informal education. In the DHSS' *Under-Fives Initiative* started in 1983, official approval but paltry resources have been given to the voluntary sector to do the work of supporting families. Mainly middle class mothers of schoolage or older children are being recruited by voluntary agencies, such as Homestart or Homeplus, to 'teach' the skills of full-time exclusive motherhood to poor or working class mothers on an unpaid basis. The Pre-school Home Visitors provide a range of help from advice on domestic and budgetting matters, to shopping itself and baby-sitting. Men cannot be recruited for several reasons. One is that the volunteers have to be able to demonstrate their own adequate 'parenting skills' by having their own clean and tidy home. Social workers vet the recruits in their own homes. Second, men are presumed to be at work, or, if unemployed, registered as 'available for work' and therefore unable to commit themselves to such long-term voluntary work. Third, there is a fear of gossip and sexual innuendo if men are seen to be visiting 'parents' in their own homes, revealing the true nature of the gender of the parents.

'Parenting skills' are also now being taught in more formal child care organisations. Family centres are the creation of voluntary children's societies but are now being copied by the statutory social services. Jan Phelan, reporting on a study of family centres established by the Church of England Children's Society claims that one of their chief characteristics was to 'help families as a whole; in practice it was found that most centre activities focus on individual aspects of the family. Some centres are more child-oriented, others more parent-oriented, some concentrate more on the family as a unit, while others focus more on women' (1983, p. 39). Phelan continues:

> 'Among specific aims quoted by individual centres are: to increase individual and collective strengths; to foster happier family relationships; to *encourage parental awareness in bringing up children*; to help people find new ways of seeing their role within the family; to *enhance women's position in the family* and society; to reduce stress; to help families through a crisis; to aid those on low incomes; to increase the range of choices in tackling problems, and to provide *support* and *generate initiatives for families*'.
>
> (*ibid*, p. 39) (my emphasis)

Education in its widest sense is understood here. Indeed many of the initiatives described provided 'parental skills'. Many local authorities have now converted their day nurseries to 'drop-in' family centres. Avon social services now includes in the job description for a nursery nurse to work in day nurseries for 'vulnerable families and children', 'to maintain and develop professionally sound interaction between families and staff and to assist parents in developing good parenting skills . . . ' It is curious that these jobs are generally filled by 18 year old girls who have just completed an NNEB and who personally have little practical knowledge of parenting. Were they themselves or their sisters to become pregnant and become teenage or schoolgirl mothers they would be treated as having broken some unwritten law about 'good parenting'.

Changes in the way schools work with families also exacerbates rather than erodes the differences between mothers' and fathers' work. Schools tend now to rely on women's unpaid work in preparing children to attend and on maintaining adequate standards for daily attendance. Schools depend upon women's unpaid work. They expect mothers to have done 'educational' work with their children before they come to school. Reception class teachers expect their new infants to be able count and to know their letters. Those children who have not already been taught a lot by their mothers need special attention to compensate. A Professor of Education has just developed video tapes for mothers of pre-school children to help them with early learning. They are curiously entitled 'Mother: Get Ready to Read'. Teachers set clear standards for what work mothers have to do to prepare their children to go outside the home and into school. Dorothy Smith provides a beautiful example:

'A little pamphlet addressed to parents published by the Ontario government makes recommendations for how children's reading and writing skills can be improved . . . the list of suggestions includes many items which are like the kinds of activities children might be engaged in in kindergarten or primary grades . . . all presuppose and make invisible expenditures of time, effort, skill and materials. Paint, crayons, scissors, paper, photographs, works of art are supposed to be available. Many of the activities suggested presuppose also some, if not considerable, preparatory work on the part of the parent in preparing photographs and reproductions of works of art, in making puppets and certainly considerable further work in cleaning up after these events have taken place. Space is presupposed in which these messes can be made without damage to household furnishings etc. Presupposed also are skills involved in knowing how to discuss works of art with your children, how to extend their vocabulary etc . . . It is the investment of mother's work and thought in activities of these kinds which prepares children for school.'
(D. Smith, 1983, pp. 16–17)

Schools are generally organised, like the health services, on the assumption that mothers will be available during the hours of the working day to take the children if necessary. For example, school closures for in-service training are announced giving little notice or respect for working mothers. The hours of the school day, in any event, do not match those of the conventional working day. Moves

Miriam David

to develop a continental school day also reduce women's opportunities for paid employment. Few schools, or LEAs, will accept the extra responsibility of caring for children out of school hours. Mothers have to make their own private arrangements. Schools expect mothers to be available at both ends of the school day, to fetch young children to and from school. When children are taken ill they are often asked if their mothers are at home or out shopping. Of course, it is recognised that some mothers do work outside the home but it is always the mother's whereabouts, not the father's that are first enquired about and her work, rather than his, which is interrupted. (As I wrote this the telephone rang with the school nurse from the children's primary school on, to let me know that one of my children had head-lice and I must take immediate action. Since my husband was to collect the children I had to ring to tell him).

Schools also rely on mothers to maintain them in their present form. For example, the Health Education Council has just begun a large-scale advertising campaign, funded publicly and displayed in health centres, schools and on television. It tells mothers to be home when their children come home from school.

'Home from School Again – A Little Dirty Maybe but Cheerful and Eager to tell you about it. Make it a time to talk. Let her tell you about her day, and tell her about yours'.

Note not only the expectation that mothers be home but that for once, it is daughters who are the more important. Either they have to learn by example how to be mothers one day or is it that the Health Education Council has learnt to be non-sexist by using girls instead of boys? Yet they have not realised the sexism implicit in their appeal to mothers?

Mothers are also, nowadays, expected to 'help' with the actual school. HMI, reporting on the effects of local government expenditure cuts on schools, ask about the 'parental contribution':

'The LEAs' provision for education is increasingly being *supplemented by parental contributions of both cash and labour*. Such contributions benefit many schools, but at the same time they also tend to widen the differences in the levels of resources available to individual schools and, in turn, the educational opportunities available to pupils. In some three-quarters of all schools visited, parental contributions were said to be moderate or substantial . . . The type of parental support varied widely and included *help in the classroom* or school library, in improving and maintaining the premises and furnishings, in supplying and maintaining school transport and *in the provision of teaching resources*. The teaching resources most frequently purchased included essential items such as micro-computers, audio-visual equipment, library and *textbooks*, PE and games equipment and musical instruments . . . in nearly half the

primary schools visited, the cash contributions received were in excess of one-third of the capitation allowance provided by the LEA'
(DES, May 1984, pp. 29–30) (my emphasis).

Although the cash contribution is great, the contribution of labour is of greater significance. 'Parental helpers' teaching reading, writing and maths as well as cookery, music, and running the bookshop are a vital feature of primary education. In Canada, such parents are called 'listening mothers'. In Britain, parental involvement is seen as more active. Yet some teachers are beginning to ponder its value. It has been described as 'the volunteer army in the firing line'. (*TES*, 1985, p. 8) In addition, it has been argued that:

> 'the increasingly high profile of parents in more than half the country's primary schools could pose a threat to the teachers' status. For centuries, teachers have been considered *in loco parentis*. Some fear that the roles are now being reversed, with parents *in loco domini*.
>
> (*ibid.*)

The HMI point to how this parental contribution increases inequalities of opportunity. It not only increases them within schools, between pupils within schools, between pupils with 'helping mothers' and 'working mothers', but also between schools in middle class areas and working class areas. In middle class areas, containing traditional families the volunteer mothers may be highly skilled – trained teachers, graduates etc. – whereas helpers in working class areas may be recruited with the aim of providing them with 'parental skills', on the model developed by the Plowden committee (1967) to improve primary education. Parental involvement clearly increases disparities between children's chances, especially those coming from lone-parent families where the necessity to seek paid employment is paramount. The Hargreaves Report on Secondary Education in Inner London found that over a quarter of children in its schools came from lone parent families, yet it advocated more parental involvement on the traditional model.

Advocates of parental involvement, parental skills and parental education do not acknowledge the ways in which their proposals build on the traditional sexual division of labour. Although the aims of some of the proposals are entirely laudable, without changes in the organisation of education and work, they can only succeed in increasing inequalities of opportunities between both social classes and the sexes. Proposals to provide equal opportunities for boys and girls in education also build on the traditional sexual division of labour and the relationship between family and work. By only focussing on providing girls with educational and training opportunities to take up 'non-traditional work' or male jobs, girls' unpaid and necessary work of caring for family members, whether their own children or siblings and dependent relatives, remains untouched. As Illich puts it, women will remain 'handicapped' in relation to the economy. He writes:

> '. . . women are discriminated against in employment only to be forced, when off the job, to do a new kind of economically necessary work without any pay attached to it . . . To a greater extent and in a different manner from men, women are drafted into the economy. They were and are deprived of equal access to wage labour only to be bound with even greater inequality to work that did not exist before wage labour came into being'.
>
> (1983, p. 46)

Most proposals for sexual equality in education do not deal with this 'handicap'. For example, the Equal Opportunities Commission in 1984 launched an initiative to involve more girls in science and technology to enable them to have better job opportunities and careers. Entitled Women Into Science and Engineering (WISE), it aimed to get girls to take up courses and obtain 'vocational skills' for jobs and careers in the new industries such as micro-electronics and information technology, vital to economic recovery and growth. The Women's National Commission, in discussing 'new directions in education and training for girls and women' only focussed on improving girls' chances in paid employment. They remark:

> 'Women at all stages of life and with all levels of qualifications (or none) need to be given insight into changes in the job market, changes in life patterns, opportunities in new technology; also to learn, by direct contact if possible, how other women have acquired confidence and found points of entry to new experience . . . We were also very much aware that informing girls and women about opportunities in non-traditional fields must go hand in hand with encouragement and a substantial amount of long-term support and counselling. Problems of self-confidence and practical problems, such as managing child-care and a career-break, have to be tackled.'
>
> (1984, p. iii).

By seeing the 'problems' of child care and a 'career-break' as confined to women, they are endorsing the current divisions between work and family. Lady Howe is right to argue to go beyond that:

> 'We urgently need a "renegotiation" of work and family. There will be disagreement on the particulars. But once there is general acceptance that caring and domestic life are the equal *practical* responsibilities of men and women then work patterns and policy and much else will fall into place.'
>
> (1984) (my emphasis).

However, such general acceptance is far from being realised. Pugh and De'Ath are unusual in their advocacy of the necessity of 'shared parenting' as a step in achieving sexual equality. Yet 'shared parenting' itself is insufficient, given the dramatic changes in 'family worlds'. As Riley points out (1983) it is obviously no solution for parents bringing up their children alone 'by force or by choice'.

Ehrensaft has, however, shown that shared parenting among a small number of relatively privileged households experimenting with the idea:

'alters the authority relations not only between parent and child but between males and females . . . shared parenting families substitute "unisex" parenting for the "instrumental-emotional" gender division of traditional families'.

(1981, p. 44)

But as she acknowledges, if shared parenting is to be a widespread solution, it needs a 'concomitant restructuring of work and politics'. (1981, p. 23) It also requires more attention to be focussed on the male than the female role. Betty Friedan has recently written that:

'We cannot hope to have complete equality if we look for changes in the female sex role alone – we must look for comparable changes in the male sex role, and a transcending of sex role polarisation . . . advanced second stage feminism as I envision it, says we should not say "equality versus that family" of "feminism versus the family". The family itself is evolving, and we cannot deny the importance of the family for human society . . . (It) will necessarily involve the restructuring of the workplace and the home . . . '

(1983, p. vii)

To achieve such changes in sex roles in the family and work, a 'radically different sex education' is a necessary prerequisite. This would entail teaching not only truly gender-neutral parental skills and child care but also a new form of sexual morality. Gender-neutral parenting assumes that both men and women are capable of providing love, intimacy, commitment and nurturance to children. As Parker (1984, p. 1) puts it:

'Most children are looked after by one or both of their parents. The crucial characteristics of that relationship are three-fold:
They are:

   (i) the unity of care and responsibility
  (ii) permanence, and
 (iii) partisan commitment-love.'

In fact, in our society these characteristics are not usually shared equally by mothers and fathers. Part of the problem for fathers has been the necessity to find forms of paid employment which require for their fulfilment, distance from children. The TUC acknowledged this, in looking at women's work opportunities:

'If women's particular role as a parent is fully recognised, and it is

accepted that women will need to take fairly lengthy periods of leave to
have children and may then work part-time afterwards, then they cannot
conform to the traditional male pattern of employment'

(1977, p. 108).

A new sexual morality requires that men and women be given equal
respect and treatment as well as opportunities in both the home and
the public world of work and politics. The Health Education
Council in the early 1980s attempted to develop a new sex education
publicity campaign. Yet it was premissed on a double standard with
'girls should say No; boys should just be careful'. Boys need to learn
to take the lessons of sexual responsibility to heart just as much as
girls. If boys were required not only to care about their families and
the children they created but that they also had to take daily
responsibility for caring for them, their attitudes to sexual activity
might perforce change.

These changes in what is taught at school about sex and parenting
could only succeed in their entirety if there were changes in the organisation of work and family life. A public commitment to the
centrality of child care and the care of family members in all our lives
would have to be made. This would have to be implemented by
giving all employees paid leave from work on the grounds of family
responsibility. This would not only be, as with current maternity
leave and pay, at the time of childbirth, but for sick or ill relatives.
The EEC is now advocating such family leave. It might also
incorporate time off for parental involvement with children's
schooling and, for schoolage parents, time out of education without
penalty to educational careers. Until it is recognised that all employees, workers, students and pupils have commitments to care for as
well as work for family members, sexual equality cannot advance
very far. True sexual equality requires that opportunities for unpaid
as well as paid 'work' be equalised by means of a social and sex education that is committed to the task. This, in turn, requires teachers
to recognise the issues and be trained accordingly. Social and sex
education need to become a core of the school curriculum: corre-
spondingly teacher trainers must include such issues in both initial
and inservice training courses in order to achieve full sexual equality
of treatment and respect.

References

Anderson, D. (1985) 'Ripe for a British Moral Majority' *The Times*,
    (15.10.85, p. 12).
Aplin, E. and Pugh, G. 1983 *Perspectives on Pre-School Home Visiting*,
    National Children's Bureau.

Berger, B. and Berger, B. 1983 *The War Over the Family*, Basic Books, (In G.B. , Penguin, 1984).

Bland, L. 1985 'Sex and Morals: Rearming the Left' *Marxism Today*, September, pp. 21–24.

David, M. 1983 'Sex, Education and Social Policy' in S. Walker and L. Barton (eds.).

David, M. 1984 'Teaching and Preaching Sexual Morality', *Journal of Education*, Vol. 166, March.

David, M. 1985 'Motherhood and Social Policy: A Matter of Education', *Critical Social Policy* 13.

David, M. 1986 'Moral and Maternal: The Family in the Right' in R. Levitas (ed.).

Davies, M. 1978 *Maternity: Letters from Working Women*, Virago.

Dyhouse, C. 1981 *Girls Growing up in late Victorian and Edwardian England*, Routledge and Kegan Paul.

DES, 1984 Report by Her Majesty's Inspectors on the Effects of Local Authority Expenditure Policies on Education Provision in England – 1983.

Ehrenreich, B and English, D. 1979 *For Her Own Good*, Pluto Press.

Eisenstein, Z. 1982 The Sexual Politics of the New Right: On Understanding the Crisis of Liberalism for the 1980s, *Signs: Journal of Woman and Culture*, Vol. 7, No. 3, pp. 567–588.

Finch, J. 1984 Community Care: Developing Non-Sexist Alternatives *Critical Social Policy 11*.

Friedan, B. 1984 Preface in Palgi *et al* (eds.).

Gilder, G. 1981 *Wealth and Poverty*, Basic Books.

Hargreaves Report, 1984 Secondary Education in Inner London, ILEA.

Howe, E. 1984 'Towards More Choice for Women', *New Society*, 27 May.

Illich, I. 1983 *Gender*, Marion Boyars.

Joshi, H. 1984 *Women's participation in paid work*: Further analysis of the Woman and Employment survey; Department of Employment Research Paper No. 45.

Levitas, P. (ed.), 1986 *The Ideologies of the New Right*, Polity Press.

Martin, J. and Roberts, C. 1984 *Women and Employment: A Lifelong Perspective*, HMSO.

Mount, F. 1983 *The Subversive* Family, Counterpoint.

New, C. and David, M. 1985 *For the Children's Sake*, Penguin.

Palgi, U. 1983 (eds.) *Sexual Equality: The Israeli Kibbutz Tests the Theories*, Norwood Editions.

Petchesky, R. 1984 *Abortion and Woman's Choice*, Longmans.

Phelan, J. 1983 *Family Centres: A Study*, The Children's Society.

Plowden Report, 1967 *Children and their Primary Schools*, HMSO.

Pugh, G. and De'Ath, E. 1984 *The Needs of Parents: Practice and Policy in Parent Education*, MacMillan.

Riley, D. 1983 The Serious Burdens of Love, in Segal (ed.)

Rimmer, L. 1981, *Families in Focus*, Study Commission on the Family.

Segal, L. 1983, (ed.) *What is to be done about the Family?* Penguin.

Smith, D. 1983 *Women's Work as Mothers: a new look at the relation of class, family and school achievement*. Unpublished paper.

Social Services Select Committee, 1984 *Children in Care*, HMSO, Vol. 1.

Social Trends 14, 1984 HMSO.

Study Commission on the Family, 1983 *Families in the Future*.

Times Educational Supplement, 1985 *Volunteer Army in the Firing Line*, April, 12, No. 3589.

TUC Working Party, 1977 *The Under Fives*, TUC.

Walker, S. and Barton, L. 1983 (eds.) *Gender, Class and Education*, Falmer Press.

Whitfield, R. 1980 *Educational for Family Life*, Hodder and Stoughton.

Women's National Commission, 1984 *The Other Half of Our Future*, London Cabinet Office.

Author Index

Abercrombie, N. 59
Adams, C. 157, 164
Ahier, J. 139
Alpin, E. 208
Anderson, D. 194
Apple, M. 34, 58, 59, 73–4, 75–95,
    100, 114
Armor, D. *et al.* 23
Arnot, M. 157, 158, 171
Aronowitz, S. 35
Ashton, P. T. 2, 22–40
Atkinson, P. 175

Ball, S. J. 117, 125, 126, 135
Bandura, A. 25
Barres, D. 115
Barnett, A. 160
Bates, *et al.* 98, 99
Barton, L. 71, 210
Bell, L. A. 132
Belotti, G. 171
Berger, B. 191
Berman, P. *et al.* 23
Bernstein, B. 96, 97, 107
Biddle, B. J. 23
Bidwell, C. E. 113
Bjorksten, E. 175–6
Bland, L. 176, 195
Blauner, R. 31
Bolton, E. 115

Briault, E. 149
Britton, E. 145
Bronfenbrenner, U. 36
Brown, B. B. 38
Brown, R. J. 139
Burstyn, J. 175

Callahan, R. 34
Campell, B. 92, 95, 192
Cant, A. 156, 164
Carchedi, G. 59
Carnoy, H. 36
Carnoy, M. *et al.* 93
Cedoline, A. 32
Clarke, J. 98, 99
Clarricoates, K. 171
Coates, R. 70
Cockburn, C. 172, 173
Cohen, J. 59
Cooley, M. 36
Connell, R. W. 94
Conveney, L. *et al.* 170, 171
Coward, R. 169, 170, 182–3
Cox, R. W. 143
Crunden, C. 177

Dale, I. R. 117, 118, 120, 121
Dale, R. 100, 140, 141
David, M. 190–210
Davies, B. 73, 96–116

Davies, I. R. 117
Davies, M. 198
De' Ath, E. 191–2, 198–9, 206
De Beauvoir, S. 186
Deem, R. 153, 171, 186
Dembo, M. 23
Dewey, J. 34, 35–6
DES 117
DHSS 202
Doda, N. 23, 32
Dreeben, R. 38
Dunkin, M. J. 23
Dunsire, A. 4
Dworkin, A. 172
Dwyer, P. *et al.* 93
Dyer, K. 172, 179, 181
Dyhouse, C. 196, 197

Edward, R. 92–3, 94
Ehrenreich, B. 197
Eisenstein, Z. 209
Eliot, T. S. 25
Elster, J. 21
Emery, F. 36
Emery, R. 36
English, D. 197
Evans, J. 73, 96–116, 117
Exeter University 117

Fenwick, K. 145
Ferris, E. 172, 181
Finch, J. 143, 199
Fletcher, S. 175, 176, 177
Flora, P. 139
Flude, M. 139
Fomin, F. 95
Forum 125
Fougere, G. 67
Freedman, S. 1, 2, 41–57
Freeman-Moir, D. F. 63
Freiden, B. 207
Freire, P. 39
Fruchten, N. 48
Fulton, O. 122, 124

Gaskell, J. 95
Gehlen, A. 30
Getzels, J. W. 23
Gibson, S. 23

Giddens, A. 5, 59, 149
Gilder, G. 194
Giroux, H. 35
Glaser, B. G. 97
Glass, G. 26–7
Glatter, R. 138
Gleeson, D. 98, 99
Glickman, C. 39
Goodlad J. 34, 35, 37
Grace, G. 69
Gray, J. 3–21
Greer, P. R. 46–7
Griffin, C. 184

Habermas, J. 5, 20
Hacking, I. 69–70
Hall, A. 181
Hall, J. 117, 121
Hall, R. E. 174
Halsey, A. *et al.* 70
Hammersley, M. *et al.* 96
Hanmer, J. 174
Hannon, V. 3–21
Hargreaves, A. 96, 100, 104, 135, 140, 146
Hargreaves, D. 154, 165, 166
Hargreaves, J. 175, 182
Harman, G. 143
Harris, K. 58, 59, 60
Headlam Wells, J. 156, 158
Herbst, P. 36
Herzberg, F. *et al.* 35
HMI Report 108, 178
Howe, E. 206
Hunter, C. 117
Hutter, B. 169

Illich, I. 206

Jackson, P. W. 23, 53
Jackson, S. 170, 173, 176, 177
Jeffreys, S. 169, 172
Jones, G. W. 4
Joshi, H. 209
Joyce, B. R. *et al.* 37
Jungck, S. 94

Kamm, J. 175
Kelly, A. 154, 155

Kelly, M. 70
Kesler-Harris, A. 52, 93
Kitzinger, S. 51
Kogan, M. 6, 8, 117, 142, 144

Labour Party 158
Lauder, H. 2, 58–71
Lawn, M. 58, 146, 148
Layton, D. 117
Leach, M. 122, 124
Lee, D. 59
Lello, J. 4
Levin, H. M. 78–9, 80
Lindblom, C. E. 143
Locke, E. 35
Lortie, D. C. 28, 29
Lundgren, U. P. 96, 107, 113

McCabe, C. 136
Maccoby, M. 36
McCrone, K. 176
MacDonald, M. 171
MacIntosh, P. 176
McKenzie, G. 59
McRobbie, A. 184
Mahoney, P. 171, 155
Martin, J. 193
Marx, K. 114
Maslach, C. 35
Metropolitan Life 31
Medley, D. *et al.* 39
Millman, V. 153, 158
Mills, C. W. 30, 33, 148
Moore, R. 98, 99, 100
Morris, V. C. 34
Mount, F. 195
MSC, 100, 123, 129, 130, 131

National Education Association
    (NEA) 22, 23, 31, 45
Nava, M. 184
New, C. 196
Nixon, J. 132
Noble, D. 92, 94
Norton Grubb, W. 93–4

Offe, C. 59, 60, 139
Okeley, J. 177
Olson, P. 92, 94, 95

Open University Course E333 141
Open University Course E353 139
Ozga, J. 58, 74, 138–150

Parfit, D. 21
Parker, 207
Parkin, F. 70
Pateman, T. 6
Payne, G. *et al.* 143
Petchesky, R. 194
Phelan, J. 202
Pickard, J. 98
Pile, W. D. 147
Pratt, J. 158
Pratt, J. *et al.* 153, 157
Pring, R. 98, 106, 107, 117, 121
Pringle, M. K. 191
Pugh, G. 191–2, 195, 198–9, 206,
    208
Pyart, B. 117, 134

Radford, J. 169, 174
Raffe, D. 110
Ranson, S. 3–21, 143, 146–7
Rawls, J. 35
Reinecke, I. 93
Rescher, N. 92
Ribbins, P. M. 139
Rily, D. 207
Rimmer, L. 193
Roberts, C. 193
Rowbotham, S. 159
Rudduck, J. 134
Rumberger, E. 78–9, 80
Rush, W. *et al.* 35

Sallis, J. 8
Salter, B. 139, 147
Sanders, M. 123, 124, 125
Sarah, E. 171
Saunders, M. 130, 133
Saunders, S. 174
Schaefer, R. 36
Schools Council 145
Schutz, A. 24, 25
Scraton, S. 169–189
Sekington, R. 117
Seed, J. 115
Segal, L. 209

214   *Author Index*

Sen, A. 8
Sharpe, R. 71
Sharpe, S. 171
Shearer, D. 36
Shaw, J. 157
Shirley, I. 71
Shor, I. 92
Sikes, P. J. 73, 117–137
Sikes, P. J. *et al.* 118, 120, 130, 132
Simpson, T. 68
Smart, B. 169
Smart, C. 169
Smart, J. 67
Smith, D. 203
Smith, M. 26–7
Smith, S. 157
Sockett, H. T. 4
Social Services Select Committee 197
Spender, D. 155, 171
Spradley, J. 25
Springhall, J. 177
Stanko, E. 174
Stanworth, M. 171
Study Commission on the Family 193
Streibel, M. 94, 95
Stenhouse, L. A. 40, 132
Stewart, J. D. 4
Stober, M. 55
Stoney, S. M. *et al.* 128

Tamashiro, R. 39
Tapper, E. 139, 147
Taylor, F. W. 55
Taylor, H. 164
Taylor, M. 132
Tesconi, C. A. Jr. 34
Thorsrud, E. 36
Tipton, B. 113–4, 138
Tomlinson, J. 147
Toner, B. 189
Trist, F. 36

TUC Working Party 207–8
Tyack, D. 55

Urry, J. 59

Valli, L. 95

Wallace, R. G. 112
Walker, P. 71
Walker, S. 71, 210
Weaver, T. R. 147
Webb, I. 175
Webb, R. B. 2, 22–40
Weeks, J. 170
Weiner, G. 154, 155, 157, 158, 159, 164, 171, 185
Weiner, R. 35
Weiss, P. 178
White, P. 70
White, p. 70
Whitfield, R. 191, 194
Whyld, J. 155
Whyte, J. 153, 155, 158, 165, 171
Wilkes, C. 71
Williams, G. 169
Willis, P. 98, 99, 185
Wilson, E. 169
Wirth, A. G. 36
Wise, A. 40, 94
Witcher, H. 158
Wolcott, H. 143
Wolpe, A-M. 171
Woods, P. 109, 132
Woodward, K. 95
Women's National Commission 154, 200, 201, 206
Wright E. O. 58, 59

Yates, L. 184
Yee, B. 2, 58–71
Young, I. 181–2

Zwerdling, D. 36

Subject Index

Accountability x, 3–20, 83
  definitions of 4–5
  forms of 6–8
  policies on 8–18
'advisory' system, for options 109
alienation, of teachers x, 30–1, 35
autonomy, in education 112–4

'beneficient mafia' 147
biological technologies 78
Boston Globe 41, 46, 50
Brunel University 138, 144
burnout, in teachers 28–9, 32, 41,
  44, 54–6

Callaghan, James 118
'capital flight' 81
Careers and Occupational
  Information Centre (COIC)
  117, 118–9
'career-break' 206
career opportunities, from MSC
  132–3
Carnegie Foundation for the
  Advancement of Teaching 50
central government, control over
  education 58–61, 144–6
Center for Law and Education Report 95
Centre for Educational Research
  and Innovation (CERI)
  192–3

child centred learning 16–17
classification 107–8
community participation 17–18
comprehensive education 125
computers
  and social class 86–9
  in school 75–7, 88–9
computer literacy 86–8
Conservative, education policy 68,
  73, 97–9, 118–9, 146–8
consultancy role, on gender issues
  155, 165
consumerism, in education 7–8,
  12–15
control
  on TVEI 104
  over education xi, 58–61, 144–6
cost effectiveness, of schools 83
Counselling and Career
  Development Unit (CCDU)
  120
CPVE 48
critical theory 143
curriculum
  computers in 83–5
  options at 14+ 107–112
  political intervention in 98–9

'deadwood' 45
'delivery' 12

democratisation, of the work place
35–7
de-powering, of teachers 74, 83–4
deskilling 49–50, 78–82
of teachers 34, 74, 83–4
DES (Department of Education and
Sciences) Reports 117, 202

'ecological' orientation 24, 34
'ecological' threats 26–32
Education Act 1944 144–5
Education Act 1980 3, 7, 8
educational administration 138,
139, 140–1
educational management 138,
144–6
educational policy, study of 96–8,
138–148
efficacy research 22–4, 25–6, 34–5
elite theory 148
equality, and gender 153–166
equal opportunities
policies 156, 161
versus feminism 159–60
Equal Opportunities Commission
206
ethnographic work 25, 143
examination results, publication of
3, 8–9

Family centres 202
Family structures, and parenthood
192–3
Feminism 159

gender
equality in schools 153–166
on MSC programmes 153, 200–1
modes of influence 155–8
girls in science and technology
project 155, 158
Great Debate 3, 118
'guidance' system, for options 110

Hargreaves Report 205
HMI Reports 108, 178

individualisation, of reform 32–3
influence, and gender 155–8

INSET programmes 131–2
and gender 157, 163–5
in-service training 124, 131–2

intentionality, by teachers 111
interview material 146–8
isolation, of teachers 28–9, 51

jargon, of MSC 119–20
job market, of the future 79–82

Labour, and work 114
Labour Party
in Britain 158, 160
in New Zealand 67–8
labour market, for teachers 60

macro level sociology 140–1
management
of education 35, 138, 143–6
of teachers 51–4
Manchester gender project, 163–5
Manpower Services Commission
(MSC) 117–35
gender policy 153, 200–1
in schools 118–20
teachers' perception of 120–34
Reports of 100, 123, 129, 130, 131
market accountability xi, 7, 12–15,
16, 17
master teachers 50–1, 52, 54–6
merit pay 54–6
Metropolitan Life Insurance
Company 31
micro/macro gap 140–1, 146
micro level sociology 140–1
micro studies 140–1, 148
Milton Keynes gender project
160–3
morale, of teachers 31–2
Moral majority 194
motivation, of teachers 22–37

National Commission on Excellence
in Education (NCEE) 47–8
National Education Association 22,
23, 31, 45
'new vocationalism' 98
networks 147

New Zealand Post Primary
   Teachers Association
   (PPTA)
   and pay 61–5
   and University Entrance 65–7

occupational families 120
Open University 139, 146, 160, 161,
   164
   for pupils 107–112
   for mixed ability groups 108–9
ownership 120

parent education 190–210
parental choice 12–15
parental participation 3, 204–5
   in option choices 111
partnership thesis 144–6, 147
physical contact, in PE 180–2
physical differences 179–80
physical education
   and sexuality 171–186
   contemporary philosophy 178
   history of 175–8
physical, ideology of 170–1
physical violence 171, 173, 174
Plowden Report 205
pluralist approach, to policy 144–6
pluralist/Marxist divide 141–2
policy analysis project 142
policy sociology 140–144
politics, and gender 155–6, 158,
   159, 160, 165
politics of education 138
power, in physical relations 172–4
powerlessness 51
   of teachers 29–30
professional accountability 6–7,
   9–12
proletarianisation 78–82
   of teachers 58–71
Proposition 2½ 42
public accountability 7–8, 17–19

Reagan education policy 42–3
relative autonomy 112, 113–4
researcher, roles for 155–6
role demands, on teachers 26–7

salaries, of teachers 27–8

schools, and gender 171, 184–5
Schools Council 145
self evaluation 7, 10–11
sexual equality, in parent education
   190–208
sexual harassment 185
sexuality, politics of 169–186
skill learning 48–9
social administration project 141–2
social and life skills courses 98
social literacy, and computers
   89–91
social science project 142
sociologists, role in schools 154
software, purchase of 84–5, 86, 88
Special Reports on Educational Subjects
   (1898) 176
standards, in girls PE 182
Stantonbury Campus sexism in
   education group 153
state control 83
state intervention, in schools 68, 73,
   97–9, 113, 118–9, 146–8
status of teachers 27–8
stress 32
strikes 61–4
structuralist view 59–60
Swann Report 163

teachers
   and gender 157, 158
   burnout 28–9, 32, 41–57
   difficulties 100
   motivation 22
   proletarianisation of 61–9
   training 131–2
technology
   and inequality 82–9
   politics of 75–7
   replacing teachers 61
   teaching 73
Technical and Vocational
   Educational Initiatives
   (TVEI) 96, 97–8, 99–101
   curriculum content 107, 131
   experimental 126–8
   gender 153, 161–2, 100
   mixed ability groups 104, 105, 108
   resources 129–30

TUC Working Party 207–8
TRIST (TVEI Related Inservice
    Training) courses 117, 119,
    126, 130
'typification' 25

unemployment 81–2

valorization, of teachers 60–1
vocational curriculum 73, 106
vocational education x, 107, *see also*
    TVEI

women in science and engineering
    206
Women's National Commission
    154, 200, 201, 206
work 114
working class
    and family life 195–6

Youth Opportunities Programmes
    (YOPS) 98
Youth Training Scheme 98, 117,
    119, 200–1